THE
HOLLYWOOD
CONNECTION

Other titles by Michael Munn and published by
Robson Books

Trevor Howard
Charlton Heston: A Biography
The Hollywood Murder Casebook
Hollywood Rogues
Clint Eastwood: Hollywood's Loner

THE HOLLYWOOD CONNECTION

The True Story of Organized Crime in Hollywood

MICHAEL MUNN

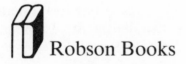

Robson Books

First published in Great Britain in 1993 by Robson
Books Ltd, Bolsover House, 5-6 Clipstone Street,
London W1P 7EB

British Library Cataloguing in Publication Data
A catalogue record for this book is available from
the British Library

ISBN 0 86051 856 6

Typeset by Spectrum Typesetting Ltd, London
Printed in Great Britain by St. Edmundsbury
Press, Bury St. Edmunds, Suffolk

This book is dedicated to

Jane

for all her support and faith

Contents

1

Hollywood 'Hit'

A black Cadillac quietly pulled up along Linden Drive, its lights and engine already switched off even before the car came to a halt, drawing up alongside the car that belonged to Al Smiley.

Smiley was Benny Siegel's good friend and associate in the Los Angeles-based chapter of Lucky Luciano's Mafia-run syndicate. Siegel ran all of Luciano's operations – the drug peddling, the gambling, prostitution and the extortion of Hollywood studios; or, to be more precise, they used to be Luciano's operations. Benny 'Bugsy' Siegel had come to California under Luciano's instructions to counteract Al Capone's hold on Los Angeles, and now Siegel had taken the questionable decision to cut Luciano out altogether, not just in California but also across the Nevada border in Las Vegas.

Out of the Cadillac emerged a man with a 30-30 carbine in his hand. The street was deserted, and using the night to cloak him, the assassin dashed silently up to the Spanish-Moorish mansion and flattened himself against the wall. Keeping low, he made his way around the house, checking at windows for signs of life inside. Finally he came to the lounge window and, looking through it, he saw the back of Benny Siegel's well-groomed head. He was sitting on the sofa, reading a newspaper. At his side sat Al Smiley.

The assassin raised the rifle, fixing the target in his sights. His finger tightened on the trigger and suddenly the 30-30 blasted the window. Siegel never heard the blast, never saw the glass smashing; a bullet thudded into the back of his head. Still crouching, the assassin pumped eight more rounds into the room, a further two of them hitting his victim, while the others just blasted the room.

Wasting not a single second, the hit man stood up and ran straight back to his car, jumped in, roared the engine into life and sped away into the night.

It was 20 June 1947. Across the border in Nevada, events regarding Bugsy Siegel's last pay-off were to finish unfolding.

It was ten-fifty at night but at the Flamingo Hotel in Las Vegas the evening was only just beginning to liven up as the dice rolled, cards were dealt and the roulette wheels spun in the hotel's popular casino. It had been six months since Benny Siegel's Flamingo suffered its disastrous opening in December 1946. It had been such a failure that within its first week it had gone into the red, forcing Siegel to close it down at once. Following two months of reorganization and reinvestment, Siegel had reopened the Flamingo in March and was now making a healthy profit.

Much of its investment had come from underworld sources. They were furious that Siegel had made no effort to repay them. They were about to claim their share of the profits.

Three men, Gus Greenbaum, Moe Sedway and Morris Rosen, walked into the lobby and made their way towards the desk.

'On behalf of the hotel's Eastern stockholders,' announced Greenbaum to the desk clerk, 'we're taking over the management of the Flamingo.'

The clerk fought to find his tongue. 'But...but...the Flamingo is managed by Mr Benjamin Siegel.'

'The Flamingo *was* managed by Siegel,' Greenbaum corrected him. 'You're all working for me now.'

Back on Linden Drive, Al Smiley picked up the phone and called Cary Grant, one of Siegel's closest friends. Grant expressed his devastation at the news; and gave his condolences, but couldn't guarantee he would be at the funeral. The fact was, he had no intention of turning up either to pay his last respects or to see his mobster friend buried.

Then Smiley called Howard Hughes, Siegel's silent partner in the Flamingo. Hughes, like Grant, chose not to pay his respects.

Siegel's brother-in-law, Chick, who had been upstairs with his girlfriend at the time Siegel was murdered, tried to get through to one of Benny's closest and most loyal film star friends, but George Raft was out.

George Raft, the movie star, screen gangster and highly publicized friend of Benny Siegel's, was distraught at the news reverberating around Los Angeles. But, like many movie moguls who had handed over thousands of dollars to Siegel, he was not totally surprised. Siegel had played too many dangerous games, although there must have been few who, like Raft, had known just how deeply in trouble with the Syndicate Bugsy had got himself.

Raft had first heard the news while playing bridge at a swank Hollywood club. Soon afterwards he drove over to Linden Drive. Police and photographers were all over the grounds of the mansion where Siegel lay dead.

On his car radio, Raft listened to the newscaster making further announcements about the fantastic gangland killing. Raft barely heard all the details beneath the continual wail of sirens, but some words came through: '...shot several times through the back of the head...half his face blown away...Benjamin 'Bugsy' Siegel, murdered by person or persons unknown...'

Raft turned off the radio and drove home. He'd hardly had time to remove his coat when the doorbell rang. He answered it and found two men from the District Attorney's office.

'We'd like to ask you some questions about the murder of Benny Siegel.'

'I don't know anything,' Raft replied blandly.

'Can we come in?'

'Sure,' said Raft and led them inside.

'When did you last see the victim, Mr Raft?'

'The last time I saw Benny was this morning,' he told them. 'I was having breakfast. He told me he hadn't slept for days. He looked pretty awful. He said he was having a lot of trouble with the hotel and the investors from the East Coast. He wanted me to have dinner with him tonight at Jack's at the Beach. He said he had something to tell me. But I couldn't make it; I had a meeting with a producer, Sam Bischoff, to discuss a three-picture deal we were putting together. The meeting finished about nine.

'I knew Benny probably wouldn't be home till maybe eleven o'clock, so I figured I could get in a few games of bridge at the club. It was around ten-thirty or so when this actor, Dewey Roberts, comes bursting into the room all excited and he says to me, "Did you hear? It just came over the radio. Benny Siegel got killed in his house." That's all I know.'

In Paris, actress Virginia Hill fainted at the news of Benny's death. There were rumours that she was overseas because of a row she had had with Siegel, and when she declined to return home, it added fuel to the fire.

One thing she was now very careful about was preserving her true identity. She didn't want the police knowing of her underworld activities, and she certainly didn't want it made public knowledge that she was in fact secretly married to the Jewish Don of Hollywood.

The power that Luciano, enthroned in Cuba away from Italian and American authorities, had wielded over the motion picture industry died with Bugsy Siegel. Since Luciano and Al Capone had first begun their power struggle over the film business more than fifteen years earlier as a climax to their battle to control the whole nation, the fight had always promised to culminate in a bloodbath on the streets of Los Angeles. All Hollywood connections forged over years of violence had come to a sudden end in a way more bloody and terrifying than any Hollywood gangster movie could ever have hoped to portray.

2

Escape from the Ghettos

James Cagney settled uncomfortably into his studio chair. He was eighty-one and making his comeback in *Ragtime* in 1980. It had been more than four decades since his early screen triumphs in the best of Warner Bros gangster films like *Public Enemy*, *Angels With Dirty Faces* and *The Roaring Twenties*.

He pointed a stubby finger at me and said, 'There were only three ways a kid from my neighbourhood could get ahead. You could become a prize-fighter, go into show business or go into crime.'

Cagney could have chosen any one of the three, for he was blessed with amazing co-ordination, and he learned how to fight; he often had to with so many tough individuals and gangs roaming the streets. He could have been a champion prize-fighter had he chosen that route. Or he could have been a prime punk, ripe for a life of crime. But his co-ordination allowed him to learn how to dance – and it was dancing that he came to love, giving him the drive and ambition to crawl his way out of the tough ghettos of New York where he had been born in 1899. By 1914, Cagney was performing in the legitimate theatre, appearing as a female impersonator in *Every Sailor*.

But his background was one that could easily have tipped the scales the other way, and if he hadn't had the breaks, he might well have gone the way of others that he knew. Like Peter Hessling, known to his friends as Bootah. 'A lot of the kids from the streets had brushes with the law,' Cagney recalled, 'but usually for minor offences. But Bootah went too far.'

Bootah ended up in jail more than once. Jimmy used to play baseball with a local team called the Nut Club. One day the Mutual Welfare League of Sing Sing Prison invited the Nut Club to play against its inmates.

Taking his place behind the homeplate on the prison grounds at Ossining while the pitcher warmed up, Cagney suddenly heard a voice calling, 'Hello, Red.' Having been told that under no circumstances should any of the boys speak with the convicts, Cagney ignored the call which he figured had to be directed at him because of his red hair.

'What's wrong, Red, getting stuck up?'

Cagney couldn't ignore that remark and turned to see Bootah. He'd ended up inside for wounding a cop in a stick-up and was now caught up in an inevitable spiral into the depths of crime that were almost impossible for a kid like him to crawl out of.

'Some years later, about 1927,' said Cagney, 'he committed the *ultimate* act. He was pulling a stick-up when a cop came round the corner. Now, this cop's wife had taken sick, see, and so the cop had been excused from his shift so he could go home and look after their four kids. He was on his way home when he came round the corner and came upon Bootah holding a gun on some guy. Bootah swung around and *Bang*! He shot the cop dead. He went to the electric chair.'

According to Cagney, Bootah was not a 'terribly wicked young man, but a victim of his own environment'. He explained, 'Of all the kids I knew who got into trouble, Bootah was the only one I felt any real sympathy for. I always found him a quiet, reasonable, decent human being.

'As a kid Bootah and his family either starved or found ways to get food. I remember seeing him one day while I was standing in front of the church waiting for communion. He came by carrying a basket and when I asked him where he was going, he said, "I'm on my way to see the priest because my family doesn't have any food, so the priest can't refuse me."

He went up to the priest's house and came back a few minutes later. I said, "How'd you make out?" He said, "The priest wouldn't give me nothing."'

It was from this kind of background that a good many of the leading mobsters came. There was, for instance, Lepke Louis Buchalter, who was to have considerable involvement in what would become known as the 'Hollywood Shakedown' in years to come. He was of Cagney's generation, born in 1897. When he was thirteen his father died and, while his mother tried to exist on charity from her relatives, Lepke took to committing petty theft.

In 1915 he was picked up for burglary, sent to the Cheshire Reformatory for an indefinite term, and was paroled. He jumped parole and, at the age of nineteen, was sent to Sing Sing for a year for various burglaries. By the time he came out, having been dubbed 'Judge Louis' by the inmates, he was prepared for bigger and even more nefarious activities, graduating his way to leadership of the Amalgamated Clothing Workers Union and, later, to being a valued member of the official Syndicate 'hit' machine, dubbed Murder Inc. by the press.

Tony Curtis, himself a native New Yorker with a background of poverty and deprivation, but of a generation later than the likes of Lepke and Cagney, developed an understanding for and an empathy with 'Judge Louis' Lepke when he researched his life to portray the mobster in the 1974 movie *Lepke*. 'He was a victim of the environment and establishment of the period,' Curtis told me. 'But look what he created. A murder force of two hundred men. When he pushed people out of windows, stuck 'em full of ice-picks, did ya see the cops running up and taking him? No way. They were on the payroll. That's how Lepke took care of business. *Put 'em on the payroll or bump 'em off.* He was a brilliant man, powerful, who had to take all of his genius and turn it into something foul and degrading, for he had to take a life in order to make his point. He had to kill to survive.

'The only area open if he was impatient and saw no other way out of his ghetto was crime.'

It was going into movies that saved Curtis, as it had Cagney. It also gave some redemption to George Raft although he originally chose the first route, as outlined by Cagney, which was the ring.

Raft was born in 1895 and brought up in Hell's Kitchen where, as a boy, he had to learn to take care of himself on the New York streets. He capitalized on his ability with his fists by becoming a professional boxer at the age of sixteen. He won his first fight but succeeded in getting knocked out seven times during his seventeen bouts. His last fight resulted in him having a broken nose, two black eyes, a puffed-up jaw, and a torn ear which required 22 stitches – and all he got paid for his cuts, breaks and bruises was $5. So he turned to pool hustling.

After a particularly profitable evening, Raft would go with his pool hustling partner Billy Rosenberg to celebrate at Lindy's, a fancy delicatessen between 49th and 50th Streets, which was frequented by Broadway stars. It was also a popular hangout for gangsters. Journalist Mark Hellinger, later to become a film producer of tough gangster pictures, rubbed shoulders there with various big-time hoods such as Arnold Rothstein and Waxey Gordon. When Hellinger began writing and producing films, he based many of his characters on the people he knew.

When Billy Rosenberg decided to quit pool hustling and earn an honest dollar as a song writer (later writing such classics as 'Me and My Shadow' and 'It's Only a Paper Moon'), Raft, with a talent for dancing, headed for the ballrooms.

He entered an all-round championship dance competition held at St Nicholas Garden on 66th Street when he was seventeen. Women in the audience, even those twice his age, were excited by his olive skin, his jet-black hair and black suit with flared trousers. A sharp, black derby rested casually over one eye. The moment the spotlight hit him, the visual impact earned him a tremendous ovation from the audience. He mesmerized the audience as his feet moved so fast that the orchestra had trouble keeping up with him.

When the dance finished, he took a bow and then went into a perfect impersonation of Joe Fresco, the creator of the jazz dance, chewing on a cigar Fresco fashion. When the number finished, the audience rose in rapturous applause and there was no argument among the judges about awarding him the first prize.

Triumphs like this ignited an ambition to become a professional dancer. He was on his way to escaping his own particular ghetto, and eventually he would become a movie star. But along the way he was side-tracked by his friendship with one Owney Madden who would lure him sideways into criminal activity. George Raft was the one major movie star who was a gangster both on and off screen.

Owney Madden was born in England and went to America at the age of eleven. He immediately took to the streets of New York with the Gopher Gang, battling opposing gangs such as the Hudson 'Dusters' and the Five Points Gang for control of neighbourhoods and the exclusive right to commit crimes there. The ensuing pitched street battles were very often too violent for the police to break up, although it was common for gangs to pay off the cops to keep away from street battles, or even to turn a blind eye when shops were burgled.

Madden graduated to become leader of the feared Gopher Gang and he thereafter became a target for other hoods. On 6 November 1912, a dance was under way at 52nd Street. Madden walked in and, like a scene from a movie, the band instantly stopped playing. Madden was feared and respected, and he savoured the moment, standing smiling for several seconds. Then he waved a hand for the band to continue.

'Have your fun,' he announced to all. 'I won't bump off anybody here tonight.'

The band played on and Madden found himself a table on a balcony overlooking the dance floor. A girl approached him, won herself an invitation to sit down, and proceeded to engage Madden who relaxed in her company.

Before he realized what was happening, eleven men had surrounded him. He remained perfectly fearless, stood up and said defiantly, 'Come on, you guys, who did *you* ever bump off?'

A gun blazed, and Madden went down with six bullets in him. He was rushed to hospital and saved by immediate surgery. He'd come close to death, yet when the cops questioned him, he told them, 'It's nobody's business but mine who put these slugs in me.' The underworld had a tradition: you never blabbed to the cops. The Sicilian Mafia have a word for it – *Omerta*, a code of silence.

He continued frequenting dance halls, and it was in such a place that his path crossed that of George Raft, to whom men like Madden were heroes; they were survivors in a competitive world who proved to be as successful as any tycoon or businessman. Such men were considered as important as any show business celebrity or politician.

'I'm having dinner at Delmonico's tomorrow,' Madden told Raft. 'Join me and my friends.'

Raft accepted with pride and the next day found himself sitting in the elegant restaurant with a group of men whose company excited him. 'This is my pal Al Brown,' Madden told Raft, indicating one of his guests. 'Al, this is George Raft. He's a dancer. And he's brilliant. He's also a good friend of mine.'

'I'll have to make a point of watching you perform,' said Brown who would later become infamous as Al Capone.

Raft got to know many leading mobsters this way. Many of them took to inviting him to eat with them or play cards at their tables, and he could include Salvatore Lucania, later to be called Charlie 'Lucky' Luciano, Meyer Lansky and the young and eager Benjamin 'Bugsy' Siegel among his circle of underworld friends. He enjoyed their company, conversing with them on subjects close to all their hearts, such as sport, gambling and sex.

Most of all Raft idolized Madden and was keen to become a member of his gang, but in those pre-Prohibition days there was little work for him, who, while he was eager, was not desperate to get in too far over his head. Madden could be ruthless, as was his army of gangsters, and Raft just didn't have it in him to become what the Mafia would term a 'made man' – someone who had killed as a matter of duty.

No other underworld figure – not even Benny Siegel in years to come – had such an influence on Raft.

'I love this way of life,' Madden told Raft. 'I'm a big shot to everyone. Even to politicians, like Jimmy Hines. I'm good for Jimmy because I can do things for him, and he's good for me because I can benefit from his success. Maybe you'll be a star one day, and if you are, we can be good for each other, George. But in this business, you gotta watch out for the guy who wants to take over, and then I ain't so nice.' As Patsy Doyle was to discover.

Patsy Doyle was having a quiet drink in a Hell's Kitchen bar when in from the snow and the freezing night stepped Willie 'the Sailor' Mott. He was a petty thug and small-time gangster ready and willing to take on any task for the right price. He caught sight of Doyle who was one step above thugs like Willie. But *only* one step. He was also a member of Madden's notorious Gopher Gang.

Mott wandered over to Doyle's table and offered to buy him a drink. Doyle accepted and, as the evening wore on, he began shooting off his mouth about how he was going to take over from Madden.

Two men sat drinking at the bar, listening intently to Doyle's conversation. One of them left his bar stool, went over to Doyle and said, 'Me and and my pal would like to buy you a drink.'

'Why is it everyone wants to buy me a drink tonight? If it ain't one two-bit punk, it's another.' Doyle glanced over at the other stranger seated at the bar. 'Small-time nobodies, huh?'

'That's what we want to talk to you about. You see, we want to move into the big time.'

Doyle stood up. 'Stay here, Willie. I won't be long,' he said and stepped over the bar.

The other stranger got off his stool, dug his hands deep into the pockets of his coat and said, 'We got something for you – from Owney.' He whipped out a pistol and pumped three bullets into Doyle's chest. The other stranger also had a gun and simultaneously fired three shots. Doyle twisted and fell heavily against the bar.

Mott had dived under the table and watched as the two gunmen pocketed their guns and walked hurriedly out of the saloon. Mott crawled out and went over to Doyle who was slumped forward over the bar. Mott turned him over and discovered he was still breathing. A red puddle had quickly formed on the bar.

Doyle suddenly lurched forward, taking several steps and falling against the door. It swung open and he staggered outside. Women screamed and people hurried out of his way as he fell dead, splattering the snow with blood.

No one might have connected Owney Madden with the murder if he had not dumped a girlfriend who, out for revenge, sang to the police. He was charged with first-degree murder.

Witnesses who had initially testified against him, however, found themselves persuaded to claim in court that they had lied, insisting that Madden had nothing to do with the murder. But there was still enough evidence to convince the jury that he had set up the killing and they found him guilty of manslaughter. Sentenced to serve from ten to twenty years in Sing Sing, he earned himself the nickname 'Owney the Killer'.

George Raft visited Owney the Killer in the penitentiary several times. Although Raft didn't know it at the time, these visits to the pen were to prove more than useful later, when he was to draw on them to portray convicts in gangster films like *Each Dawn I Die*. More than that, though, he would later find out exactly what it was like to be a gangster on the streets of New York during Prohibition, for while inside Madden told him, 'You're a good guy, George. When I get outa here, I'll put some work your way.' It was invaluable experience to him as an actor.

While he waited for Madden to be in a position to keep his word, Raft went to work, during 1912, in discreet cafés, or 'tea rooms', where tea was the last thing on the minds of the frustrated housewives who frequented them. During the afternoons he worked at Churchill's where, dressed in a tight suit with his black hair slicked down with Vaseline, he danced with women who paid him two dollars a time. He made more money later in the privacy of their homes.

After Churchill's, he went to the Sunken Galleries to dance with and fondle women for money until 5.30. He got into what he called 'a happy rut', dancing by day, getting laid by night, all of it paying his rent.

Unlike Cagney, or Curtis years later, George Raft embraced the seedier, more nefarious side of life. His eventual move to Hollywood was all part of Owney Madden's plan and if it had not been for his gradual emergence into show business, there is no knowing exactly how he would have turned out. No doubt he would have continued to dance and might even have become a great star on Broadway. But had he remained in New York he would never have been able to escape the influence of the likes of Al Capone, Lucky Luciano, Bugsy Siegel and Meyer Lansky; four of the most notorious names in criminal history.

Even in Hollywood he was unable to entirely avoid the activities of his four friends who were not only to shape the underworld into an organized syndicate but who were the brains, and the brawn, behind the Hollywood connection.

3

Young Hoods

In Italy at the turn of the century, several organizations made up the underworld – the Neapolitan Camorra, the Sicilian Mafia and the Calabrian Carbonari. Italian gangs were established in America along the same lines, although there were an increasing number of independent operations which embraced a broader ethnic membership. These criminal elements attracted the many truants who hung around on street corners. For them, the tough street life of the ghettos was their only diversion, and any kid with aspirations of becoming a big shot had every opportunity to do so. As it did for Alphonse Capone.

He was born in New York on 17 January 1899, the son of Gabriel and Teresa Capone who had escaped the slums of Naples, Italy, for the slums of New York City. The Capone family lived in a tenement block on Navy Street in Brooklyn, the centre of the biggest Italian ghetto in the city. Gabriel Capone was a barber and only slightly better off than the usually illiterate immigrants, many of whom learned they could turn a quick buck by being in service to the underworld.

In 1907 the Capones moved to 38 Garfield Place, which was in a neighbourhood where young thug Johnny Torrio was prominent. His so-called social club, 'The John Torrio Association', was an induction centre where youngsters like Al Capone were drawn into underworld activities.

Capone was no dumb kid. At school he maintained a B average up to sixth grade. But he fell behind as his truancy increased. During his second year in the 6th grade, he punched a female teacher and received a beating from the principal for it. That day Capone left school and never went back.

He took a job in a candy store, then became a pin setter in a bowling alley, and for a while he was a paper and cloth cutter in a bindery. During his free time he bullied school-children and extorted their lunch money. Before long he met Torrio who introduced him into the notoriously violent Five Pointers Gang which roamed Manhattan's Lower East Side.

The Five Pointers was run by Paolo Antonini Vacarelli, known as Paul Kelly, who used his New Brighton Dance Hall in Manhattan's Great Jones Street as his headquarters. He commanded some 1,500 Five Pointer thugs and offered a number of services. The size of the job was reflected in the fee: $2 for punching, $4 for both eyes blackened, $10 for nose and jaw broken, $15 for a knock-out, $19 for a broken arm or leg, $25 for a shot in the leg, $25 for a stabbing, and $100 for 'the big job'. Kelly enjoyed protection from the corrupt officials of Tammany Hall in exchange for the enforcement of votes at election time.

In one of the many cellar clubs used by young hoods, Capone, calling himself Al Brown, met a tall Irish girl named Mae Coughlin. As a rule, the Italian and Irish communities didn't mix. Italian boys knew it was expected of them to find a wife early in life, while the Irish boys preferred to wait until they were settled in their occupations. So marriage-eager Irish girls were attracted to the Italians and within weeks of meeting, Al and Mae were married, on 18 May 1918.

The following year Mae gave birth to their first and only child, Albert Francis Capone, affectionately known as Sonny. The boy's godfather was Johnny Torrio.

During Capone's days as a Five Pointer, something happened that would have repercussions which were felt all the way to Hollywood more than a decade later. It was an incident that proved to be the catalyst for the hatred between

Capone and fellow gang member Salvatore Lucania, later to be known as Charles 'Lucky' Luciano.

Salvatore Lucania hurried along with a hat box in his hand. It was the spring of 1916, he was nineteen and he worked for the Goodman Hat Company, a women's haberdasher owned by Max Goodman who had taken it upon himself to take this young Sicilian under his wing. Salvatore was nine when he left the sulphur-mining town of Lercara Friddi in Sicily to come to America with his family in 1906 expecting, as did most European immigrants, to find the streets paved with gold. Instead, they found the streets teeming with pushcarts and people.

Their neighbourhood on Manhattan's Lower East Side was a melting pot of Sicilians, Calabrians, Irish and Jews, all suffering as much, if not more, deprivation and poverty than they had experienced in their homelands. Salvatore learned to speak broken English and began organizing his own gang, pooling all their profits so that each member had equal shares. When he wasn't playing truant, he noticed that some of the smartest kids in his class were either Jews or mainland Italians. Consequently, he sought associations with Jews and Italians, as well as Sicilians, meeting with them at the Victoria Movie Theater which was a neutral zone for gangs. One such Italian hoodlum he befriended was Francesco Castiglia, and their friendship was to last a lifetime. Castiglia would later emerge as Frank Costello.

On his way to deliver the hat, Salvatore had one other customer waiting, but not for any kind of headwear. This extra delivery had been supplied by George Scanlon, the pioneer of the gutter business of drug trafficking. Scanlon hand-picked his errand boys after observing them in gang wars, pushcart raids and all the other street activities that made a kid rise in the esteem of his peers.

Lucania was just the kind of kid Scanlon had been looking for. He had approached Salvatore and said, 'How'd you like to make a few bucks runnin' errands for me?'

'What kind of errands?' Salvatore asked in his broken English mixed with his acquired New York accent.

'Just deliverin' my stuff.'

Lucania knew that 'stuff' meant anything from dope to heroin. And when Scanlon told him there would be ten, maybe twenty dollars a day in it for him, he accepted the offer.

Salvatore was to run many such errands for Scanlon, and carrying hat boxes for legitimate customers made for a good cover. He arrived at the first stop-off point which was a bar. The customer, a man, smiled as Salvatore took from the hat box a vial of heroin and passed it to him. Then Salvatore held out his hand.

'You pay now, mister,' said Salvatore.

'What's the hurry, kid?' asked the man.

'Got a delivery to make,' replied Salvatore, patting the hat box.

'You're not going anywhere, kid,' said the customer. 'You're under arrest.' To Salvatore's horror, the customer produced a badge that identified him as a Federal agent.

And so it was that, on 26 June 1916, Salvatore Lucania was sentenced to a year at the New Hampshire Farms Correctional Institute, where he was visited by a distraught Mr Goodman. He was bitterly disappointed in Salvatore.

'I thought you were different from the other kids,' he berated Salvatore. 'That's why I gave you the job. Three years you've worked for me, and what do I find? That you've been moonlighting for this drug peddler. I really thought you had it in you to make something of yourself.'

'I have, Mr Goodman,' said Salvatore with deep sincerity. 'You wait and see. I'll be outa here in no time. I'm gonna be a model prisoner.'

'I'm glad to hear you say that,' said Mr Goodman.

Salvatore was as good as his word and was released after serving six months. He'd learned a great deal in prison, and it had nothing to do with selling hats. He'd already gained an education from local thieves and loan sharks in how to escape from his own particular ghetto, and, not surprisingly, he had turned to petty theft. His education was furthered by the loan sharks, the drug peddlers, the gang leaders and the all-round punks he met inside.

On the outside once more, he promptly returned to his criminal ways, forcing his exasperated father to throw him out of the house. He did make one significant change in his life. He hated the name Salvatore – he felt its diminutive, the familiar 'Sal', was a girl's name. He took on a new name, Charlie Lucania.

He also joined the Five Pointers, and there he met Al Capone. They hated each other from first sight, not least because of the centuries-old hatred between Sicilians and Neapolitans.

One summer afternoon they were patrolling a neighbourhood, seeking out rival gangs when they saw two boys from another mob running down an alley. Lucania and Capone gave chase, caught them and, drawing their knives, engaged in a bloody fight. The two rival thugs dropped dead, their throats cut.

Capone was arrested and charged with murder but claimed that it was Lucania who had done the killings, insisting he was happy simply to enjoy a good fight. He claimed that Lucania came up behind each of the boys and slashed their throats. The police did not believe his story.

He swore vengeance upon Lucania; it was a vendetta that would later be fought on the streets of Hollywood.

Capone managed to escape conviction when he realized that the police were not so much interested in throwing him in prison as they were in being paid off. He bought his way out and learned the lesson that he taught others; that anyone can be corrupted and that anything can be fixed for a price.

Meanwhile, Lucania's eligibility for membership into the Mafia, as a son of Sicily, had been noted, and under the auspices of Giuseppe (Joe) Masseria he was introduced into the 'Family'. Lucania, now truly 'connected', was ready to begin his rise to become the Mafia Boss of Bosses, whose final triumph was to take over Hollywood.

Meyer Lansky was born and bred in New York's East Side in a ghetto of ugly tenements that were adorned with miles of washing lines. Like Charlie Lucania, he had learned how to overcome the frustrations of poverty by emulating the local crooks. But unlike Lucania, and a lot of other hoods, Lansky was a somewhat quiet and generally intelligent young man. His younger friend, though, was a small thug; Benjamin Siegel, a good-looking Jewish kid born in 1905 who, at the age of twelve, vaunted his flashing teeth and beautiful baby-blue eyes.

He also had an appealing charm about him which belied an undercurrent of sexual chemistry and violence. Teenage girls were attracted to him and he responded, despite his young years, by trying to kiss and penetrate them. Any girl who resisted his advances aroused his violent temper; he simply raped her. It was a case of be nice or pay the consequences. It was a general principle that he practised when he became the crime lord of Hollywood.

On Jewish holidays the righteous and orthodox Jews locked up their shops and Hebrew stores and flooded into the streets, heading for the local synagogues. Groups of bearded men in black suits, black hats and white prayer shawls gathered on street corners to greet each other, while boys in skull-caps danced along the gutters, cutting through the steam rising from the drains. Once they were all in the temple and the streets were deserted, Benny Siegel came roaming, picking out which store he'd break into this time, ensuring that some honest Jewish store keeper would return when the holiday was over to discover his premises damaged and many of his goods stolen.

Hardly more than twenty years later, deprived New York kids would still be following the same lifestyle, as Tony Curtis told me. 'There were two or three street gangs and I was quite involved in it all, sure. We were a group of young boys

– about seven or eight of us – and we used to play havoc in our neighbourhood and steal cases of Coca-Cola, cigarettes, anything.

'We didn't steal so much because we needed money, because *everybody* was flat broke in those days. It was the excitement, because life was rather boring in the ghettos that we lived in. Our visions were really very limited. The fantasies and dreams we have now were nothing when we were kids. You really had no idea what the world was like, so you lived in these little ghettos and you needed something to distract you. A lot of us were unhappy in our home life – I wasn't particularly – but two or three of my chums were, so we did that sort of thing.

'Old ladies weren't the things we hit because old ladies where we lived woulda knocked you down. But there were candy stores who had their supply places out back where they used to put their cases of Coke, boxes of chewing gum and cigarettes.

'We'd get away with some of it, keep it in a certain place, and sometimes we'd get caught. We never went out with guns. I don't know if we woulda stepped up to that. But as Bugsy Siegel said, "We only kill each other," so when we were kids in New York we only used to really steal from each other. Once the big hauls were made, the gangs would try and knock off each other.'

Meyer Lansky had a much clearer vision than Benny Siegel of the bigger and better ways to make easy money. His ideas began to take shape when he and Benny met up with Charlie Lucania in 1917.

Charlie Lucania liked Jews. Few Italians, or Sicilians, did. Charlie admired their penchant for handling business. In Meyer Lansky he found the kind of Jew who could fulfil his ambitions, and in Benny Siegel he saw a tough but likeable kid. There was an immediate rapport between the three young hoods.

'I never want to become a crumb,' Charlie told the other two. To him anybody who worked legitimately for a living was a 'crumb'. 'You two wanna be crumbs, or you wanna be somebody in this world?'

Benny and Meyer were unanimous. 'We're gonna be somebody.' They were sworn everlasting friends and comrades. The embryo of what was to become the most powerful and organized criminal association ever had been formed. Within two years they had a gang of twenty members who terrorized East Harlem and Manhattan, robbing small banks, stores and warehouses. But despite these criminal activities, Charlie Lucania had a sense of honour and loyalty as far as his friends were concerned, and perhaps in his own mind he saw himself as a sort of Robin Hood. Not that he necessarily gave to the poor. But he didn't turn a blind eye to an elderly Sicilian widow in need or a beggar on a street corner.

Tony Curtis, as a young boy, knew hoods of this ilk. 'There was a guy called Herbie that I admired a lot. This was around 1933 when I was seven or eight years old. He was about eighteen, wore double-breasted suits and every now and then he'd come around the neighbourhood in a convertible. That used to blow everybody's mind, particularly if it was winter time because he'd have a topcoat on, his hat pulled down but still he'd come in the convertible with the top down.

'He was always nice with the kids around the neighbourhood. I had occasion two or three times to be in a house where he was in, and ya know, he always seemed to me like a gentleman. Never rough or crude. But there were all kinds of stories about him. He was quite a well-known character in the neighbourhood.'

Lansky and Siegal too had their gallant side. They had formed themselves into the infamous Bugs and Meyer Gang which they originally formed to protect Jewish kids from the Irish gangs. This was a service performed outside of their association with Lucania, but as greed later became their dominating motivation they changed their policy to ensure that their protection service was making profits.

Lucania's Italian pal, Francesco Castiglia – now calling himself Frank Costello – had joined the mob. He had been born in Calabria in 1891. He had four sisters and one older brother. His parents brought the family to America in 1896 and settled in East Harlem in New York, living, like most of the Italians who dominated the streets between Fifth and First Avenues, in a slum. Italian families struggled to survive. It was Costello's older brother, Eddy, who introduced young Frank to gang warfare.

Frank, unlike his thug of a brother, had a cunning criminal mind. When he was fourteen he broke his leg when he fell from a tree on his aunt's farm in Astoria. One night, with his leg in bandages, he got out of bed, got dressed and slipped out of the farmhouse. A week earlier he had heard his mother tell the landlady she had no money to pay the rent and the landlady had screamed back that she was two months behind and the family would find themselves out on the street.

Knowing that the landlady got up early every morning to clean the stairs and backhouses and that she always carried her money in her enormous bosom, Costello headed for home in East Harlem, limping his way to the 92nd Street ferry which took him across the East River. Half an hour later he was hiding out in the tenement block with a black handkerchief tied around his face.

He heard the landlady descending the stairs, and hid back in the shadows. At the first opportunity he threw himself at her, swung his arms round her neck, plunged a hand into her bosom, grabbed the money and hobbled away as fast as he could.

The landlady recognized him and rushed to his mother, screaming, 'Your son is a thief. He stole my money.'

Frank's mother screamed back, 'You're lying. My son is not here. He is with his aunt in Astoria.'

The landlady complained to the police, and some officers later drove out to the farm where they found the boy, his leg tightly bandaged, lying in bed.

It was his clever criminal brain that made him the perfect choice as chief executive officer of the 'Buy-Money Bank' run by Lucania, Lansky and Siegel. They also branched out into bookmaking and gambling. In time they would all have a finger in the Hollywood pie. Before all that, however, something happened that provided the likes of Lucania, Siegel, Costello and Lansky with greater profits; Congress passed the Volstead Act on 27 October 1919. On 20 January 1920 the Prohibition Amendment went into effect.

4

New York

Joe Adonis was a silent, suave and resourceful Italian who had settled in the South Brooklyn waterfront area where, as a youngster known as Jo Doto, he'd sought out the companionship of delinquent gangs and set about looting stores. As he rose in the esteem of his followers, he reverted to the name of Joe Adonis.

He was, it was said, the one crime lord who looked like the movie version of the Big Shot Mobster. He was handsome in a sinister way with his hair greying at the temples. When Humphrey Bogart once saw him, his immediate reaction was, 'That's the fellow I'd like to play in a movie.'

Adonis kept to the code of *Omerta*, working quietly and efficiently, raising no dust or fuss. When he needed to do any heavy thinking, he preferred not to be surrounded by others. He took few people into his confidence and concealed his activities under a shroud of secrecy. So when he came to see Charlie Luciano – people found Luciano easier to pronounce than Lucania – and his cohorts one day in 1920 with a proposition, it had to be important.

Their headquarters was a Tenth Street East Side apartment. Benny Siegel stood on guard outside, a cloth cap fitting snugly on his youthful head. He might only have been fifteen, but few came tougher than Benny. He had a temper that erupted in an instant, striking fear in men much older than himself. So they called him Bugsy, but never to his face. And he was never so called by his friends.

The Bugs and Meyer Gang, acting under the cover of an

auto-rental agency, had developed into a crack corps of gunmen. Siegel and Lansky supplied fast cars, skilled drivers and
expert gunmen to anyone willing to pay. Lansky was the executive and Siegel the field commander. They were a formidable team. Lansky liked to keep to the shadows. Siegel
– handsome, aggressive, ready for action – loved the spotlight. It was cheaper for Luciano and Costello to make them
partners rather than pay their fees, so now Lansky and Siegel
worked only with them.

Joe Adonis arrived, allowed Siegel to frisk him, and then
followed the young Jew in to see Luciano, Lansky and Costello. They all listened with cautious interest as Joe told them,
'Some local boy who made good – name of Al Capone – has
brought news from Chicago.'

The name of Al Capone sent revulsion through not only
Luciano but Frank Costello too. 'I hate that bum,' said Costello. 'I've always hated him.'

'What's the news?' asked Luciano.

'Bootlegging,' Adonis answered. 'They're running bootleg booze and people are buying it by the gallon. They're
raking in huge profits and it's giving them power like you can't
believe. Charlie, Benny, Frank, Meyer, I got a proposition.
Why don't we combine our forces to ship in booze? I got
control of the waterfront. You got the muscle.'

Competing with the Chicago mob appealed to the New
Yorkers. So Luciano and Adonis agreed on a deal that was to
make them all rich and break Luciano's gang into the bootlegging racket.

To many citizens, as well as the gangsters, bootlegging was
a victimless crime, a service that was welcome. Even some
police proved unscrupulous enough to be easily persuaded,
through pay-offs, to ignore Luciano's activities. Meyer
Lansky suggested a profitable and influential formula for
success in bootlegging; buy the best pure liquor and sell it at
premium prices to the highest social classes. That way they
made money and gained support from society people with
influence.

As the organization grew, each member began to specialize. Luciano was in a sense the overseer of the organization, handling recruitment and negotiating with other gangs. Meyer Lansky and Benny Siegel organized protection crews for the ships and vans transporting the liquor. Frank Costello dealt with gambling and pay-offs – or, as he preferred to call them, 'influence payments'. As for Joe Adonis, he raked in profits for the organization from various sources including loan-sharking and prostitution.

Other racketeers who joined the organization included Albert Anastasia, a ruthless killer who had only recently been released from Sing Sing. He became Luciano's 'enforcer'. Meyer Lansky brought in his Jewish friend Lepke Louis Buchalter whose protection racket in Manhattan's garment trade was used by the organization as a way of channelling bootleg liquor throughout the district. Frank Costello managed to form an alliance with the Bronx Beer King, Dutch Schultz. Two Big Shot racketeering partners in New Jersey, Abner 'Longie' Zwillman and Willie Moretti, also joined the organization.

There was another who came in with Luciano – Arnold Rothstein. This legendary gambler and son of a highly regarded Jewish family was quick to get in on the bootleg trade. He set up contacts in Scotland to deliver real Scotch to a point just off the New Jersey coast, beyond the US territorial boundary. He then made a deal with Irving Wexler, better known as Waxey Gordon, to arrange for the pickups by speedboat and subsequent distribution throughout America. Luciano had much the same deal going with Waxey Gordon, and it seemed only good business sense for all of them to co-operate.

One night in 1921, Charlie Luciano, wearing his customary camel-hair coat and grey fedora, stood at the corner of Sixth Avenue and 50th Street, waiting for a new girl in his life. A car pulled into the kerb and a bunch of men jumped out, grabbed him and hustled him into the car.

As the car moved off, the men began grinding their heels

into his face, arms and legs. Some hours later, Luciano was found, cut and bleeding, wandering along Hylan Boulevard in the Princess Bay section of Staten Island. Although Luciano and his close associates always firmly denied it, he was, according to initial reports, knife-wounded in several places, had his right eye closed, his wrist slashed and a face muscle cut. Word quickly spread that Luciano had been hacked at by gangsters with ice-picks and hung by the thumbs.

However, Frank Costello told his attorney, George Wolf, who from time to time also represented Luciano, that the attackers were cops. They were trying to force him to reveal the whereabouts of the gangster Jack 'Legs' Diamond. Luciano was not overfond of Legs Diamond, but apparently the fugitive was hiding out at Luciano's place and Luciano intended to keep his whereabouts a secret. That was Costello's version.

There is another 'cop' theory that claims the police were 'making a point' on behalf of a New York detective whose young daughter had been the subject of Luciano's advances, and since Luciano had failed to take the initial warning, he was now taking the consequences.

Whatever the real truth and whoever the attackers were, everyone, including his pals Benny, Meyer and Frank, agreed that to 'go for a ride' and return alive, he had to be incredibly lucky. So he became known as Lucky Luciano. For the rest of his life, he scowled at newspapermen who called him Lucky. He hated the name. Costello told George Wolf, 'I never heard nobody call him Lucky, not even behind his back.' To his friends he remained, always, Charlie.

To complement his growing success, he wanted to emanate class, and so Rothstein taught him dress sense as well as etiquette. It was Rothstein who was the inspiration of many of Damon Runyon's stories. He was a man who'd bet on anything at all, for anything from ten to ten thousand dollars. In 1919 he won several hundred thousand dollars gambling on the World Series when the Cincinnati Reds beat the Chicago Black Sox. However, an investigation determined that eight members of the Chicago Black Sox received $100,000 to throw the game. Although he was never proven to be the pay-off man, Rothstein was widely believed to have fixed the game.

When he ran an illegal crap game, the players were likely to include Luciano, Al Capone (but not when Luciano was present), Waxey Gordon, Bugsy Siegel and George Raft. At that time, Raft's prominence and reputation as a dancer on Broadway was growing along with his billing. Stanley Burns, a one-time acrobatic dancer and now a showbiz entrepreneur, caught George's act and booked him to dance with Elsie Pilcer and Dudley Douglas at the Orpheum and on the B.F. Keith Circuits. Raft travelled with Pilcer and Douglas from coast to coast, establishing himself as a star; and after the tour he had no problem getting bookings in top Broadway clubs.

Through his association with Owney Madden, Raft was a favourite entertainer among gangsters. They came to watch him dance, and it always pleased him when a mobster such as Luciano or Siegel patted him on the back and said, 'You're an OK guy, George. Join me for drink.' Raft would sit down, order a fruit juice and engage in small talk, or so he always claimed. For most of his life, Raft never admitted just how involved he was with the underworld. But he did admit it to his friends, like James Cagney. In his autobiography, Cagney wrote how, during the making of the film *Each Dawn I Die*, Raft told him that 'when he was working for the clubs, he was really working for the Mob – capital M'.

When Raft joined in one of Rothstein's crap games, he was certainly no stranger to the Big Shots at the table. A round-up by police of these gamblers would have resulted in half the underworld losing its leadership. So Rothstein paid policemen to tip him off in advance of any raids. But it was only the Big Shots who would get the word to vanish out the back. Other players were rounded up and arrested, including George Raft who on one occasion was hauled off to the local precinct. He gave the police a false name, but as someone somewhere was pulling the right strings, the charges against him were dropped.

Rothstein came to operate a legitimate casino in association with Luciano, the Partridge Club in New York, as well as casinos on Long Island and in Saratoga. He was the gambling king of Broadway, indulging in drug trafficking on the side. The end for him came in 1928 following a two-day marathon poker game in which he lost vast sums to racketeer George McManus. With no ready cash at hand, Rothstein promised to pay McManus but made the serious mistake of welshing on the debt. McManus met with Rothstein at the Park Central Hotel and shot him. Rothstein died later in hospital but, true to the code of *Omerta*, he didn't name McManus as his killer.

Benny Siegel stood by a Ford truck, checking his pistol and machine-gun. Men in Luciano's employ loaded the truck with 'hams', large burlap bags lined with straw into which bottles of Scotch were packed.

Tony Renni walked with Costello to the truck, saw Siegel climb into the front of the truck, and stopped. Renni had ridden as an armed guard on numerous liquor runs, and knew what it was to run into trouble. Three times he had been the victim of hijackings from rival gangs. The first time, he'd been lucky to be left alive and tied up along with the other guards while the hijackers got away with their prize. The second time, he failed to stop the hijacking when he was shot in the arm. The third time, he and the other guards succeeded in fighting them off. His distraught wife begged him not to accept any more protection jobs; she told him 'You'll get killed, Tony. it only needs to be just a single bullet, just one more job. Give it up, *please*.'

'Look, honey, I'm earning five hundred dollars a time from Luciano and Costello,' he told her, and left for work.

Now, seeing the young kid they called Bugsy, he felt insecure. He knew the kid had a reputation for being tough, but could he handle this kind of a job? Renni clearly didn't know

Siegel personally. It was just that the 'Bug' was only nineteen, too young for Renni's liking. He grumbled to Costello, 'He's just a kid. And a touch crazy too, I hear.'

'If you run into trouble,' said Costello, 'you'll be glad Benny's on your side. You have nothing to worry about.'

Renni wasn't convinced. He climbed in the back of the truck, clutching his pistol and machine-gun. Costello leaned against the front of the truck, talking to Siegel. 'Don't forget, if there's any trouble, fire the flare gun. I got men planted along the road to Hoboken who'll come to your aid. And don't worry about the police. There won't be a patrol car on that road tonight. I made sure of that.'

Siegel was riding shotgun. The driver climbed in and turned on the ignition, and the Ford rumbled off into the night towards Hoboken. Siegel glared into the darkness ahead, showing no sign of nerves at all. He was in his element, looking for action and ready for it if it came. He cradled the pistol on his lap while the machine-gun lay at his feet.

They hadn't travelled very far when Siegel saw the vague outline of a car ahead, parked across the road.

'Roadblock!' yelled Siegel. The driver slammed on the brakes, bringing the heavy truck skidding half-way around as it came to a halt. 'Back it up!' Siegel shouted. He didn't wait for the driver to get the car into reverse before grabbing his machine-gun, throwing open the door, diving out onto the road and racing into the woods.

The hijackers opened fire with machine-guns. Before the driver could slam the gears into reverse, the truck was peppered with bullets, several of them slamming into the driver's forehead, jerking him back lifeless into his seat.

Renni kicked the back door open and leapt out, the flare gun in his hand. Keeping low, he ran towards the trees and had almost made it when a flashlight lit him up, allowing a burst of machine-gun fire to concentrate on him. He fell forward, sprawling on the road, dropping the flare gun and groaning in agony. The flare gun lay beyond his reach.

Siegel scrambled among the trees, and stopped to catch

sight of Renni laying in the road, and the flare gun a few yards from him. Men moved silently through the woods. Siegel froze and lifted the machine-gun. He aimed towards the flashlight and fired. There was a shriek of pain and terror and the flashlight dropped to the ground.

'Switch off those fucking torches,' someone yelled, and all the lights suddenly went out.

Siegel quickly shifted to one side as machine-gun fire tore into the ground where he'd just stood. He slipped through the trees and came to the road side. The flare gun still lay there. He sprang towards it, scooped it up and disappeared into the bushes beyond just as machine-gun fire ripped up the road.

Gasping for breath, he lifted the flare gun and pulled the trigger. Nothing happened. He tried again. This time a flare shot up into the sky, lighting up the whole area so that he clearly saw one of the hijackers coming up on him from behind, trying to hide behind a tree as the sudden light took him by surprise. Siegel aimed and fired, cutting the man down with a shower of bullets.

The woods suddenly became alive with machine-gun fire, spitting bullets as Siegel threw himself to the ground. He returned fire, spraying a whole area with his machine-gun, knowing that any moment someone would be upon him and that would be that.

Just then, Siegel saw headlights approaching and hoped it was a car full of Costello's men. It ground to a halt fifty feet up the road. Startled for a moment by the arrival of the car, the hijackers allowed a moment's ceasefire, giving Siegel all the time he needed to scramble to his feet and run through the woods towards the car. He reached it and swung open the door to discover, not a crew of armed men, but a terrified old man.

Some of the hijackers, thinking reinforcements for the other side had arrived, ran for the truck, the rest heading for their car. It looked now as though they would certainly escape with the liquor. With a blast of his gun, Siegel brought down one of the guys running towards the truck which lurched forward and began pulling away. Siegel brought it to an abrupt halt by shooting out the right rear tyre.

Then he looked inside the car at the old man and coolly shot him dead. He jumped in, pushed the body aside, took the wheel and sped towards the truck, careering around it, almost driving into the woods, and headed straight at the hijackers' car. He rammed the front end of it, sending it half spinning across the road and turning over onto its side.

The impact made Siegel's chest slam against the wheel, but despite the pain he was out of the car in an instant, training the machine-gun on the four men who clambered out of the overturned car.

At that moment further headlights appeared and a car approached. It screeched to a halt, and an armed crew jumped out. They were Costello's men.

One by one the problems were dealt with. The hijackers were promptly disposed of. The burst tyre on the truck was replaced. And Tony Renni was attended to. He was lucky to be alive. And he knew now that Frank Costello had been right about Siegel. Renni much later told George Wolf that he always treated Siegel with respect following that.

Not surprisingly, when Lucky Luciano was later to organize an élite assassination squad, known as Murder Inc., he would include Bugsy Siegel as one of the prime hit men.

Dabbling on the outskirts of the underworld, George Raft continued to visit Owney Madden in the pen, consolidating a long-lasting friendship. In time Madden would do Raft favours, and Raft would return in kind. But for the most part Raft was concerned with his rising career, and while many men of his age were married, he considered that marriage meant a time-consuming lifestyle he couldn't afford.

He had all the women he needed for countless one-night stands. However, there was one girl who especially appealed to him. Grayce Mulrooney was one of his ballroom partners and, unlike all the other women who threw themselves at him, she was a devout Catholic who came from a fine family.

Her mother was a probation officer, and her uncle was a ranking police officer who later, under Mayor Jimmy Walker, became the Police Commissioner of New York City. There was something about her that he liked, and he began dating her. But he never slept with her.

Grayce had become a social worker on Welfare Island and was usually unable to go on tour with Raft. But when he told her he was to tour the Keith Vaudeville Circuit with Pilcer and Douglas and would be gone for almost four months, she asked if she could travel with him for the first three or four weeks. Raft agreed and she took time off from work.

After the late show at Scranton, they drove to Wilkes-Barre and arrived around two in the morning. They hadn't made hotel reservations, and Douglas tried to book a double room for himself and Elsie, and two single rooms for Raft and Grayce. But there was a convention at the hotel and only two double rooms were available.

'It's no problem,' said Raft, 'I'll sleep in the car. Grayce can have a room of her own.'

'I couldn't let you do that,' said Grayce. 'The room has twin beds. I don't mind sharing the room with you.'

After they had unpacked and settled down, Raft kissed her goodnight, and they went off to sleep in their separate beds.

At four in the morning the phone rang. George answered it and heard an angry man shouting, 'I want to talk to Grayce!' Thinking it might be her father, Raft woke Grayce and passed her the phone.

'Hello?' she said and then put her hand over the phone. 'It's a man I know – he's having me followed.'

'What man?' asked George in amazement.

She began crying down the phone. 'Please, Joe, we didn't do anything. George didn't do anything. Don't do that to him. He's innocent.'

She hung up and sat on the bed crying.

'What the hell's going on?' asked Raft. 'What's it all about? What's he going to do to me? Who is it?'

Grayce explained that she had gone out with another man.

'I went with him because I was lonely. You were gone so much.' She explained that he was a New York Big Shot who had become obsessed with her and had her followed everywhere. She couldn't get rid of him and was frightened because he'd threatened to follow her on this trip.

'Did you sleep with him?' asked Raft.

'What kind of a girl do you think I am?' she cried.

George held her and said, 'Everything's all right. There's no need to worry.'

'But he says he's going to cause you trouble. He will get you on the Mann Act. You can't take a women across a state line for immoral purposes. You could get twenty years in prison.'

It was dawn and Raft was too exhausted to think straight. He said something virtually on impulse that he regretted for the rest of his life. 'We'll get married. That will solve the problem.'

'Only if you really love me,' she said.

'Look,' he said blandly, 'I really love you.'

But the truth was, he didn't. He took the threat seriously and saw himself going to prison if he didn't marry her. He'd seen his pal Owney put behind bars and he had no intention of joining him.

Straight after breakfast they went down to the City Hall to get a licence and were married at four that afternoon.

That night he did two shows. When they got back to the hotel Grayce went to the bathroom while he waited for her, ready to make love to her for the first time. But it was an hour before she emerged from the bathroom, her eyes red from crying.

'George, I got something to tell you,' she said. 'That man raped me, and then I began sleeping with him almost every night. I'm no virgin!'

Raft's double standards took over and he felt as though he'd been slapped hard in the face. It didn't bother him that he'd slept with more girls than he could remember. He felt tricked. He could say no more to her. He climbed into bed and lay there, furious, unable to sleep.

The next night, Saturday, they drove back to New York where Raft left Grayce with her parents and then went on to Ohio. A few days later his mother wrote to him, telling him that Grayce had been seen with two men in the Long Beach Club. According to Raft's account, he waited 'a few weeks' before he called her on the phone, accusing her of being unfaithful. Why he waited so long, he didn't say. She told him to calm down since she could explain everything better in person. He insisted she get on the train and come to him in Philadelphia.

She watched him do his late show and then he took her to a speakeasy where she explained that the two guys she had been with were just old friends. Raft didn't believe her and thought she was acting like a drunken floozy. They began arguing. He ordered a soda to drink – he never touched alcohol.

As they continued yelling at each other, he gulped back his drink. It tasted awful. When the waiter came back to take a further order, Raft asked him, 'What the hell kind of soda is this?'

Smiling, the waiter said, 'You're drinking the finest home brew.'

Raft was furious. 'I ordered a soda.'

'Sure ya did,' said the waiter. 'And some folks ask for coffee, but this is what they really want.'

Raft stood up, his anger boiling over. He kept himself in check. He later said, 'I could've killed the son-of-a-bitch.'

By the time they got a Raft's hotel room, he was almost blind from the bootleg liquor. Grayce, also drunk, undressed and put on a négligée. He couldn't see what she looked like, but he could feel the soft, silky fabric. He grabbed her and kissed her roughly. No longer concerned with his blindness and more drunk than he'd ever been in his life, he fell with her onto the bed. He fumbled to undo his trousers, pushed them down and in a moment he was inside her.

For the first time they shared a few moments of lust without passion and intimacy without love. Neither of them knew much of what they were doing. Raft certainly didn't care. When he awoke the next morning, he knew that he had penetrated his wife for the first and last time.

They stayed together for just a few weeks until Raft walked out on her, ending the marriage before it had had a chance to begin. When he asked Grayce for a divorce, she said, 'We married till death us do part. That's what my Church teaches, and that's how it's going to be.'

No doubt Grayce hoped he would come back, but Raft blamed her for wrecking the marriage. As he said many years later, 'In those days there were two kinds of girls – those who did and those who didn't. And Grayce definitely didn't.'

In 1923 Owney Madden was released and returned to a criminal world that had been dramatically restructured by Prohibition. The once roaming street gangs had become efficient organizations and networks. Mob leaders set boundaries and sometimes merged with other racketeers. Ties with politicians and policemen were tightened, and Madden had no problem adjusting to these new underworld rules. Despite his ruthlessness, he was a cordial man who numbered among his friends influential columnist Walter Winchell, crime writer Damon Runyon, and noted journalist and short-story writer Mark Hellinger. Madden also knew every ranking cop and politician in town, including Mayor Jimmy Walker. And he had a close friend in George Raft.

Madden's business headquarters was in the Publicity Building on the corner of Broadway and 47th Street. It also housed the offices of many vaudeville booking agents, lawyers and boxing promoters. Actors, singers and hoofers, fight managers and fighters, along with gangsters and thugs, mingled outside the building throughout the day and into the night.

George Raft was a regular visitor to Madden's office, often pulling up outside the building in Madden's own black Packard. He was immediately recognizable as one of the sharpest dressers on Broadway, in spats, high trousers, wide lapels and a black shirt with a white tie. A pearl-grey hat was usually pulled down over one eye.

He was popular with most of the guys who hung around on that corner, and whoever opened the car door for him usually received a few bucks. Among them was Mack Grey, a struggling fight manager who later became Raft's close friend and confidant in Hollywood. Raft liked to stop and chat to Gray about the boxing world, although Gray always figured that Raft was there for reasons that had nothing to do with the ring, or dancing.

One particular day, Raft came in answer to Madden's call. 'I got an assignment for you, George,' Madden announced. 'But first you're gonna get a lesson from Feets. You know Feets Edson? Good, because he's gonna teach you how to drive a big car – gangland style.'

Raft was delighted to have been chosen and he followed Feets Edson out to the waiting car. They went on a bizarre drive through the streets at high speed, careering round corners and speeding down narrow alleys, just as they might do if armed men were lying in wait for them. Then they headed for the Third Avenue El where Raft learned to drive at breakneck speed, avoiding the broken-up pavement and driving along the trolley car tracks all the way from 59th to 110th Street.

After that, Raft happily obliged Madden by driving vans that were part of Madden's fleet of beer trucks. And in case any rival mob should try and hijack the vans, Raft carried a gun. He was sworn to help protect the fleet, and he was proud to do so. He once admitted, 'If I had any ambition, it was to be a Big Shot in my pal Owney Madden's liquor mob … I had a gun in my pocket and I was cocky because I was working for the gang boss of New York.'

By 1925 the Phoenix Brewery plant on Tenth Avenue had passed into Owney Madden's possession. It was constantly being raided and closed by Prohibition agents but, each time it closed, Madden reopened it, using his influence with the police and the politicians. His influence, through generous pay-offs, was so effective that on one occasion when Federal agents tried to raid the plant, it was protected by a squad of city cops who fought them off. From these premises, Madden supplied the East Coast with several hundred thousand gallons of beer which bore the personalized name of 'Madden's No. 1'.

Not only did he have his own brewery, but he owned several nightclubs, including Harlem's Cotton Club. Madden wasn't unique among mobsters when it came to owning clubs. Just about all the top gangsters owned their own places of entertainment because it gave them a place to meet and do business without arousing suspicion.

According to Vincent Teresa, a third generation mafiosa, most mobsters liked to be in the limelight, having grown up in poverty and finally making it big. When they had money, fancy clothes, fast cars and beautiful women, they wanted everyone to know that they'd made it. 'When a mob guy owns a club,' he wrote in his book, *My Life in the Mafia*, 'it's like a guaranteed success – they draw business and broads and entertainers like flies. Maybe it's the excitement of mingling with mobsters. Maybe it's something else.'

Entertainers, according to Teresa, are worse than girls for going 'nutty over mob guys'. This is because the mob has for years owned some of the best nightclubs in America. Entertainers were never too shy to come into a club and 'get cosy' with gangsters before asking them for help in getting a spot at these clubs. 'It was good for our business to have them,' said Teresa.

Entertainers were paid union rates, although the top stars were paid what they were worth. But a good many of them were gamblers, and the mob guys often ensured that what entertainers gained for performing was lost at the gaming tables. Teresa cited Fats Domino as one particular entertainer who earned $12,000 a week and then lost the entire amount in a rigged dice game.

As well as nightclubs, Madden also held substantial interests in several Broadway shows and clubs, perhaps most notably the El Fey Club where the star attraction was Texas Guinan, the most famous cabaret hostess of the decade. It was the Jazz Age, speakeasies were booming, and Texas Guinan was New York's unofficial hostess. Her speakeasy, the El Fey, was named partly after her partner, Larry Fay, but spelt Fey. He was a gangster and friend of Madden's, involved in numerous rackets and gangland activities.

When Larry Fay wanted Madden to supply protection for the club, Madden sent over a squad which included George Raft. Texas knew of his reputation as a dancer and as a lady's man. 'I got a better use for you,' she told him. 'I'll give you $150 a week to dance. There'll be extra money for you when you entertain my lady guests.'

'What do you mean, *entertain*?' asked Raft, feigning naivety.

'I think you know what I mean. But if you're having trouble understanding, let's put it this way; they fuck you, they pay me, I cut you in. We both make money and you get all the pleasure.'

Each night her show opened around midnight when she walked out and called, 'Hello, suckers.' That brought the house down every time. Then she got up on chairs and sang, keeping the show going until around five in the morning.

The El Fey Club was the 'in' place to go, decorated in gaudy red and gold but in all respects a real dive. Raft quickly became a main attraction. Ruby Keeler was another dancer there who later became a star, although Keeler was only fourteen at the time and working illegally.

Awful champagne and booze were served in coffee cups. The El Fey's clientele included royalty – the Vanderbilts, the Astors, the Whitneys, kings and queens – established showbiz stars like Fred Astaire and George Gershwin, and well-groomed gangsters from Brooklyn, Jersey, Harlem and the Lower East Side. Among these were Lepke and Benny Siegel who welcomed Raft at their tables. His friendship with Siegel was particularly strong.

With so many exciting lawless men sitting at the tables and

with such superb entertainment, the club attracted anybody who could afford the exorbitant prices, and was filled to capacity night after night.

Almost every night, Texas pointed out some glamorous society woman to Raft and said, 'She's crazy about you and wants to take you home.'

In the beginning he protested. 'Christ, no,' he told her. 'I'd much rather pick someone myself.' He preferred chorus girls, or any girl who didn't know him, but he hated society women. He branded them 'real bitches'.

'The customer is always right,' Texas reminded him, 'and Larry would be awfully upset if you turned down a guest.' Raft had no choice but to play the male whore again. He also had to help Fay with other jobs, like hijacking a rum-running ship anchored in the harbour and risking Federal arrest.

He was earning $5,000 a week dancing, often working in four different clubs or theatres in a day. He wanted to leave his nefarious life behind now and concentrate on his dancing which was turning him into a Broadway star. Apart from having to perform privately for the 'rich bitches', he thoroughly loved his life. Just around the corner Hollywood waited. But he wouldn't be there just to make movies.

A rush of hijackings had cut short Luciano's supply of bootleg booze, and in desperation he paid a visit to Enoch 'Nucky' Johnson, the 'king of the Jersey Coast'. They called him Nucky because of his fondness for using brass knuckles. Luciano gave him ten per cent of all profits from bootlegging while Prohibition remained in force, in return for allowing, and protecting, shipments of liquor being landed on his coast. It was to prove a profitable treaty for Luciano's mob. But Nucky Johnson wasn't a man to be crossed, as George Raft knew. And Raft was worried.

Hilda Ferguson was considered to be one of the most beautiful of the Ziegfeld Follies girls, and Raft found her to be an exciting lover. They met in secret at each other's apartments for some unbridled lust. But there was a problem of which Raft was only too acutely aware. Hilda was Nucky Johnson's girlfriend.

Raft knew Johnson personally – Raft sometimes danced at Nucky's Silver Slipper Club in Atlantic City. As a friend, Johnson was generous and valuable. But his fierce reputation put the fear of God into his enemies.

The time finally came when Raft decided he'd risked his life long enough for the excitement this girl gave him. He awoke by her side one morning and told her, 'Look, if Nucky gets to know about us, he's likely to have me bumped off.'

'Who's going to tell him, Georgie?'

'That isn't the point. You know he'd kill me if he found out. He's done as much to people for lesser things.'

Hilda wasn't impressed. 'I'm surprised that a man like you could be so scared.'

'It ain't a case of being scared. I admire and respect Nucky. I don't want to clash with him. It's better if we didn't see each other no more.'

Hilda was furious. A few weeks later Raft and a couple of good friends – Walter Winchell and Mark Hellinger – were in the Hotsy-Totsy Club. Hilda was dancing with Johnson. She saw Raft and said to Johnson, 'There's our good friend Georgie.'

'Let's dance over and say hello,' said Johnson, and they swung towards Raft's table. Hilda came right up to the table and said, 'Hello, Georgie.' And as she spoke, she reached out her hand as though to stroke Raft's face. Deftly and slowly, she raked her nails across his cheek while Johnson assumed she was just giving him a gentle, friendly caress. Then they danced away.

Nucky Johnson wasn't the only gangster Raft knew and refrained from ruffling. Dutch Schultz definitely had a screw or two loose, certainly not the kind of man to argue with as he was as likely to run a knife through you as look at you. Late one night, at about four in the morning, Raft was having dinner with a friend in a Third Avenue speakeasy following a late show at the El Fey. In walked Dutch Schultz and two of his cronies. Dutch saw Raft, nodded in greeting, and took the table next to him. No words were exchanged and Raft continued chatting with his friend.

The buzzer that warned that the police were about to raid the place sounded. Alcohol was speedily disposed of. Dutch took two guns from his men, got up and went over to Raft and, without a word, placed the guns, including his own, under Raft's overcoat which lay across a chair. He knew the police, aware that all the booze would have disappeared, would search for weapons. Raft just sat in silence and watched helplessly as Dutch returned to his table. He didn't dare protest, or say anything at all.

The cops came in and began frisking people. Raft remained seated, scared that he would be discovered with three guns under his coat. He was not about to put the finger on Dutch Schultz who obliged the cops by standing with no resistance to be frisked. Everyone in the place was searched – except for Raft. He could only assume that the cops recognized him.

The cops left. Dutch got up, came over, collected his guns and returned to his table without a word of thanks. Raft was furious, but said nothing. He knew better than to complain.

5

Chicago

Marino Bello was a swarthy, well-dressed 'man's man' who boasted of an endless stream of sexual conquests. His jobs were numerous and dubious. He was at times a waiter, but mostly he was a wholesale food salesman whose wares were not necessarily legitimate, and a seller of unlisted five-and-dime stocks. He was also a small-time pimp. Like a good many Italian gangsters, he was far from shy, and when he saw a pretty, plumpish blonde eating alone at the College Inn, he had no hesitation in approaching her and politely asking, 'May I join you?'

Jean Carpentier was a stranger to Chicago and she was nervous but relieved that somebody as well-mannered and sophisticated-looking should show seemingly sincere interest in her. She allowed him to join her and before long was carried away by his smooth, slick sophistication. For Bello, she was one of the easiest pick-ups he'd come across.

Her only reason for arriving in the Windy City in 1922 was to escape her autocratic father, Sam D. Harlow, a wealthy Kansas City property dealer. When she and her husband, Dr Montclair Carpentier, a dentist, had a daughter, Jean's strait-laced, ultra-conservative father decided that nobody knew better how to raise his granddaughter than he. 'Jean didn't know what the hell she was doing,' he was to say, and he was determined that he would raise the child, called Harlean, in a strict fashion.

'She should go to the *right* kind of school,' he told Jean and Dr Carpentier, 'so she can meet the *right* kind of little girl.'

Against Dr Carpentier's wishes, Harlean was consequently enrolled in the stultifying Barstow School for Girls.

Grandfather Harlow managed to take over the young girl's life completely during her most formative and impressionable years, forbidding her to bring home any friends. 'You might catch something,' he told her. She always had to be meticulously groomed and, although he lavished gifts on her, he denied her any kind of normality in her childhood.

Partly due to this tyrannical approach to their lives, but also because their marriage had always been hopelessly dull, Jean and Montclair parted. They had tried to make it work 'for Harlean's sake', but when Harlean was nine they divorced 'with no hard feelings'.

Jean was too vapid a woman to stand up to her father and she told her parents, 'I'm going to visit some cousins.'

'Where for God's sake are you going?' demanded her father.

Jean then told him the truth. 'To Chicago. I'm going to have some fun, maybe get a job.'

Leaving Harlean in the care of her grandparents, Jean left for the Windy City where she met Marino Bello. Here at last was a man who promised the fun she sought, and she discovered a sexual appetite she'd never known before.

When Sam Harlow heard about his daughter's relationship with Bello, he became hysterical. Checking up on Bello, he yelled, 'I refuse to allow that Italian gangster in my house.'

Harlean begged her grandfather to allow her to see her mother. Jean desperately missed Harlean, but Sam Harlow told his daughter to 'stay away'. Harlean saw little of her father too. Sam Harlow had accused him of plotting the marriage breakdown, and the outraged Dr Carpentier refused to come to the house. Harlean only ever saw him at his office.

Like most Italian men, Marino Bello believed it was a mark of respectability to find a wife, so he courted Jean, waiting for her divorce to become final. To the Italian, even a gangster like Bello, family was everything. Virtually all of the leading mobsters married and had children.

Frank Costello had a non-Italian wife. She was a Jewish German called Loretta Giegerman whom he met and fell in love with when he was twenty-three. Her parents were wealthy and lived on upper Park Avenue. Like Luciano, Costello liked and got along with Jews. When he met Loretta (whom he affectionately called Bobbie), he felt it was like meeting one of his own people. They were happy in each other's company although both their mothers disapproved. Costello's mother felt he should marry a nice Italian girl. Instead, he married his Bobbie in 1914. Until then he had still been using his real name, Francesco Castiglia, but on the marriage licence he signed himself for the first time as Frank Costello.

Charlie Luciano, on the other hand, was that rare Italian who enjoyed little about family life. He hardly ever saw his own parents after his father threw him out, although years later during an uncommon Christmas visit to his family, he admitted that 'for a few hours I almost wished I had a nine-to-five job'.

Even the non-Italian gangsters found the urge to get married. Benny Siegel's poor wife, Estelle, took a back seat in his life, giving him children but having little else to do with him as he embarked on one love affair after another. Far more moral, relatively speaking, than Benny was Meyer Lansky who married a devoutly religious girl, Anna Citron. Her father was in important man in the produce business, and Lansky was able to take advantage of his father-in-law's legitimate business for his own illicit enterprises.

Marino Bello also took advantage of his father-in-law-to-be. Sam Harlow detested Bello, but because the Italian gangster was loath to work for a living, Harlow found himself having to bail Jean and Marino out of financial trouble from time to time. And that certainly suited Bello who installed Jean in various second-rate hotels and apartments.

That year, 1922, Chicago's Boss of all Bosses, Big Jim Colosimo, took a bride. Dale Winter shared in her husband's ill-gotten riches while Jean had to make do with what Bello came up with. But Dale had entered a far more dangerous world than Jean.

Dale had come into Colosimo's Restaurant looking for a job as singer. The Restaurant was the most celebrated nightclub in Chicago; its bootleg booze was the finest, and the whores alluring. Movie stars, politicians and celebrities of every kind flocked there.

Dale's only previous singing experience was in a church choir but Colosimo hired her immediately, and very soon the news swept through the Windy City that Big Jim had fallen for a 'little choir kid'. Not long after, they were married.

It was 11 May 1922 and the honeymoon was over. Jim Colosimo was making love to his lovely young bride when the phone rang.

'Forget it,' Big Jim whispered in her ear. But unable to bear the constant ringing, she answered the phone.

'Lemme speak to Jim,' said the caller, Johnny Torrio, Colosimo's lieutenant. Dale handed the phone to Colosimo.

'OK, I'll be there,' said Big Jim, and hung up. 'Got a delivery of two truckloads at the club at four this afternoon.'

'Let Torrio deal with it, honey.'

'Not this time. It's a special shipment of whiskey from Canada, and the boys from there will only deal with me.'

Colosimo promptly arrived at the restaurant at four o'clock. It was virtually deserted. As usual, he wore a bright red rose in his lapel. He waited for a while in the lobby and then strolled into the club. The cleaning ladies were making sure the place was ready for the evening.

At half-past four he was too mad to be kept waiting any longer and stormed into the lobby. Just before he reached the door Frankie Yale stepped out of the cloakroom. Yale was the twenty-five-year-old head of the Unione Siciliano, a 'charitable organization' that included many

Italian gangsters. He was also the owner of the Harvard Inn on Long Island where Al Capone had been a bouncer. Johnny Torrio had hired Capone as his lieutenant, but for special jobs Torrio used Frankie Yale.

Standing in the lobby of Colosimo's Restaurant, Yale had a .38 pistol in his hand. He aimed and fired. The bullet ripped through Colosimo's right ear and entered his brain. Big Jim twisted as he lurched forward, dropping dead onto the lobby floor. Yale fired again, just to make sure.

The former Dale Winter was now a widow and Johnny Torrio was Chicago's new Boss of all Bosses. Al Capone was his right-hand man. Despite all the frenzied activities of men like Luciano and Madden, it was 'Scarface' Al Capone who became the symbol of the Roaring Twenties, or what was otherwise called the 'lawless decade'. Throughout the twenties, it was Capone's name that frightened ordinary citizens, and with good reason. It was his city, Chicago, that earned the name of Mobtown. It was a place so violent that Lucky Luciano called it 'a real goddam crazy place. Nobody's safe in the street.' By comparison Johnny Torrio was a reasonable man.

As Torrio's deputy, Capone made plans to remove Dion O'Banion, boss of Chicago's Irish Syndicate. On 10 November 1924, a car pulled up outside the flower shop from where O'Banion ran his organization, and from where he sent flowers to those who had departed this life – on his orders.

O'Banion was in the shop as Frankie Yale and two men stepped out of the Cadillac and into the shop. O'Banion held out his hand in greeting to his old friend Yale. Yale grabbed his hand, jerked his arm and pulled him into his arms, holding him tightly, making him momentarily helpless. It was just long enough for the two men to draw their pistols and fire several times into O'Banion's head.

When Torrio heard about O'Banion's demise, it came as a complete surprise. He had not ordered the 'hit'. It had come directly from Capone. O'Banion's death resulted in a street war across the city. Torrio tried desperately to make peace as the war claimed more than five hundred lives before a truce was called.

Johnny Torrio was helping his wife and the chauffeur carry some packages from the limousine into their apartment house. Torrio encouraged his wife to take these shopping expeditions because he was so devoted to her, and she publicly called him 'the greatest husband in the world'. Presumably it didn't bother her that he owned the largest chain of brothels in Chicago.

As Torrio grabbed the two remaining boxes and began walking towards the apartment house door, a car screeched to a halt and out jumped two men with machine-guns. They were sixteen-year-old Sam Giancana and Leonard 'Needles' Gianola.

Smoke and spurts of flame spewed from the barrels as Torrio jerked hideously under the hail of bullets which blasted apart his face, chest, groin and arms. Then the gunmen ran back to the car, and it roared away up the street, leaving Torrio lying on the ground, blood pouring from his wounds.

Ann Torrio was screaming and pulling him by the arms, dragging him towards the house. He was still alive and crying over and over, 'Mamma mia, mamma mia.' On that day, 24 January 1925, the gunmen had made a terrible mistake. They didn't ensure the job was done. Torrio was operated on and he survived.

After three weeks in the hospital, he announced that he was retiring. He left for New York where one of the first people he contacted was Frank Costello, by now considered one of the shrewdest and richest of New York's gangsters. With Luciano's blessing, Costello set Torrio up in a little bootlegging business.

Despite the fact that Torrio had not been finished off, Al Capone was impressed by Sam Giancana's cold-blooded enthusiasm. Giancana was known as 'Mooney' because he was considered the craziest, or 'mooniest', of the young thugs working for Diamond Joe Esposito, leader of one of the Chicago gangs. Capone continued to give Giancana occasional jobs.

Giancana knew no loyalty. A few years later he would chase Diamond Joe out of town and join Capone who now ruled the whole of Chicago while New York was controlled by Luciano. They would both soon look to ruling Hollywood. Even young Sam Giancana would leave his mark on the movie capital.

During Christmas 1925 Jean Carpentier was permitted by her father to return home to visit Harlean. It was the second Yuletide running that Sam Harlow had permitted Jean home. She had not seen Harlean since the previous Christmas, and was pleasantly surprised to find how much her daughter had physically developed. As far as Sam Harlow was concerned, the fact that his granddaughter was growing into a young woman only served to make him even more protective of her. 'Goddamned if she's going to go out with boys before she's eighteen,' he said. 'And when she does, *I'll* pick the boys.'

During Jean's visit of 1925, she developed a bad bronchial condition, and to her father's dismay and disapproval she had to remain there on doctor's orders for several weeks. 'OK,' Sam Harlow snorted, 'but that boyfriend of yours stays away!'

Marino Bello was still in Chicago, where things were getting a little too hot with all the tension between Capone's and Torrio's supporters. Bello had had dealings in the past with both Torrio and Capone, and he knew that right now wasn't the time to start taking sides. And in case he should find himself in a position where he was forced to make a decision as to whom he gave allegiance, he decided to take a vacation and get away from the Windy City for a while. With a sudden burning desire to be with Jean while she was ill, and with the violence increasing in Chicago, he flew out to join her.

Sam Harlow was white with fury. He called Bello an 'oily Latin', a rebuff that Bello shrugged off as he settled down to the comforts of Harlow's home, immersing himself in 'business deals' such as selling dubious stocks and getting involved in undiscovered gold mines. All the insults and rebukes that Sam Harlow threw at him made no impact; Bello knew when he was onto a good thing.

His active sex life with Jean continued under Sam Harlow's roof as soon as Jean felt well enough. She had become insatiable and kept her father awake with her loud moans of ecstasy night after night.

Sam Harlow asked Bello naively after his first night listening to his daughter's strange noises, 'What were you doing to my daughter – beating her?'

'No, fucking her,' replied Bello nonchalantly.

Harlow didn't ask again.

Screenwriter Jesse Lasky Jr, who later befriended Harlean Carpentier, told me, 'Marino Bello was delighted to discover that his stepdaughter was turning out to be so beautiful, and he desired her, probably more than he desired her mother. He set about wooing her, winning her confidence by teaching her to waltz and do the tango. He even went to the strange extreme of showing her how to apply lipstick in such a way, he told her, as to make a man want to kiss her. And of course, he did kiss her, if only in a fatherly way. He enjoyed playing with her mouth, but not like a couple of girls who say "I'll put lipstick on you and then you put mine on," and there is nothing sexual in it at all. For him, this was all foreplay, and he looked forward to the day when she would fall for him, or so he believed.'

Jean's divorce from Carpentier became final, and on 10 January 1927, Bello, forty-three years old, married Jean, thirty-six. Somewhat surprisingly, Dr Carpentier saw in Bello a welcome influence on his daughter that contrasted with the kind of tyrannical guidance that Sam Harlow offered, and Carpentier voiced his appreciation to Bello.

'I do what I can,' said Bello. 'A girl that age needs a father, not a grandfather.'

This kind of support gave Dr Carpentier the impetus to

confront Sam Harlow. 'Marino will be leaving with Jean soon,' he said, 'and the best thing for Harlean would be to get her out of this house. It's about time that Harlean was given the opportunity to grow up.'

Harlean was sent off to a fine and highly respected school, Ferry Hall, in Lake Forest, Illinois. 'I think it was Dr Carpentier who managed to prise his daughter away from Sam Harlow and enrol her at a private boarding school, Ferry Hall,' said Jesse Lasky Jr. 'She told me that she was totally miserable. She had hardly any friends and she wrote to her mother and grandparents every day begging them to bring her home. But by then her mother was too preoccupied with Marino Bello and didn't want her living with them. 'I don't believe that Jean Bello had realized that her husband had designs on her daughter and therefore wanted her away from him, because later all three lived together and Mrs Bello had no qualms about her gangster husband and beautiful, sexy daughter being under the same roof. But I have no doubts that Jean Bello did regret neglecting her daughter and tried to make up for it, for mother and daughter were devoted to each other.'

Grandmother Ella, a quiet, caring woman, begged Jean to consent to Harlean's return to their home. But Marino, Jean and Dr Carpentier declined, 'for the sake of the child'. The 'child,' in fact, was now a beautiful young woman with smooth skin, blue eyes, full lips and blonde hair.

Her parents, and stepfather, swore that Harlean would, under no circumstances, be allowed to return to the clutches of her grandfather. Yet neither the parents nor the stepfather seemed to want to be saddled with her either. They told her she would have to remain at school. Harlean took desperate measures, as Jesse Lasky explained: 'In an act of utter desperation, she wrote to her family, saying that she had met a young man, Charles McGrew, at a Saturday afternoon dance. He was twenty-one and the son of wealthy Chicago business people. She wrote that she liked him better than anyone she had ever met and he had proposed to her. She told her family that she would marry him if she was not allowed to leave school and return home. She knew that married women were not allowed to attend that school.'

Jean and Marino rushed to Chicago to see Harlean and Charles before the 'baby' did something that 'a good girl shouldn't do'. Tearfully, Jean assured her mother, 'I still am a good girl. But to ensure that I stay that way, Mamma, please take me out of school.'

'I'll try, sweetheart,' said Jean, lying. 'But you know your grandfather.'

A week later Jean phoned Harlean and said, 'We've decided that we will take you out of school at the end of the year.'

'No, I want to come home now, *please,*' Harlean cried.

Feeling betrayed, and determined to carry out her threat, she eloped with McGrew in March 1927. The school wired the news to her grandparents, asking them to 'remove your rebellious granddaughter at once'. As soon as Charles's parents heard the news, they whisked him away to relatives far from Chicago.

Marino Bello came to collect Harlean and took her back to Kansas where Grandfather Harlow decided, 'I've had enough of the whole bunch of you and I want you out of my house.'

To Bello's delight, Sam Harlow gave them enough money to last a year, so Jean and Marino packed their bags and took the still tearful Harlean off to Los Angeles. They settled in a small, furnished two-bedroom apartment and Harlean began to enjoy the feeling of being part of a real family again. She found Bello, at that time, sympathetic and understanding, and he always seemed to know the right things to say to cheer her up. But she did not then know what kind of man he really was, as Lasky told me. 'He was always wheeling and dealing in various nefarious activities, but he never made much money. He refused to get a real job so Jean had to become the breadwinner, selling cosmetics door-to-door and working in a restaurant. For some reason, Marino decided he was perfect star material and set about trying to become an actor. Every day he showed up at studio gates hoping to be discovered. The best he ever did was to get some work as an extra. So did Jean who did better at being an extra than he did.'

Jean often took Harlean to studios and it wasn't long before an agent took a look at Harlean and decided she could be a star. About that time, Bello discovered that there was a thriving business in Hollywood known as the 'husband business' whereby men actively sought to marry beautiful women who were already movie stars or who were one step away from movie stardom. Those men then used their wives to gain them entry into influential circles, and even allowed men into their wives' beds in return for special favours. Bello was astute enough to realize that, while his wife was never going to amount to anything important in Hollywood, his step-daughter might. Photographs of her in the nude began to circulate.

An agent, Arthur Landau, took notice of the young blonde bombshell and took her to see Hal Roach, who ran his own studio, specializing in comedy and turning out all the early Laurel and Hardy silent two-reelers. Roach took one look at her and thought she was photogenic and had a great body, and by early that afternoon she had a contract with the Roach Studio.

A further touch to her blossoming career was a name change. Harlean didn't care for her married name of McGrew, and she didn't like Carpentier either. And she certainly didn't want to be called Bello. She was, and always remained, deeply attached to her mother, so she took her mother's first and maiden names, becoming Jean Harlow. To avoid confusion with her mother, she was forever after known as Baby Jean and her mother became Mama Jean.

Later that year, 1927, a former associate of Marino Bello's turned up in Hollywood. He was the feared Al Capone, known nationally as 'Scarface' because of the scar that marred his chubby left cheek.

In Chicago things had been getting a little too hot as Mayor 'Big Bill' Thompson ordered the police to clamp down on

Capone's operations. Capone was furious that an administration into which he had poured so much money should turn on him. But Thompson had become very ambitious and had aspirations of becoming the President of the United States. So he now turned on his former ally, and Capone decided it was time to leave town for a while. He turned up in Los Angeles, much to the consternation of the 'Combination'.

The 'Combination' was a group of men who wielded much control over the city, paying off law-enforcement agencies and providing protection for a variety of illegal activities, from gambling to prostitution, in return for tributes which amounted to around $50 million a year. The men who controlled this feudal system enjoyed the support of a large segment of the Los Angeles press in city hall.

The Hollywood Syndicate had some links with the mobs in New York and Chicago, but by and large they were a law unto themselves, making huge profits from bookie and gambling dens and more than a thousand brothels. Many government officials who were elected by the public to stamp out all were happy to receive handsome payoffs in return for turning a blind eye. Some attempts at reform were made, but the genuine law enforcers were outnumbered.

Capone had at least one trusted Hollywood contact he knew he could count on. This was Joseph P. Kennedy, founder of the Fitzgerald-Kennedy dynasty of Boston (and father of the future President, John F. Kennedy). His ambition had been to become wealthy and powerful. He was a Harvard graduate who at the age of twenty-five became Boston's youngest bank president. During Prohibition he had worked with the likes of Frank Costello in the bootlegging business, importing the finest Scotch and Irish whiskies and French champagne, which he distributed from secret warehouses on the East and West Coasts.

Kennedy owed Chicago. When he brought liquor through Detroit without permission from the city's Jewish gang, known as the Purple Gang, the Jewish dons put a contract on his head. Kennedy had gone straight to Chicago and met with

Diamond Joe Esposito. Diamond Joe, Paul Ricca and another associate, Murray Humphreys, enjoyed themselves immensely as Kennedy positively begged them to save his life. Esposito finally agreed to the request and from then on Kennedy was in their debt.

In 1926 Kennedy purchased the Hollywood-based Film Booking Offices of America Inc. Studio which turned out small pictures which never played at the big city theatres. Kennedy managed to persuade a major theatre to show a Fred Thomson cowboy picture and it proved an enormous success. Joe Kennedy was now a major force in Hollywood. But it seems he did not exactly make it on his own. Ricca, Humphreys and Frank Nitti had apparently backed his entry into the world of motion pictures.

When Al Capone went to Hollywood in 1927, he booked into the Biltmore Hotel. The local press flocked to his suite and fired questions at him.

Did he sanction the deaths of men he might consider to be his rivals?

'I'm a businessman,' he told them, 'and getting people murdered is not good business.' He laughed and the gathered newspapermen laughed with him.

Was he in Los Angeles to supply booze?

'Let me tell the good citizens of Los Angeles this. They should get their own booze.' There was more laughter. Capone made for good copy, and he enjoyed the attention paid to him by newspapermen.

After the press had left, detectives turned up, sent by the Combination who were terrified that the Chicago mob had designs on their rackets. Capone greeted the detectives warmly, offering them coffee.

'Gentlemen, I understand the concern of the men you come here representing,' he told them. 'The truth is, I've heard so much about California that I figured I had to see it for myself. I assure you, I'm leaving here tomorrow.'

The next day Capone was on a train heading back towards Chicago where Bill Thompson was soon to repair his friendship with the powerful mobster. After Capone had left Los Angeles, the detectives' visit to his hotel room was leaked to the press and the next day newspapers were emblazoned with such headlines as CAPONE TOLD TO BLOW; GANG CHIEF ROUTED.

Whatever he may have told them, Capone had satisfied a certain curiosity. Hollywood had much potential for any number of shakedowns. Previously, he had shown no interest in the movie business as a racket, although he had always been fascinated by film stars.

In New York, Charlie Luciano and Lepke had gradually taken over the projectionists' union, raking in thousands of dollars by collecting membership fees. Capone had always ignored that particular racket, considering the control of movie theatres as something unworthy of him.

He concentrated on the unions that controlled factories, bars and trucking companies among other things. His lieutenant, Frank 'the Enforcer' Nitti, led his goon squads into factories, warehouses and businesses, taking over on behalf of Al Capone and, at gunpoint, persuading everyone to sign his union petitions.

With so much to be gained from unions, it was therefore surprising that Capone ignored the Chicago projectionists' union, known as Theater Operations Local 100. It was run by an Irish hood, Tommy Maloy, who knew how to keep his members in line with the use of guns. The union had originally been run by crook Jack Miller who had been shot dead in 1920.

After Maloy took over, he held his first business meeting in 1924 which turned into a riot when the membership rose up to threaten strikes, chaos and even death. Maloy had his goons fire several rounds of machine-gun fire into the ceiling, and the meeting settled down to conclude peacefully.

Membership of the union grew under the leadership of Maloy who offered non-union projectionists a choice; either join up or expect a cracked skull. Most were happy to go along with Maloy's sham. The job itself was a well-paid one. Many projectionists earned up to $175 a week, compared to the average wage of around $5 or $7. Members only had to pay $3 a week to the local and another dollar to the international union. But non-members, who would be hired by the day and issued with work permits, had to pay up to ten per cent of their weekly salary. It paid men to join the union and both they and Maloy were happy.

Capone had shown no interest in taking over Maloy's racket. But by 1927 he was sizing up the movie industry and his short vacation in Hollywood whetted his appetite. His big problem was how best to deal with the 'Combination'. Capone decided to bide his time.

6

Hollywood

With every step up the tinselled ladder of success, Jean Harlow was closely followed by Marino Bello. He was behind her evolving career, or so he claimed, taking credit for her achievements, beginning with her first role for Hal Roach. It was a bit part in Laurel and Hardy's *Double Whoopee*. The script called for Jean to step out of a taxi just as Stan Laurel slams the door, catching her skirt and tearing it off.

Before filming the scene, the director called Jean over. 'You are under-dressed, aren't you?'

'Of course,' she replied.

The cameras began turning and the actors went through their paces. Laurel slammed the taxi door and off came Jean's skirt. There was suddenly great excitement among the crew as Jean stood there in only her panties. Harlow couldn't figure out what the fuss was all about until someone told her that she was supposed to be wearing flesh-coloured tights beneath her underwear, and that's what the director had meant by being 'under-dressed'. By pure accident, Jean Harlow had caused a sensation and was suddenly Hollywood's latest sex symbol.

The news spread fast that a new screen siren had made her debut. The word didn't stop before it reached the ears of Grandfather Harlow who entirely disapproved of the movie business. He got straight on the phone to Hal Roach.

Jean was summoned to Roach's office. 'I've had word from your grandfather,' he told her. 'He doesn't like you working in the movies. So I'm suggesting we just tear up your contract so you can return to Kansas where I believe your husband is waiting for you.'

Since Harlow and her family were still, if only in part, dependent on her grandfather, she felt she had to accept a release of contract, and she returned to Kansas in 1928.

After spending an unbearable year with her grandfather, Jean Harlow decided to take her life in her own hands and, defying the old man who promised to disinherit her, returned to Hollywood to join Mama Jean and Marino Bello. Hollywood was still interested in her and she landed a small role in *The Saturday Night Kid* with Clara Bow and Jean Arthur.

Bello would have been glad to be away from Chicago that year, because on St Valentine's Day, 1929, things came to a head for syndicate leaders.

George 'Bugs' Moran had inherited the O'Banion gang and was causing Al Capone trouble. Capone decided that the only solution was to dispose of the whole gang in one go.

Seven of Moran's henchmen were lured into a garage, believing they were to await a shipment of illegal liquor. A police car roared into the garage and screeched to a halt. Out jumped two uniformed policemen and three plainclothes cops carrying machine-guns. But they were not cops at all. The two in blue were Sam Giancana and Leonard 'Needles' Gianola, and the others were Fred Burke, Alberto Anselmi and John Scalise, all members of Capone's army. The Moran boys were lined against the wall and the three plainclothes men opened fire, tearing the whole gang apart.

Bugs Moran was on his way to the garage when it happened, and escaped the fate of his entire gang. But he didn't hesitate to proclaim to the newspapers, 'Only Capone kills like that.'

Sam Giancana's participation in the event was significant in that he had become to Capone what Bugsy Siegel was to Luciano – a trusted killer. But when it came to loyalty, Giancana was fickle. He really belonged to whoever was the stronger. And following the St Valentine's Day Massacre,

Capone was a marked man. The killings had really stirred up the Feds, both in Chicago and New York.

Waiting in the wings to take over Capone's rule was one of his lieutenants, Paul Ricca, although it was generally believed that Capone's most trusted lieutenant Frank Nitti would take charge. All Giancana had to do was wait and see who would eventually become Capone's successor.

To combat Capone, Federal Agent Eliot Ness would soon be sent to Chicago. Capone thought he could buy off Ness but discovered that Ness and his special force of hand-picked agents would accept no amount of money. Ness and his force became legendary as the 'Untouchables'.

Lucky Luciano figured that something had to be done to keep things quiet in the underworld and give the Feds no further reason to stir things up. Meanwhile, he had some business to take care of in Los Angeles where the drugs racket had become ripe for a takeover.

Drugs had been widespread in Hollywood since its earliest days. Wallace Reid, Alma Rubens and Barbra LaMarr were just a few of the stars known to have become hopelessly addicted to hard drugs. Movie junkies such as they were relied on studio-based fixers. On the Sennett lot there was an actor whose name was never to become a legend but he was forever remembered as 'The Count' due to his elegant manner and dress sense. His biggest source of income was peddling drugs to film stars. He was typical of the drug pushers in Hollywood who operated independently. They would soon find themselves in competition with none other than Lucky Luciano.

Luciano needed someone to front for him; someone acceptable to the Hollywood community. He chose Pasquale 'Pat' DiCicco, a rich, handsome and charming Italian playboy who possessed a violent temper when angered.

He associated with Luciano in New York, simply enjoying the thrill of being in the company of gangsters while not getting himself involved in actual crime. Before Luciano had thought of him as his front man, DiCicco had established himself in Los Angeles, where he set himself up as an agent. He had a number of clients, although none of them were major stars, got invited to the best parties, met the right producers and became a much-liked personality with many in the film business.

He gave generous tips to studio guards who let him through the gates. He became a familiar face on the film sets even though he hardly ever had anything to do with the pictures being filmed. His charm and good looks won many over, especially the women, who were smitten by him. He got to know people like The Count and learned which stars were clients.

When Luciano arrived in town, he looked DiCicco up and, eager to renew their acquaintance, DiCicco took to introducing his friend around Hollywood. Not that Charlie Luciano needed introducing. His face was as famous as those of the movie stars he met, many of whom knew of his reputation as a big-time gangster and were thrilled to shake his hand.

Much about Luciano's dealings in Hollywood has not been widely recorded and until recently little of it was known outside certain circles. I obtained material from a source in California whose family was connected to Luciano during the twenties and thirties. Mr Volonte – not his real name – revealed to me how extensively Luciano was involved in the Los Angeles drugs racket, as well as other things which are related later in this book. Of Luciano's first visit to the Hollywood community, Mr Volonte said, 'There were men in Hollywood – men who ran the studios – who had connections of their own to the underworld. But they mostly knew Capone in Chicago and his men. However they had heard of Charlie Lucky and a lot of film stars liked to meet him. He was a celebrity and he was charming to them so they liked him. It became impossible for them to believe this man was a killer because he was a man who smiled, spoke gently and was gracious to everyone, especially women. But they didn't know that while he was engaging them at big Hollywood parties, his men were charging into places with machine-guns where the drug racketeers were hiding their stocks of cocaine and heroin, and taking over for Luciano. I don't know for sure if men were killed, but Luciano was not a man to walk away when someone told him "no". If they were smart, they either got out of town or accepted Luciano's offer to go on the payroll. That's how members of my family got involved. They were pushing drugs on the streets and the next thing they were working for Luciano. To Luciano it was all business. He was not a man who killed because he was homicidal. It was all business. And he liked good business. But with Capone, there were problems which Luciano had to deal with.

'People say, "Why didn't the law do something to stop Luciano?" He paid off the law. He had spies everywhere.'

Luciano even had men in the office of District Attorney Buron Fitts who was one of the most corrupt DAs Los Angeles ever had.

Howard Hughes had just made a silent picture called *Hell's Angels,* a World War One saga about the Royal Flying Corps, which starred Ben Lyon and James Hall. They played a couple of Oxford undergraduates who become pilots. Greta Nissen, a Norwegian actress, had the role of the middle-class English girl who loves them both. Just as the film was nearing completion, sound in movies became established and Hughes decided to reshoot the whole thing as a 'talkie'. But he had problems. Lyon and Hall could get away, barely, as Oxford undergraduates but Greta Nissen, with her strong Norwegian accent, couldn't hope to be believable as a middle-class English girl. So Hughes sought a replacement.

A blonde actress, Thelma Todd, had finished a film, *All Tied Up*. During filming she had collapsed on the set and been diagnosed as suffering from 'chronic exhaustion'. So she took a cruise to Catalina Island as part of a three-month vacation, during which she met film director Roland West. He had made several successful films and was involved with United Artists, the company financing *Hell's Angels*.

West wasn't particularly good-looking, and, at forty-four, he was nineteen years older than Todd. But she was instantly attracted to him and there began what she probably supposed would be just a holiday romance. But when the cruise was over, he pursued her. She was impressed by his sincerity and by his understanding of her aspirations to become a serious actress instead of just another dizzy screen blonde. West promised that he could get her the female lead in *Hell's Angels*.

While she waited for the call from Howard Hughes, she returned to work for Hal Roach where both she and Jean Harlow were under contract. Three weeks passed and Todd began to wonder if West had simply been making empty promises. Then she got a call from him asking to meet her at the Brown Derby Restaurant. She arrived to find West sitting with Joseph Schenck, chairman of United Artists, and Howard Hughes.

'Mr Schenck and Mr Hughes agree that you're perfect for the part,' West told her. She could hardly contain herself.

Schenck spoke up: 'You will have to start immediately. Hal Roach will have to release you.'

Hughes said very little but joined them in drinking a toast. Thelma drank heavily, as usual, and was giggly and drunk when she left the restaurant, thinking her future looked glorious.

The next day she was back on the Roach set, filming a scene for a three-reel Charley Chase musical, *High Cs*. During a break, she went to see Roach to ask for his permission to make *Hell's Angels*. But he had already heard the news and was furious that she had not told him immediately.

'I know all about *Hell's Angels*,' he said, 'and I'm damned disappointed I didn't hear about it from you. I've worked hard promoting you as a Roach comedienne, not as some flyer's tramp. I will not release you from your contract here.'

'I don't need your permission,' she retorted. 'I can just walk out.'

'You do, I guarantee you'll never work again. No studio will take on anyone who's in dispute with their studio.'

She stormed out, holding back the tears, and managed to

finish her day's work. Then she went home and knocked back a bottle of Scotch before falling sleep for the night. The next morning she was awakened by a phone call from West who was furious.

'Schenck's madder than hell,' he told her. 'He says I wasted his time pushing you when you weren't available. Why won't Roach release you?'

'He will,' said Todd. 'Can you put Schenck and Hughes off for couple of days until Roach calms down?'

'I'll try,' said West, and for the next three days he personally tried to persuade Roach to allow her to do the film.

Meanwhile, Ben Lyon went wandering through the Roach studio and came across Jean Harlow. He later said, 'I'd never seen anything like her in my life. She had silver hair, a fabulous figure and a very tight-fitting black satin gown which showed every curve in her body. I went over to her and said, "How would you like to play the lead in *Hell's Angels*?"'

'What do I have to do and to who?' she asked cautiously.

'You merely have to meet Howard Hughes,' Lyon told her and promptly took her to Hughes who, upon hearing her accent, said, 'She doesn't sound much like a middle-class English girl.'

Nevertheless Lyon persuaded him to give her a film test. That evening Harlow made her screen test. Hughes thought she looked so superb that he forgot all about her accent and gave her the role. Hal Roach had no qualms about releasing her, possibly to teach Thelma Todd a lesson, and the next morning Hughes signed Harlow to a three-year contract. Thelma Todd was inconsolable and took to the bottle.

By the time Harlow began working on *Hell's Angels,* she had developed an image of sexuality that more than made up for her acting limitations. She dispensed with bra and panties, and wore white, tight dresses. She even dyed her pubic hair to match the bleached hair on her head, and it was said she rubbed her nipples with ice to make them stand out against her tight dresses.

Howard Hughes's publicity men were hard at work on her

promiscuous image, sending her on a series of personal appearances during the release of the film, which opened at Grauman's Chinese Theater on Hollywood Boulevard in June 1930.

Publicity men mingled with the press, asking questions to which Harlow gave quick, witty and often outrageous answers.

'Jean, are you wearing a brassière?'

'That sounds like a near-sighted question.'

'How do you like to wake up in the morning?'

'I like to wake up feeling a new man.'

'Miss Harlow, would you steal a husband?'

'Wouldn't that be like shoplifting in a second-hand store?'

Before long Jean Harlow was hailed as 'America's new Blonde Bombshell'. Marino Bello saw his future secure. He promptly fired her agent, Arthur Landau, and took over as her personal manager (Landau was rehired later at the studio's insistence). He was to put his own version of the 'Husband Business' into action. Screenwriter Frances Marion, in her autobiography, *Off With Their Heads*, described Bello as 'Jean's philandering stepfather [who] slyly pointed out her assets to men who were in a position to further her career.'

As far as Harlow herself was concerned, she was willing to go along with his schemes, which in turn aroused Bello. He wanted to possess her completely and he began leaving suggestive notes in her bed; pathetic advances she kept secret from Mama Jean as she didn't want to upset her. She felt she could deal with Bello. She had, after all, learned how to grow up fast under Bello's guidance. And under his guidance, she would learn much about the underworld, as, through him, she found herself having to fraternize with some of the biggest of the Big Shots.

Thelma Todd would also become involved with a man associated with the Mafia, and he was soon to become the Boss of all Bosses.

'George Raft was the closest to a gangster than any other

actor I ever met,' James Cagney told me. 'Which wasn't surprising because when I made *Each Dawn I Die* with him, he told me that when he was working for the clubs in New York, he was really working for the Mob – with a capital M.'

Every way Raft turned, he found himself caught up in Mob business, whether he liked it or not. On the one hand, he was one of Owney Madden's protection crew, and on the other he was employed by Larry Fay to dance at the El Fey Club, and Fay was in league with Madden and other underworld leaders. His partner, Texas Guinan, although herself in business with Madden, avoided anything to do with big-time crime and she nagged Fay to follow her example. He insisted he was just a businessman, and he could prove it by citing the fact that he poured his share of the profits from the club into the ownership of a legitimate taxi business. But he still did business with the underworld and this caused friction between Fay and Texas. She attracted the Park Avenue crowd and objected to Fay's gun-carrying hoods who often sat at the tables with their guns in view.

One night George Raft witnessed an argument when Texas discovered Fay with a bunch of hoods in the downstairs bar, making plans that Texas didn't like the sound of. She flew into a rage and told Fay to get rid of them, fearing that a shoot-out would close the place down.

Finally, after a series of federal raids, her fears proved to be well founded, and the club was closed down in 1928. Around this time Raft began working on Broadway in a Dillingham show which, up to that time, was the high point of his career. It looked all set to end there, as Cagney recalled.

'Poor George, thought he had finally made it, but the Mob had other plans for him. Madden told him he was going to Miami, Florida, to open a new nightclub there, and George told them he couldn't leave the Dillingham show. That got "the boys" mad at him, and he agreed to go down to the train to see them off for Florida. But when they got to the station, they grabbed him, took off his overcoat, his shoes and hat and hid them until he agreed to get on the train. So he said, "You win" and got on the train but as they pulled into North Philadelphia, he jumped off and ran in his stockinged feet through the snow to catch a taxi back to New York.'

The way Cagney remembered it was not quite the way it happened. Madden didn't order Raft to Florida, nor did he have Raft hijacked. It was Texas who invited him to join her in the new club she and Fay were opening in Miami. But Raft told her he was staying in New York. She accepted his decision, but Larry Fay didn't. He tried to persuade Raft to change his mind. Raft was adamant.

'I've got too much going for me here,' he told Fay. 'I see no reason to leave.'

Fay was furious. He had a fearful temper when spurned, but he checked his anger and decided there and then that Raft would not get off so lightly. He appeared to calm down. 'At least come and see me and Texas off on the train tomorrow,' he insisted.

Raft knew he had come close to a violent confrontation. He breathed a sigh of relief and said, 'OK, the least I can do is say goodbye.'

The next day Raft turned up at Penn Station, still wearing his tuxedo and dancing shoes, and followed Texas and Fay into their private compartment. He kissed Texas goodbye, and then he left the compartment with Fay. He reached out for Fay's hand to shake it. Fay suddenly dealt him a swift and crunching blow to the head, and he crumpled unconscious to the floor.

When he came to, he found himself in a compartment. The train was in motion, heading for Miami. His shoes and coat were gone. He could hear Texas laughing in the adjoining compartment, and he wondered if she had been involved in this kidnap plot. Then he realized that she would never have anything to do with such a criminal act. This had been Larry Fay's plan, and Raft was damned if he was going to sit out the ride and end up in Miami.

He stayed quiet and waited until the train rolled into North

Philadelphia. The platform was on the opposite side of the train to his compartment. He picked up a metal water-bottle, smashed a window, and climbed out. It was bitingly cold without his coat, and snow soaked and froze his stockinged feet. He crept along, keeping low, passing beneath the window of Fay and Guinan's compartment. The whistle blew and the train began pulling out. He was safe. He ran to the road where he waved down a car.

'Get me to New York and I'll make it worth your while,' he told the driver.

'Sure, jump in,' said the astonished driver.

The man drove Raft all the way to New York, and Raft paid him very handsomely for his trouble.

Some time later, in 1929, Raft got a call from Texas. 'Hey Georgie, I'm just about to leave for Hollywood where they're going to film my life story. There's a part in the picture for you, if you want it. All you gotta do is play yourself, do some dancing.'

What helped Raft make up his mind to join her in Hollywood was Owney Madden. He knew Raft could prove useful to him in Hollywood as a front. 'Take the offer, George,' he said. Raft did as he was told.

The film was called *Queen of the Night Clubs*. It was no great picture, but it put Raft in Hollywood where Madden wanted him. His associations with the underworld in New York gained him access to certain circles. But he didn't realize then that those associations were known to the police.

Texas had rented a house at 572 North Camden Drive in Beverly Hills where she threw a huge party. There were many gorgeous women, and Raft was struck by one in particular. She was Molly O'Day, the star of such films as *The Patent Leather Kid*, *The Lovelorn* and *The Little Shepherd of Kingdom Come*. She was only seventeen and Raft was now twenty-three. She was instantly attracted to him, and they began seeing each other regularly. He said he found her to be one of the sweetest, most gentle women he'd ever met. When he wasn't spending all his money at the races, he was spending time with Molly.

One day he won a considerable sum on the horses, enabling him to afford a room at the Mark Twain Hotel on Wilcox Avenue. When he began running out of cash, he sold one of his expensive suits for $30 to one of the hotel's guests.

Two days later he was walking through the lobby when two detectives stopped him. 'Your name Raft?' they asked.

'Yeah.'

'What's your business here in Los Angeles?'

'I'm an actor. I just made a film here.'

'We'd like to know where you were last night.'

'I was sitting right there in the lobby.'

'All evening?'

'Yeah. If you don't believe me, just ask the clerks.'

'We will.'

Within minutes the clerks had confirmed his story. 'So what's this all about?' asked Raft.

'There was a stick-up last night. We figure it's the same guy who's pulled at least a dozen jobs. We know he's been staying at this hotel and he was careless enough to leave his jacket behind. It had your name sewn in the inside pocket.'

Raft explained how he had sold his suit to some guy. The detectives said that he was in the clear – for now. As they left, one of them said, 'We hope you're not going to get yourself into any kind of trouble. We've now got your name in mind.'

Raft needed to find further acting work if he was to remain in Hollywood without arousing suspicion. Texas Guinan had gone back to Miami, and he had no luck landing a further film part throughout 1929.

In Atlantic City that spring, Raft's pal Benny Siegel was about to rise in power, thanks to Al Capone and the St Valentine's Day Massacre; he would reach the zenith of his power several years later as the Jewish Don of Hollywood.

7

Crime Organized

Benny Siegel watched the girls parading in their bathing suits along the white beach of Atlantic City, the summer playground of New York. But there was no time on this warm sunny day in May 1929 for playing around, with so much important business to deal with.

'Take a look, Benny,' said Torrio, pressing a page into his hand. Siegel tore his gaze from the girls and scanned the names on the sheet of paper. It read like a *Who's Who* of the underworld; all the crime lords who had accepted the invitation to the convention.

Siegel read aloud the names: 'Lou Rothkopf and Moe Dalitz from Cleveland. King Solomon from Boston. John Lazia from Kansas City. Joe Bernstein from Detroit. Sam Lazar from Philadelphia. Al Capone from Chicago. They are coming?'

'All of 'em,' said Torrio.

Siegel passed the list to Frank Costello who sat on a bench. 'If the Feds had hold of this list...' mused Costello. 'How's Capone going to react, I wonder?'

'He thinks this whole thing is aimed at him,' said Siegel.

'I hear he's thinking of leaving,' said Torrio.

'He'll stay,' said Frank.

Siegel gazed out to sea. 'Well, if he's got any objections,' he said, 'the ocean makes for a good dumping ground.'

Frank Costello had spent many nights talking to Charlie Luciano and Johnny Torrio about what to do with Capone. They'd decided on inviting all the crime lords to a convention at Atlantic City to establish a unification of all the mobs and so stamp out further random killings – most especially, to clamp down on Al Capone without starting the bloodiest war of all.

Siegel went back to the President Hotel to check on the security arrangements. On his way through the lobby he met Meyer Lansky and his new wife, Anna. 'What a honeymoon you two are having,' said Siegel. 'Virtually every one of your business associates is here, Meyer.'

He entered the large conference room where he found Luciano watching as preparations were finalized. Above the rich mahogany tables and chairs hung a crystal chandelier.

'Frank's concerned how Capone's going to react tonight,' said Benny.

'He's not our only worry,' said Charlie. 'We still got Joe Masseria to deal with.'

Joe Masseria was the biggest of New York's mafiosi. Luciano had formed a treaty with 'the Boss' back in 1927. But Luciano had purposely neglected to invite Joe the Boss to Atlantic City. And he expected trouble to come of it. He would deal with him later, however, as he would with all the 'Moustache Petes' as the old school of Mafia leaders were called. This was just the first stage in Luciano's rise to overall power, and in his rise, he would, he thought, deal with Al Capone once and for all. But this would prove not only to be a single step on the route to power, but also to the final showdown in Hollywood.

'I been talking with all the other delegations and they all agree that Capone's gotta be stopped,' said Luciano confidently.

That evening the crime lords sat in the conference room. Near one end of the table sat the Chicago delegation – Frank 'the Enforcer' Nitti, Jake 'Greasy Thumb' Guzik, bodyguard Frank Rio, and a grim-looking Al Capone.

The New York delegation sat at the other end with Charlie Luciano at the head. He was flanked by Frank Costello, Johnny Torrio, Joe Adonis and Benny Siegel.

Torrio, as the 'elder statesman', rose and spoke first. 'The reason we called this meeting is because it's time we got organized. Everybody's working on his own and that makes for rivals. And we got independent guys muscling in, and that's got to stop. What we need is a nationwide combination with each boss in charge of his own city, but we all work with each other.'

Torrio finished his speech, sat down, and Costello rose to continue. 'We gotta get organized and put ourselves on a business basis. Because that's what we're in, a *business*. We got to stop the kind of thing that's going on in Chicago right now.' The focus of everyone's attention suddenly shifted to Al Capone. Costello continued, looking straight at Capone: 'You guys are shooting at each other in the streets and innocent people are getting killed. That ain't good for business because the people start crying to the Feds to get off their tails and start cracking down on us. And you know what that means. Now, we got a business where millions of dollars can be made just getting people what they want. If we got all the people behind us, we're able to stay in business.

'But if the people are made to feel afraid of us, then they're going to turn the other way and start yelling at the government to clean us out. That means the Internal Revenue boys, the FBI, the drugs squads, and every DA in the country'll be on our backs. Ask yourselves, is it worth it?'

Every eye now fell on the formidable figure of Charlie Luciano as he stood up and spoke. 'We're gonna have a national commission with every family represented. From now on, nobody gets killed without the approval of the commission. No boss will be attacked unless the commission says he has to go. No one gets hit without a hearing from his own boss.

'The old way, when a guy who's in your way gets killed, is no good any longer. If we run a business like this, we'll get respect and all the dough in the world. If we keep the fireworks goin', we'll all be out of business in a year.' He sat down.

The other gangsters were vastly impressed – except for Capone and his delegation. Torrio got to his feet and looked down the length of the table at Capone. 'You're going to jail, Al,' he announced.

'What?' Capone smiled sardonically.

'We have to smooth this thing over right now. You go back to Chicago after that Valentine Day shoot-out and there'll be more bloodshed. And the heat'll just get higher. We think you need a vacation, Al.'

Capone simply looked at Torrio and said, 'Tell me when I'm supposed to laugh.'

'It's no joke, Al,' said Frank Costello. 'We got too much invested for you to ruin. Make it easy on yourself. Think of a way to get yourself out of circulation for a while. Just a while, that's all. Until things cool down.'

Capone's anger erupted. He got to his feet, throwing his chair to the floor. 'I'll let you know,' he bellowed, and with his boys close behind, he stormed out.

Capone later checked out the other bosses and discovered they were all behind Luciano and Costello. He knew he had no choice but to make the necessary arrangements. Two days later, while he was in Philadelphia, he and Frank Rio were picked up for 'carrying a gun'. They were taken into custody by Detectives James Malone and John Creedon. A year before, both had been guests at Al Capone's luxurious house in Florida. They were on the payroll and the arrest had been carefully set up.

Capone and Rio were sentenced to serve a year's imprisonment for carrying concealed weapons. The legendary 'Scarface', who had never been arrested in his life, became number 90725 in the Holmesburg County Jail.

In New York, Joe 'The Boss' Masseria had developed a loathing for Sicilians born in the area of Castellammare del Golfo. He wanted them all disposed of, especially Salvatore Maranzano, the most important of the Castellammarese Dons. The first to go, on 26 February 1930, was Tommy Reina, a Castellammarese family leader. Capone, safely tucked away for an easy spell in jail, smiled as war broke out between Masseria and his rivals. Both sides took shelter in hideaways, sleeping on mats, unable to go out on the street without risking their lives.

Frank Costello had to stay away from his office and let others run his flourishing bootlegging operations. He, Luciano and Vito Genovese, another rising Mafia leader, were not Castellammarese but they were against Masseria's pointless war.

The very thing they had tried to put a stop to was happening on the streets of New York.

In Hollywood, during the summer of 1930, George Raft finally got his break. He was with some friends at the Brown Derby Restaurant, where he was seen by Rowland Brown.

A former Detroit newspaperman, and at the time a rising director, Brown came over and introduced himself to George. 'I saw you dance in vaudeville in Detroit,' he said, 'and I liked your style.'

'Well, you know, I made a picture with Texas Guinan,' Raft told him. 'I'm hoping to get some more film work.'

'Listen, George, come over to the Fox studio tomorrow and I'll test you. I'm going to direct a film, *Quick Millions*. It's the story of a truckdriver who becomes a ruthless gangster. We got a new star for the main role, name of Spencer Tracy. But I think you might be perfect as Tracy's bodyguard.'

The next day Raft arrived for the screen test. A scene was set up where he came into a room full of tough guys and said to one of them, 'This town ain't big enough for the both of us and I'm not gonna leave, so you better get out.' Then he walked out. But he finished it off in his own style by simply touching his hat in a cocky way.

Then they set him up for a scene in which he sat on an office desk and said to the secretary, 'Say, honey, whaddaya do with your nights off?'

'I go to wrestling shows,' she replied.

The screen test was a success and Raft got the role in *Quick*

Millions. He was perfect as a screen gangster, and similar parts quickly followed. Of course, nobody knew just why he seemed so experienced at playing screen gangsters.

After *Quick Millions*, Raft was set for a part in *Hush Money* with Joan Bennett, and was receiving other offers. But the police were still keeping an eye on him.

He was at Wrigley Field enjoying a ball game, when a husky, red-faced man sat next to him. He was a police lieutenant known as Lefty James. Raft was sure he'd seen him hanging around the studio. James flashed a gold badge that read 'Los Angeles Police Department' and said, 'I'm Lieutenant James. We want to talk with you at the station.'

Raft was driven downtown and taken to the office of Police Chief Taylor. 'Have you seen Molly O'Day lately?' Taylor asked bluntly.

'I haven't seen Molly for around six months,' answered Raft.

'But you used to be involved with her.'

'Sure. But Molly and me didn't really get on. So we agreed to disagree. Just what are you guys driving at?'

'Miss O'Day was robbed in her apartment at the Garden of Allah of all her cash and most of her jewels. You're our number one suspect.'

'What kind of a guy do you think I am?'

'We *know* what kind of a guy you are. We've been watching you for a couple of weeks, and you don't look so good. You're a New York hood, which is reason enough for not liking you in our town. Since there are plenty of trains going east, I hope you've got enough for a ticket.'

'I'm no hood,' said Raft, controlling his temper. 'I'm an actor. Check it out.'

'We know that, and more.' Taylor wasn't letting on that they had been told by a New York source that he was there not just as an actor but as an agent for Owney Madden.

Joe Masseria treated Luciano like a son. Charlie Lucky was Masseria's criminal mastermind, and as the trouble with

Maranzano escalated, Masseria's demands on Luciano increased until, finally, Luciano loudly complained, 'What more do you want from me, Joe? You're swallowing up all my time these days.'

Masseria flew into a rage. 'I'm not only going to swallow all your fucking time, but your fucking whiskey business too. I think you gone crazy, Charlie. You let that bastard Costello invite everyone into the organization. Costello's got no Sicilian blood. And Sicilian blood is all that matters. Why didn't you stop him, Charlie? Look what we got now, fucking Jews. That Bugsy Siegel and Lepke, and Lansky too. Sicilian blood, Charlie, and the *right* Sicilian blood! The Castellammarese are trying to take over my rackets, but we'll deal with them.'

What Masseria didn't know was that Luciano was already planning to deal with him, as well as Maranzano. Years later Luciano said, 'All us younger guys hated the "Old Moustaches" and what they were doing. We was trying to build a business that'd move with the times and they was still living a hundred years ago.'

One night Charlie Luciano, Frank Costello and Vito Genovese met at Luciano's hideaway on Broome Street in Lower Manhattan. They had to move fast, even without the valuable advice of Meyer Lansky who was preoccupied with domestic traumas. His wife, Anna, had given birth to a crippled child, prompting her to upbraid him in no uncertain terms for his lifestyle which she disapproved of. She was certain that the crippled child was God's punishment, and her distress was such that she had a complete nervous breakdown. Lansky took his family out of New York to a secret and safe place for a while. But he had already stated his position quite clearly, saying, 'All we have to do is eliminate the two roadblocks [Masseria and Maranzano] and from then on Charlie sits on top. That's what he wants, isn't it?'

Joe the Boss was beginning to feel the strain. Luciano showed understanding and said, 'Let me treat you to a long lunch at Scarpata's.' Scarpata's was a great seafood restaurant in Coney Island. 'It will help you to relax,' said Luciano.

On 15 April 1931, they sat down at Scarpata's to enjoy linguini with red clam sauce, fresh lobster, rich Chianti wine. Joe was fat and greedy, and he ate too fast. His meal was over before Luciano's ultimate plan could be completed.

Joe stretched and said, 'Let's get back to the city.' It was two-thirty; Luciano had to stall him for another hour. He summoned a waiter: 'Bring a deck of cards.'

'What's with the cards, Charlie?' asked the fat boss.

'I just figured that a pleasant game of rummy was just what you needed. All through lunch you've talked of the things that have troubled you over the months. You gotta relax and forget the tension.'

'Good boy, Charlie. You're a good boy.'

The cards arrived and they began playing. After an hour Luciano excused himself and went to the men's room in the back of the restaurant. He was washing his hands when four men with pistols came into the restaurant and found Joe Masseria sitting with his back to them. They fired twenty times into his head. Luciano heard the gunshots. He continued washing his hands, dried them and came back into the restaurant to find Joe Masseria lying face forward on the table, the cards covered in blood.

Luciano, Costello, Genovese and even the Jewish mobsters were now welcomed by the Castellammarese group headed by Don Salvatore Maranzano. He was obsessed with ancient Roman history, particularly the life of Julius Caesar whom he appeared to consider the first Italian Boss of all Bosses. On hearing of Masseria's demise, he announced, 'The organization needs a Boss of all Bosses, which is myself.'

He gave Luciano the Masseria family to preside over, with Genovese as his underboss.

Everything seemed to settle down into the form of organized crime that Luciano and Costello had hoped for. But then came a disturbing rumour. Maranzano had drawn up a 'kill' list – Costello, Capone, Luciano, Genovese, Dutch Schultz, Lepke, Siegel and almost fifty others were scheduled to be executed.

Word of Maranzano's murder list had been spread by a Maranzano thug named Angie Caruso during a drunken spree at an establishment owned by racketeer Nig Rosen in Philadelphia. Possibly, Maranzano had got wind of the plot Luciano was hatching to become the Boss of all Bosses.

Costello and Luciano discussed how they should best deal with Maranzano. 'There's no way Maranzano can be lured to a deserted restaurant,' reasoned Luciano, 'and especially not by me.'

'I think we got an expert to settle this matter,' said Frank. He gave Benny Siegel a call and explained their predicament.

That very day Maranzano called Luciano. 'Charlie, I want you to come to my office tomorrow afternoon – say, two o'clock.'

Maranzano hung up, pleased with his plan. He had contracted Vincent 'Mad Dog' Coll, one of the most ferocious killers in the history of crime, to arrive at ten minutes past two. Maranzano was sure that Charlie Luciano would not leave his office alive.

At precisely two o'clock the next day, four men entered Maranzano's office at 230 Park Avenue and found Maranzano with his secretary and five bodyguards. One of the men flashed a badge that identified him as a Federal tax man as his colleagues disarmed the bodyguards.

'What is the meaning of this?' demanded Salvatore Maranzano.

'We would like to check your books. You'd be unwise to refuse us.'

'Come this way, gentlemen,' said Maranzano, leading the way into his private office. Two of the Feds remained with the secretary and the bodyguards. The other two entered the private office and slammed the door shut behind them. Then they stabbed and shot Maranzano to death.

The two killers burst out of the private office. Already the secretary and bodyguards were fleeing the building. The 'Feds' raced down the stairs and on the way came face to face with Vincent 'Mad Dog' Coll on his way up. One of the killers stopped just long enough to say, 'Get lost, Vincent.'

A little later Benny Siegel called Luciano. 'Maranzano's dead,' he said. 'I had a few Jewish pals of mine pay him a visit.'

Luciano knew that Maranzano's assassination would arouse the hostility of the old-guard mafiosi – the Moustache Petes – who would seek to form a coalition in order to avenge Maranzano. Luciano had made contingency plans.

Within twenty-four hours of Maranzano's death, about fifty old-time mafiosi were put down across the United States. Never before, or since, had there been such an organized and extensive programme of executions within the Mafia. It was known as the Night of the Sicilian Vespers.

Luciano called those who had been spared, the younger mafiosi, and, as he told it, 'I explained to them that all the warhorse shit was out. I told them we was in a business that had to keep moving without explosions every two minutes. Knocking guys off just because they come from a different part of Sicily – that kind of crap – was giving us a bad name, and we couldn't operate until it stopped.'

Lucky Luciano was now the undisputed Boss of all Bosses. And under him, the modern Mafia was formed, with regional families and rules against indiscriminate killings.

To carry out contracted executions, a special organization was set up which became known in the press as Murder Inc. It operated its courts and sentences under the cloak of the so-called 'Borough of Churches'. No execution was ever carried out without the approval of one of its top enforcers, Albert Anastasia. Lepke shared Anastasia's authority and power, and among the actual executioners commissioned to carry out countless murders were Benjamin 'Bugsy' Siegel, Mendy Weiss, Benjamin Goldstein and 'Pittsburgh' Phil

Straus. Another was Harry Greenberg, also known as Big Greenie Greenberg or Big Harry. Because almost all those involved in Murder Inc. were Jewish, it also came to be dubbed 'Kosher Nostra'.

Such men as Siegel were, according to Vincent Teresa, 'experts with a variety of guns and other weapons. They are cool under pressure. They also have no emotion.' They were a special breed. And they were well paid. 'They handle killings as though they were selling insurance.'

One of the gang's chief hatchet men was a Gentile, Abe 'Kid Twist' Reles; squat, thick-lipped and with long arms that dangled like a gorilla's. He was referred to later by King County Judge, George Martin, as being 'more vicious than Dillinger'.

Later, Benny Siegel had to sacrifice his compulsion to 'go where the action is' when Luciano told him, 'I've got bigger things planned for you,' and appointed him one of the chief lieutenants. However, Siegel still committed his fair share of killings, although it was a small percentage of the grand total of Murder Inc.'s jobs, which was estimated to be no fewer than one thousand.

One of Siegel's victims (as revealed later when Abe 'Kid Twist' Reles squealed loudly) was a minor league gambler in the Borough park section of Brooklyn called Flat-Nosed Puggy because of his mushroom-shaped proboscis.

Siegel, Reles and Greenberg got together to decide on how best to dispose of Puggy. 'Where are we going to get him?' Reles asked.

'Take him to your house,' said Greenie.

'Why my house?'

'You're moving anyway,' Greenie laughed.

'My wife is going to meet your wife to go to the movies,' Siegel told Reles, 'so I don't think your wife is going to be home. That's settled then.'

'Benny, ride him around an hour,' said Greenie. 'Make believe you're looking for Tiny. Then bring him to Abe's.'

'OK.'

The three arrived at Reles's house and Siegel asked, 'Have you got a rope and an ice-pick?'

Reles went into the kitchen to look, then went to the bedroom where his wife was sleeping. He woke her up, asking, 'Where's the rope we used up at the lake last summer for the washline?'

'Down in the cellar,' she replied sleepily. Reles soon returned to the bedroom with the rope and asked, 'Where's the ice-pick?'

'In the pantry.'

His wife got out of bed and followed him into the pantry where Greenie was helping himself to some milk. He looked at her and said, 'Why don't you go back to sleep?' She knew something was going to happen, and did as Greenberg suggested.

Later that day Reles's wife and Estelle Siegel went off to the movies. Reles and Greenberg waited in the house while Siegel and Ralph Dukey, the driver, collected the unsuspecting Puggy and drove him round, as planned. While Dukey waited outside by the car, Siegel took Puggy into the house. Before he knew what was happening to him, Greenie came up behind him and threw an arm around his throat, causing him to gag. Then Greenie threw the terrified victim onto the sofa.

'Don't hit me, don't hit me!' Puggy screamed. 'I got the money.' But nobody wanted the money and his pathetic pleas were making no impression on the cold killers.

Reles turned up the radio and went to get the rope. Siegel stood back and watched with some amusement as Greenie tried to hold the struggling Puggy down. Puggy sank his teeth into one of Greenie's hands. 'The bastard!' shouted Greenie, laying his full weight across Puggy in an effort to stop him kicking and struggling.

Reles gave one end of the rope to Greenie and they began trussing up Puggy like a chicken. He kept his head down, trying to stop them from getting the rope around his throat. Siegel grabbed him by the hair, yanking his head back, and

Reles slipped the rope around his throat, pulling it tight. Then he and Greenie exchanged ends, crossing the rope and tying a knot. Reles ran the rope around Puggy's throat again.

With Siegel holding him by the feet and Reles and Greenie grabbing his head, Puggy was pulled to the floor and turned as Greenie continued to tie him until his head was forced down against his chest, his knees folded up against his chest and his hands in between his knees. It was impossible for him to move. If he struggled, the rope tightened around his throat.

Exhausted, Greenie gasped, 'We better burn this bum up, so nobody will know him. Benny, go get some gas.'

Reles helped Greenie to carry Puggy out of the side door and into the car where Ralph Dukey waited. 'Take the bum down to the dumps – down on Flatfields Avenue,' Greenie told Dukey. 'Nobody will know the difference if you put a match on him there. The dumps are always burning.'

Siegel and Dukey drove down to Flatland Avenue. They pulled up and dragged Puggy from the car, into a deserted slum. 'Keep the motor running, and stay on the wheel,' said Siegel.

He poured an entire can of petrol over Puggy who spat and choked and cried for mercy. Without a second thought, Benny Siegel lit a match and threw it on Puggy who was quickly engulfed in flames. Siegel didn't stand around to watch Puggy being burned alive. He jumped into the car and Dukey sped off.

Occasionally, killings were averted by quick action, or even a phone call in the right place. It was lucky for Gary Cooper that George Raft was in Hollywood.

8

Connected in Hollywood

It wasn't unusual for George Raft to be called upon from time to time by old acquaintances from New York. This particular call was an 'emergency job'. One of the major mobsters back east was looking for his missing girlfriend and had finally traced her to Hollywood.

'She's crazy about a young actor,' Raft was told. 'If you want to save this guy's life, Georgie, you'll find the girl and hustle her out of town. Otherwise this actor winds up on a slab.'

'OK,' said Raft. 'Who is he?'

'Gary Cooper.'

Raft got straight on the phone and called a man named Wilson Mizner who knew everyone in town. Mizner called back the next day and gave Raft the girl's address. Raft drove at high speed to her apartment.

'Pack your bags, you're going home,' he told her.

'Who do you think you are, telling me what to do?'

'I'm just someone doing your boyfriend back east a favour.'

'Well, don't do *him* any favours.'

'OK, I'll do your boyfriend here a favour. It's Gary Cooper, right? Listen, baby, Cooper is a dead man if you don't get on the next train back east.'

She quickly changed her mind and in no time at all she was packed. Raft drove her to the station and got her on the first train going east.

As for Gary Cooper, this sudden loss of his girlfriend led

him into a romance that was to have its own repercussions on Benny Siegel's love life just a few years later.

Cooper was very much a lady's man, despite his bashful, golly-gee, screen image. The year 1931 marked a crossroads in Cooper's life. Since 1929 he had been involved with the fiery actress Lupe Velez, the 'Mexican Spitfire', but after two years the flames had become embers. Cooper was exhausted by Lupe's tantrums, which no doubt led him into the dalliance with the gangster's moll.

The full life he was leading was proving a little too much for him, and he began losing weight and contracted anaemia and jaundice. He once said, 'When I went to Hollywood I had no talent for acting. I had gone there full of zip and energy, ready to take on any assignment no matter how rugged. Now I was approaching thirty – not really old – but what energy I had was gone. I felt like an old man. Hollywood had burned me out and I hadn't even begun to act. I felt like throwing in the towel. I was very depressed.'

His doctor ordered him to rest so he decided to take a holiday in Europe. He went first to Paris and then to Italy where he visited Venice. One day, while sitting in the hotel lobby, feeling lonely and depressed, he received a letter from his friend, producer Walter Wanger. It read:

> Gary
> I think you'll find yourself getting lonesome by yourself in Venice ... I suggest that you take a run down to Rome and visit a friend of mine, the Countess Dorothy di Frasso, who has a place called Villa Madama. ... I'm sure you'll have an enjoyable time. ... She runs a sort of open house for celebrities, dignitaries, royalty on the go, and other congenial characters.
> She'll welcome you with open arms.

Cooper followed Wanger's advice and took off for Rome. There he arrived at the Countess's villa, only to find that she had gone away for several days. He was made comfortable by the servants, however, and some days later she returned with her entourage. As she entered the beautiful reception hall, she saw for the first time the tall, handsome and splendid Gary Cooper.

That weekend, visitors to the villa included Prince Umberto, Barbara Hutton, and the Duke of York (the future King George VI). Yet even with such illustrious company, di Frasso took it upon herself personally to keep Cooper happy.

The Countess had been born in New York, the daughter of an American millionaire, Bertrand Taylor, one-time president of the New York Stock Exchange. According to legend, he left her twelve million dollars. Her first husband was British adventurer Claude Grahame-White who apparently owned the first petrol-driven motor car in England, and had one of the first British pilot's licences. Her next husband was Count Dentice di Frasso, a close friend of Mussolini. Her acquired title and inherited wealth turned her into a Roman socialite whose jewels and international circle of glittering friends were legendary.

'She felt that the presence of young and beautiful people around her might help to keep at bay the passing years,' David Niven said to me. 'But she was a truly generous person and absolutely loved to give pleasure and provide fun for those less well off than herself.'

Cooper spent several weeks in the Countess's company, and when his strength had returned enough to prompt him to go on a hunting safari in Tanganyika, she went with him. Some maintain that during this time a change came over him. Up until then he had been very much a Montana man. But Dorothy gave him a touch of sophistication. She sent him to the best tailors in Rome, took him on visits to other countries and bound him over with such generosity that he began to feel he was now a citizen of the world.

David Niven, however, refuted this. 'Dorothy di Frasso spent a great deal of her time and money polishing Coop, who was to her like a rough diamond, but Coop resisted and remained his own man. But he greatly enjoyed his long liaison with Dorothy.'

Whether or not his relationship with the Countess affected his life, it did lift his depression about Hollywood and acting, and he returned to the United States, resolved to be an *actor* and not just a presence on the screen. He began filming *A Farewell To Arms* with Helen Hayes, who fell in love with him. Dorothy was constantly on the set, making sure that Helen kept her distance. Dorothy di Frasso was as smitten by him as he was by her.

Helen Hayes was unimpressed with the Countess. She described her as 'a very possessive and terrifying woman'. Understandably Miss Hayes never had a good word about the Countess and noted that 'after the romance with Gary broke up she had a fling with a gangster in Palm Springs, Bugsy Siegel. That doesn't reflect much style and taste, does it?'

Actually, before the Countess was to embark on her wild fling with Siegel, she was to become romantically involved with smooth-as-silk emerging movie star Cary Grant. He and di Frasso were mentioned in just about every gossip column and were seen at every night spot. Both of them would later become close to the eventual crime lord of Hollywood, Benny 'Bugsy' Siegel.

There were many in Hollywood who, like George Raft, fraternized with gangsters and indeed were often on extremely friendly terms with them. Among them, according to screenwriter John Lee Mahin, was director Howard Hawks who 'knew a number of big-time gangsters in Chicago'.

Not that there is any evidence that Hawks was ever a gangster himself. He had moved from his home town in Goshen, Indiana to California at the age of ten in 1906, but later attended school in Pasadena and finally in Massachusetts at the Philips-Exeter Academy. It was hardly a background which would introduce him into elements of the underworld. He'd studied engineering and from the age of sixteen he was a professional racer of cars and planes, and served as a pilot with the Army Air Corps during World War I; later he worked in an aircraft factory as a designer and flyer. During summer vacations at school he had worked in the props department of the Famous Players-Lasky studio, and he finally decided to return to Hollywood and began working as a cutter, then assistant director, casting director and story editor before turning to directing in 1922.

There had been little, if any, opportunity for Hawks to make underworld contacts, but it is certain that during the filming of *Scarface* in 1932, his contacts proved useful, ultimately bringing him into close proximity with the man who inspired the picture, Al Capone.

'Capone got wind that a film was being made that was supposedly based on him, which of course it was but at the time nobody was going to admit that or the film might never have got past the censor,' said John Lee Mahin. 'So he sent spies down to the studios to find out what Hawks was up to.' Ironically, the film was not originally intended to be about Capone.

Howard Hughes had bought the screen rights to a novel by Armitage Traill about two brothers, one of whom became a gangster and the other a cop. He took the property to Hawks, but before long Hawks had an idea for a different kind of gangster movie. He had heard an anecdote about how Al Capone staged a big party at which he made a long speech and, towards the end, became so enraged that he beat a traitor to death with a baseball bat. In that one act, Hawks saw a man of such wild violence that he seemed to be something of a modern-day Cesare Borgia.

Hawks called Ben Hecht, the playwright, who had won the first Oscar given to a screenwriter for *Underworld*, and asked him to write *Scarface* with him. Mahin, who was later brought in to collaborate on the screenplay, thought that Hawks might have made his underworld contacts through Hecht, who had been a columnist in Chicago and New York during the twenties and had probably come across men like Capone and Luciano. In fact, his first screenplay, *Underworld*, was, under

Josef von Sternberg's direction, the first movie to look at crime from the gangsters' point of view. It was unlikely, according to Mahin, that Hecht would ever repeat himself: 'Ben Hecht never wanted to write another gangster story as long as lived. But Howard persuaded him, saying that he had this idea of basing it on the Borgia family but making it about Al Capone and set in Chicago. That got Hecht interested, so he and Howard started writing it. They called it *Scarface*, and together they completed a shooting script in eleven days. Then I was brought in to work on the script.

'When Howard Hughes read the finished script, he said to Howard, "Where's the brother, the cop?"

'Howard said, "We don't have the brother. There is no cop."

'"But you got rid of the whole book," said Hughes. Then he said, "But you've got one hell of a story".'

Paul Muni was given the title role. Ann Dvorak played his sister, based on Lucrezia Borgia who had had an incestuous affair with her brother, Cesare Borgia. And as the unforgettable coin-flipping Guido Rinaldo was George Raft. It was the role that was to make him a star. Hawks considered it typecasting; he claimed that Raft had moved to California to 'carry a gun for the gangs'. Hawks seemed to know much about Raft's dealings with the underworld. It's possible that Raft gave Hawks a number of contacts, although this seems unlikely, because Hawks only ever seemed to call Chicago, and Raft's dealings had been in New York. Nevertheless, when Capone's spies began turning up in Hollywood, Hawks used his own contacts to find out who they were.

'Strange men kept turning up on the set, asking if they could watch the filming. Howard knew they were gangsters,' Mahin told me.

One day a guy introduced himself as George White. Hawks said to him, 'Look, I'm so goddamn busy today, come in tomorrow morning, OK?' Then he wired to Chicago, where he had a friend, to find out as much as he could about this George White. It turned out that this guy was known as Puggy

When Charles 'Lucky' Luciano became the New York Mafia Boss of Bosses he focused his sights on the movie capital, Hollywood. *(Popperfoto)*

Glamorous film star Thelma Todd began a deadly love affair with Lucky Luciano and paid the ultimate price for knowing too much. *(Popperfoto)*

Luciano's life came to an end when he suffered a massive heart attack in his native Sicily. *(Popperfoto)*

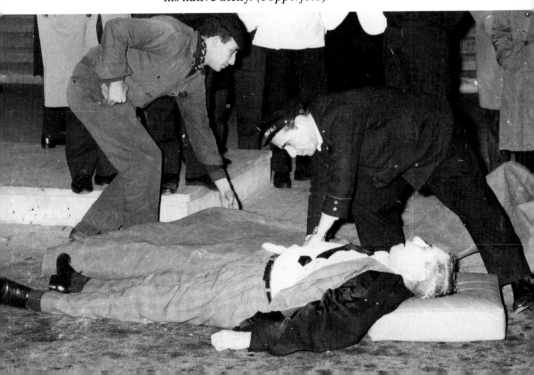

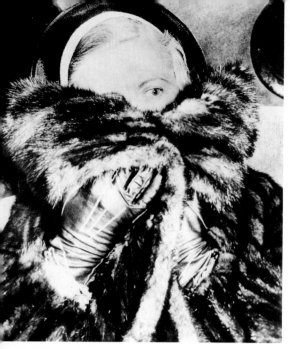

The former Mae Coughlin had good reason to hide her face from the camera; she was the wife of Chicago boss Al Capone. *(Popperfoto)*

Al Capone was Luciano's Mafia rival, and in their personal vendetta both wrestled for control of the Hollywood unions. *(Popperfoto)*

As a result of Bugsy Siegel's murder in Hollywood, the Mafia were investigated by the Kefauver Committee. Among those investigated was Frank Costello (below) who had been Luciano's right hand man and one of Bugsy's closest friends. *(Popperfoto)*

White, a member of Capone's gang. When White turned up the next day, Hawks said 'Sit down, Puggy.'

'How'd you know my name?' asked the surprised gangster.

'I know a lot more about you,' Hawks, replied. 'You're a pimp and you carry a gun and you've killed a dozen men.'

'Howard told me,' continued Mahin, 'that White didn't mind being a called a killer, but he did object about one thing. White said, "I have never been a *pimp*."

'He then gave Hawks a graphic description of a killing. Hawks said to me, "I want you to write it as a scene."

'We put things in that film that had actually happened. Such as the scene where men with guns were hidden in a hearse which they drove to a restaurant which they shot up. It was an incident that actually happened in Chicago.

'In those days, they didn't use blank bullets for films, so the scene when we shot it was like the real thing, with even a little real blood. Real machine-gun bullets smashed the real glass windows and tore up the tables and walls. One actor, the brother of Harold Lloyd, ignored a warning to keep off the set. He went around the back to get a better look and lost an eye from a ricocheting bullet.

'We had a scene in which Raft and Muni brought flowers to a rival gangster in hospital who'd been shot badly. They pulled their guns out of the flowers and killed their rival. That had happened in Chicago.

'During the editing of *Scarface*, three or four gangsters came into the studio and found Howard. They said, "The boss wants us to look at the picture."

'"Your boss? Who would that be?" Howard asked, knowing full well it was Al Capone. Then he told them they could wait until the film was at their local movie theatre when they could see it for a dollar.

'One of them said, "You don't scare easy, do you?"

'Howard said, "No. Look, why didn't you just come up and ask me if you could see it? I'll screen it for you if you tell me what you think of it."

'So he showed it to them and he told me that they were so amazed at the realism, they wanted to know how we had found about all those things. Howard told them, "I can't reveal my sources".'

At that time in 1931, Capone was battling to maintain his freedom. A grand jury had returned an indictment against him, due to raids on his bootlegging warehouses by Federal Agent Eliot Ness and his famous 'Untouchables'. Capone and sixty-eight members of his organization were charged with 5,000 separate offences relating to the Volstead Act. But the District Attorney was having trouble making the charges stick with the few key witnesses suffering a high mortality rate. So the Feds were trying to find evidence against Capone of tax evasion.

Capone decided to take a brief break, and turned up in Hollywood. Hawks sent him an invitation to come and see the rough cut of the film.

In a studio preview theatre, the feared Al Capone sat and watched a movie that was clearly based on him. Howard Hawks sat with him, although Howard Hughes was not there. Hawks probably thought better of letting Hughes, or anyone else, in on the fact that Al Capone was at the studio watching *Scarface*.

When the lights came up, Capone looked at Hawks, gave a little smile and asked, 'Now, tell me, where did you get some of that stuff?'

'Look, Al,' said Hawks, 'don't you have some things that you don't tell people?'

Capone thought for a moment. He laughed and said, 'Yeah, you're right there, Howard. Well, that's a great film you've made. Of course, I don't know anyone like that character Paul Muni played. And that Rinaldo guy, always flipping a coin – he looks familiar.'

'That's George Raft. He was a dancer in New York before he became an actor.'

Capone knew Raft well and had actually recognized him in the film. But he was curious to know what he was doing in films. He knew he was Owney Madden's man.

Capone reciprocated Hawks's hospitality by inviting him for a visit to Chicago. Hawks went to the Hotel Lexington, Capone's headquarters, and told Capone's male secretary, 'I'm Howard Hawks from Hollywood. Al told me to look him up.'

'It's a pleasure to meet you, Mr Hawks. I saw that film you made. I know the boss liked it. I'm afraid he isn't in. I'll be sure to let the boss know you're in town.'

Later that night Hawks was visited at his hotel by some of Capone's men. One of them said, 'Mr Capone sends his regards and asked us to take you to dinner and then show you around since he can't.'

Hawks followed them out into the street and was about to get into the big black limousine they indicated when he paused. 'Where is Mr Capone?' he asked.

'Well, there was a killing last night. And he had to go out of town on business.'

Hawks had a vision, like a clip from a gangster movie, of the limousine being riddled with bullets by some rival out for vengeance. He said, 'I'll meet you at the restaurant because I'm taking a cab.'

The mobsters just laughed and said, 'OK.'

When Hawks arrived at the restaurant, he found that all of Capone's men sat with their backs to the wall. They had some beautiful blondes with them.

The next day Hawks left for New York but returned to Chicago a week later, when he received a personal call from Capone inviting him to a cocktail party in his honour. The huge bash was held at the Hotel Lexington where Capone, dressed in a morning coat and striped trousers, played host. There seemed to be women everywhere, as were the cream of Chicago's criminal society. Hawks was struck by how cordial and polite they all were.

The high point of the evening came after dinner when Capone presented Hawks with a small machine-gun as a special gift. That was the last time Hawks saw Capone.

As *Scarface* went on release throughout the country, Howard Hughes sent George Raft on a personal tour, appearing at theatres showing the film. The Chicago opening was delayed until a clip was added to the film featuring a city official talking about the evils of the underworld.

After the Chicago première, a tough young hood, with a gun bulging under his coat, showed up at Raft's hotel room and said, 'Raft, the boss wants to see you.'

'OK,' was all Raft could think to say, and he followed him out of the hotel and into a big black limousine. He was driven to the Hotel Lexington and there had to pass through security checkpoints where armed guards gave him deadpan looks. Then he entered Capone's private office.

Capone was seated behind a huge mahogany desk which was adorned with various trinkets and oddments – a fancy gold inkstand, a small carved Chinese chest, a clock in which little quails and cuckoos sounded the quarter- and half-hours .... On the walls hung oil portraits of George Washington and Mayor 'Big Bill' Thompson.

'Georgie, so you been playin' my bodyguard, Frank Rio, in this *Scarface* picture,' said Capone.

'Yes, I did, Al,' said Raft. 'But it's nothing personal. Actors do what they're told.'

Capone rubbed the long scar on his face. He looked deadly serious. 'Well, you tell them guys in Hollywood that they don't know Al Capone. They bumped me off in the end and nobody's bumpin' Al off while he's running Chicago. Yeah, you tell 'em that.' Then Capone laughed.

They spent some time talking about people they'd known in New York and the old times. Finally Raft said, 'Well, Al, I gotta go.'

He was about to walk out when Capone said, 'Wait a minute, Georgie. I see you tossin' a coin all through the picture.'

'Just a little theatrical touch.'

'A four-bit piece, yeah?'

'No, it was a nickel.'

'That's worse. You tell 'em that if any of my boys are tossin' coins, they'll be twenty-dollar gold pieces.'

'I'll be sure and convey the message.' Raft turned to leave. Standing in the doorway, he asked, 'You like the picture, Al?'

Capone was flattered with the attention the movie had brought him, and with the name *Scarface* on marquees across the country. 'Yeah,' he said, 'I liked it.'

Not long after, on 17 October 1931, Capone was found guilty on three counts of tax evasion and two counts of failing to file a return. Capone was sentenced altogether to eleven years in prison, with fines totalling $50,000 and court costs totalling $30,000.

Probably no other Hollywood figure was as well connected as George Raft. Determined to put his seedy life behind him, he sought to build his film acting career and set aside the little jobs Owney Madden gave him from time to time. But it was difficult for him to escape his past completely. He was still Madden's man in Hollywood, and in the early thirties, Madden came to Hollywood.

Raft was his host and took him on a tour of Californian nightclubs, giving gossip columnists a field day tying in George Raft, the growing screen star, with gangsters. This concerned the various studios Raft was working at and did nothing to dissipate the suspicions of the Los Angeles police department.

When a cop saw Madden and Raft in a club, he arrested Madden, suspecting him of violating his parole by leaving New York. Madden was jailed while a check was made on the conditions of his parole. When Madden became hungry, Raft bribed the jailers with $150 to bring Madden some sandwiches.

The police confirmed that Madden had violated his parole, and the gangster was immediately returned to New York. By this time Madden's political connections had waned and there was no one who was able to pull the correct strings to prevent him from going back to prison. Consequently, Madden returned to Sing Sing to complete his original sentence.

For Raft, it seemed as though a door had closed behind him, and he got on with his career which at this stage wasn't damaged. He was becoming hugely successful at portraying gangsters in pictures, and the fact that he seemed to somehow live up to that image in his real life simply boosted the public's interest in him. He couldn't know that both Capone and Luciano were making inroads on the West Coast and would eventually infiltrate Hollywood, bringing Raft once again back into association with the underworld.

While raking in thousands of dollars shaking down movie theatres through his projectionists' union, Tommy Maloy had made use of the introduction of sound to movies to increase his profits even more. At first, when soundtracks were reproduced on gramophone records to be played in synchronization with the film, he insisted that theatre owners hired technicians, known as 'faders', to operate the equipment. When sound was put directly onto film, Maloy forced theatre owners to pay $1,100 to the local for each fader they dismissed, which was cheaper for the owners than keeping the faders on the payroll.

Still Capone ignored the projectionists' union, but nevertheless felt it was time to start moving in on Hollywood. So he sent his brother, Ralph – commonly known as 'Bottles' because of his brewing and bottling operations – out to the West Coast.

Lavish restaurants were sprouting up all over Los Angeles and its suburbs, including Hollywood, and movie stars and moguls were spending thousands of dollars eating out. While Luciano's men were taking over the LA drugs racket, Ralph Capone was bringing restaurant owners under his dirty thumb.

Film stars who owned restaurants were prime targets. Whenever possible, Capone put restaurant employees on his payroll. Books were cooked more thoroughly than the steaks which were usually switched for cheaper cuts for the same price. Before long, the owners found themselves unable to make a profit. Then Capone would step in and offer to buy them out for an extortionate price. Those who refused the offer found their doors locked and customers frightened away. Eventually, they had no choice but to sell up, allowing Capone's mob to move in.

By 1931 Ralph 'Bottles' Capone had become established in Los Angeles. Also by that year, according to Mr Volonte, Luciano was making occasional visits to the West Coast.

'There were always gangsters around and they knew where to find young men like me to recruit. I didn't want to be a gangster, I wanted to be a stuntman and I was lucky to get the break. But some of my relatives – my cousins – they were keen to run errands for people who worked for Luciano, and they were initiated into his Mob.'

During one of Luciano's visits, he went to the Brown Derby, which he part owned, and saw, sitting at a table, Ralph Capone. Luciano flew into a fury and grabbed Pat DiCicco by the collar. 'What the hell is that pig doin' here?' he ranted. 'That slime is supposed to be in the pen. Who did he pay off? The president?'

'What are you talking about, Charlie?' asked DiCicco, trying to calm him down.

'I'm talking about that fat pig Al Capone.'

'But Charlie,' said DiCicco, 'that's *Ralph*, his brother.'

Luciano checked his temper. They took their table, but still he was ruffled. 'What's he doin' in Los Angeles anyway?' he mumbled.

Bothered by Capone's presence, Luciano put out feelers, and it didn't take too long to discover that Ralph was shaking down the restaurant business. He was still working under orders from his brother, who continued to issue his commands from behind bars. Luciano subsequently began taking over establishments himself, installing illegal gambling casinos into many of them.

Los Angeles and Hollywood were fast becoming a potential

battleground between Luciano and Capone. Their rivalry was not to do just with business competition, but with mutual hatred too. Then, in May 1932, Capone was transferred to Alcatraz from where he was unable to transmit his orders. With Al Capone completely out of the picture at last, Luciano believed that Hollywood was his for the taking. The women of Hollywood also became his for the taking.

Pat DiCicco managed to get himself invited to most Hollywood parties, including one thrown by Hal Roach in celebration of his new comedy team, Thelma Todd and ZaSu Pitts, a sort of female version of Laurel and Hardy. All of the Roach contract stars were there at the Palace Theater, including Laurel and Hardy and Charley Chase. There were also moguls like Louis B. Mayer and Adolph Zukor. Jean Harlow was also there along with such major stars as Clark Gable and Gary Cooper.

Pat DiCicco had never met Thelma Todd before, but the moment he saw her, he made a beeline for her, took her hand and kissed it. She was quite overwhelmed by this handsome stranger.

'I am Thelma Todd,' she said, a little breathless.

'I am Pasquale DiCicco,' he replied. 'And it is a pleasure to meet you.' That was the beginning of a passionate affair.

DiCicco lavished gifts on her, took her to expensive restaurants and to cosy little hotels for intimate weekends. She had heard all the rumours about his association with Lucky Luciano. Her father had been a cop, and she had taken to playing with his gun. She had always been fascinated by men who were surrounded by danger, and to be with a man like DiCicco was the most exciting thing that had happened to her. But what she wanted most was to know about Luciano.

DiCicco was enraged that she was digging into a part of his secret life, and she discovered the violent temper he possessed. 'Who do you think you are, pressing me like this?' he ranted. 'You goddamn bitch!'

He suddenly slapped her hard across the face, bringing up a huge swelling that kept her off work for four days. Despite this, Thelma continued to be mesmerized by him and after he calmed down she gladly forgave and forgot.

On 18 July 1932, the couple travelled secretly to Prescott, Arizona for a quick marriage ceremony before the Justice of the Peace, with only the sheriff's wife for a witness. Thelma Todd had had a father who connected her to the world of crime. Now she had married a man with truly powerful underworld ties. She was as well connected as any movie star could be. She would shortly come into even closer proximity with the Mafia.

9

Blondes and Big Shots

Marino Bello was without doubt the most pernicious influence in Jean Harlow's life. Yet she seemed willing to follow
his advice and guidance. She did, however, reveal to friends
at the studio that he kept leaving suggestive notes in her bed,
still intent on bedding her himself.

'You should tell your mother,' they urged her.

'It would only hurt Mama. I can handle him – I've had
plenty of experience with jerks. I just laugh in his face.'

Howard Hughes had lost interest in her and was loaning her
out to other studios. In 1931 she co-starred with James Cagney in the film that began the popular cycle of gangster films
at Warner Bros, *Public Enemy*. She made a number of films
at Columbia, including *Platinum Blonde* which established
her as *the* platinum blonde. Then Hughes loaned her out to
MGM for *The Secret Six*, which starred Wallace Beery and
featured Clark Gable in a major supporting role. Gable and
Harlow hit it off immediately, becoming firm friends. She was
particularly thankful to have such a good friend on the set
since she and Wallace Beery despised each other.

'She's a dumb broad,' complained Beery to an assistant
director, 'and she can't act. Keep her out of my way.' The
animosity between the two seems to have arisen from her
having refused his invitation to come to his dressing-room.

Marino Bello was a constant visitor to the set, taking on the
role of Harlow's protector. He took Beery aside and told him,
'You touch my stepdaughter just once, and I'll see to it that
your arm will be ripped from your body.' Bello was well able

to carry out his threat. He maintained contacts with gangsters and knew he could find someone willing to take Beery apart, even kill him, for the right price.

Beery stayed away from Harlow throughout the rest of filming. Although Beery hated Bello, Gable liked him. They were both 'men's men', and became good buddies. It's doubtful that Gable was aware of Bello's notorious background.

Despite her popularity, Hughes still declined to cast Jean in any of his own films. Her agent persuaded him to sell her contract to MGM in 1932 with the stipulation that Hughes would have the right to use her in two of his own pictures over the next five years, although he never took up that option. MGM started her off with a salary of $1,250 a week, rising to $5,000 by the seventh year.

Accompanied by Bello, Harlow went on a series of personal tours throughout the country. During one such tour to New York, Bello introduced Jean to his old friend from New Jersey, Abner 'Longie' Zwillman, who was instantly attracted to twenty-one-year-old Baby Jean.

Zwillman made a deal with Bello to court her. In return, Bello hoped for a piece of Manhattan where he could operate in the illegal booze trade. He dreamed of becoming part of the Meyer Lansky corporation, or even Luciano's empire, and running his own speakeasy. Bello's version of the 'husband business' looked set to make him a Big Shot at last, although in reality what he was doing was little more than pimping. Yet Harlow seemed willing to go along with this, excited by the company of Zwillman. Mama Jean, however, knew nothing about any of it.

Zwillman was a frequent visitor to Hollywood, claiming to have business interests in Los Angeles. He rented a bungalow at the Garden of Allah, and took every opportunity to be with Harlow.

It would appear that she was genuinely fond of Zwillman, and for the rest of her life she wore a platinum bracelet which he gave to her. From it hung tiny objects, including a pig, which was a jokey reference to her eating habits, and a miniature man of the world, which represented himself. This was much admired by her friends, and seems to have started the charm-bracelet craze.

Harlow also gave gifts to Zwillman; strands of her pubic hair which Zwillman put into small gold lockets and gave to his friends. Somehow, Mama Jean heard about the lockets and flew into a rage at Bello, demanding he stay away from the Mob, threatening him with divorce. Bello may have been willing to allow her to carry out her threat, but he didn't want to lose his influence over Harlow. She was his meal ticket for life. Unable to bear the thought of losing both Mama and Baby, Bello gave up the idea of becoming an active member in the Syndicate – for the time being – and began concentrating instead on becoming a successful agent. Even his underworld associate Frank Orsatti had become an agent.

Orsatti was an amiable, not too bright bootlegger whom MGM executive Eddie Mannix had introduced to Louis B. Mayer in 1931. Meyer told Orsatti that the country's opposition to Prohibition was so intense that repeal was only a matter of time.

'You're in a dying business,' Mayer warned him. 'Get out while the getting is good. Be an agent. Every ten years the agents pocket one full year's income of the talented people who work here in my studio. And that's going to get bigger as salaries move up.'

It was good advice. In 1933 Prohibition was repealed. The whole underworld had to find other ways to compensate for this loss in revenue. Orsatti became an agent and also accepted the post as Mayer's permanent bodyguard. LB could tolerate hoods, as long as they paid him tribute.

News of Bello's underground connections reached the ears of MGM's echelons, thanks to Los Angeles gangster Eddie Nealis. He met for a Sunday game of golf with his friend, MGM executive Eddie Mannix. 'You know, don't you, that Baby Jean Harlow's screwing around with Longie Zwillman,' said Nealis as Mannix teed off.

'For chrissake, what's she playing at?' Mannix asked.

'It's that stepfather of hers. Come on, Eddie, don't tell me you guys don't know that Bello's from Chicago.'

'One of Capone's men, you mean?'

'Maybe not one of the big shots, no, Eddie, but the man's been around men like Capone a long time. Now he's getting in good with Longie. They made a deal so long as Longie can fuck the Baby.'

'Jesus Christ! LB's gonna have a heart attack when I tell him. What the hell else has Harlow been up to?'

'Don't you know anything about your own stars, for chrissake? She's so oversexed, that girl, she'll willingly go to bed with anyone Bello tells her to.'

'I don't believe that,' said Mannix. 'It's all an act. She's supposed to be sexy, but she doesn't sleep around, I'm sure of it.'

'You sure about that?'

'Do you know different? Have you had her?'

'I never laid a hand on her,' said Nealis. 'Movie stars are just a headache. Give me a waitress any time.'

Mannix duly reported his findings to Louis B. Mayer. 'I always knew she was a slut,' said Mayer. 'But I never knew that about Bello.'

Mayer and his cohorts had tolerated Bello because he was Harlow's personal manager, but they knew that beneath the slicked-down hair and behind the waxed moustache lay a character of dubious quality. Basically, they knew he was no legitimate agent, but until now they did not know what he actually was.

Unable to rid themselves of him, MGM continued to tolerate his presence, but Mayer wanted to waste no more time on him, despite the fact that Bello never gave up trying to form a friendship with him. He even persuaded Clark Gable to act as a go-between, but Mayer had no use for Bello and didn't mind letting him know it.

Bello continued to show up regularly at the studio, usually around ten o'clock, parking his car outside Harlow's dressing-room. When Harlow was on the set, Bello usually took himself first to the studio barber for a shave and to read the trade and fan magazines. He also spent hours in the commissary with casting directors and trying to impress producers and directors. But once Harlow's exclusive contract with MGM was signed, the studio had little need for him at all.

Her affair with Zwillman and Bello's failed attempt to be a Big Shot in the Mob awakened Jean to her stepfather's manipulations. She began seeking a way of escaping his influence.

She could now afford the luxuries in life, and so she bought a Spanish-style house in West Los Angeles. Mama Jean and Marino Bello moved in with her and Bello, seeing himself as his stepdaughter's financial adviser, began spending and investing her money in dubious ways that brought her little profit, and leaching off her and her mother. She usually curtly referred to him in public as 'Bello', but she put up with him simply because she loved Mama Jean so much, despite the fact that Mama Jean had deserted her during her childhood.

'Somehow,' said Jesse Lasky Jr, 'Jean was able to overlook the pain of the past and didn't object when Mama Jean behaved more like her sister instead of her mother. I always thought that Mama Jean was living out her own fantasy vicariously through her daughter, and enjoying Jean's fame and fortune as though it were her own.'

As for Marino Bello, Jean's success meant that he could work little, and when he did earn money, the nature of his work always remained dubious.

During the filming of *The Secret Six* Harlow met Paul Bern, right-hand man to Irving Thalberg, Metro's head of production. Bern was forty-two with receding hair and hardly attractive, but Harlow fell in love with him which, in years to come, became something of a mystery – a mystery, however, that only grew out of a fantastic cover-up masterminded by Louis B. Mayer. More than likely, Harlow was always looking for a father-figure to replace the real father she had hardly known, and the stepfather she wished she'd never had. But there never was a real question as to why a woman fell in love with a man twice her age.

Paul Bern was known in Hollywood as a 'Father Confessor', because film stars, especially women, confided to him their most intimate problems. However, according to the myth that sprang up following his tragic death, he was supposedly impotent. But that was all part of the cover-up

As the romance between Harlow and Bern progressed in early 1932, he took over Bello's position of her guiding force. Bello found himself having to stand back and watch another man take more and more control of what was after all Bello's richest commodity. He hated Bern and hoped the affair would come to nothing.

Bern wanted Jean to take the lead in the studio's up-coming *Red-Headed Woman*, but Irving Thalberg, Mayer's boy wonder, wasn't convinced that Harlow was right for the role, not least of all because Jean was blonde and not red-headed. Bern argued that she was absolutely perfect and to prove his point he decided to make a secret film test. While the test was being shot, Bern, who was wise to Bello and despised him, had him barred from the set.

Bello whisked Harlow off to do another tour on the East Coast. Each day Bern called Harlow, telling her to be patient while he waited for his chance to show Thalberg her test. Thalberg was being inundated with suggestions as to who should play the role. Bern came up with an idea but he needed Bello's help.

He managed to reach Bello backstage at a New York theatre where Jean was appearing. He told him his idea, and they agreed to join forces to get Harlow the title role in the *Red-Headed Woman*. From 8 April through to the 12th, Bello sent a series of telegrams to Thalberg, reporting that Jean had been asking audiences if they wanted to see her in *Red-Headed Woman*. 'EVERY HOUSE RESPONDS WITH ENTHUSIASTIC APPLAUSE,' he said in each telegram.

On the day that a decision had to be finally made, Bern showed the test to Thalberg. Also watching were director

Jack Conway, writer Anita Loos and cameraman Hal Rosson. Each voted for Harlow. Thalberg gave in and awarded Harlow the role.

When the news was made public that Harlow had got the part, Bello wasted no time in letting everyone know that he had personally engineered the casting. He took all credit as the guiding light in her rise to stardom, and in so doing became so unbearably arrogant that Paul Bern didn't even waste breath disputing his claims.

'Let him have the last word,' Bern told his assistant Al Lewin. 'I've got the last laugh.' His last laugh was to ask Harlow to marry him, promising her the deeds to his dream house on Easton Drive. She accepted.

Meanwhile, Marino Bello was continuing to wheel and deal his way into legitimate business. He attempted to handle important clients but was saddled with a style of running a business that would have served him better back in Chicago. One of his plans was to try to take over management of boxer Max Baer who had been brought to MGM by his fight manager Ancil Hoffman. The studio was preparing a story about the ring called *The Prizefighter and the Lady* as a star vehicle for the boxer.

While Hoffman was busy engaged in negotiating the final details with Mayer, Bello took the opportunity to take Baer aside and suggest that Baer fire Hoffman and take up with him. He promised the fighter that he could get him more bouts, and a larger percentage of receipts and bookings on big-time Vaudeville circuits between fights. He would also arrange coast-to-coast personal appearances with Jean Harlow. He had not thought to discuss this with Harlow first, or with Bern.

Baer told Hoffman he didn't need his services any more as he was taking up with Bello. Hoffman acted quickly to retain Baer with L.B. Mayer's help. The movie still needed months of preparation, so Hoffman took Baer far away from Hollywood, and away from Marino Bello, until they were ready to begin filming.

In July 1932, Harlow and Bern were married, much to Bello's dismay. He saw the control of Jean's money and business affairs passing completely from his hands into Bern's. This would undoubtedly have been a major incentive for Harlow to marry Bern, as part of her plan to escape the influence of Bello.

She appreciated the way Bern treated her like a lady. She was used to the groping and manhandling of Bello's gangster friends and the young studs of Hollywood.

The wedding reception took place the day after the ceremony. Bern himself said that Marino Bello, who only outwardly approved of the marriage, shook Bern by the hand as the bride and groom said their farewells, and whispered menacingly, 'Better take good care of my baby.'

On the night of 4 September 1932, Bern was shot to death.

The official story is that Paul Bern stripped himself naked, doused himself in Jean's favourite perfume, sat before a mirror at their home and shot himself.

Marino Bello and Clark Gable had supposedly 'gone fishing' on the day Bern died. Actually they had gone to a Mojave Desert retreat with a pair of attractive females. They had found time to fire off a few shots at some passing birds, but their prime reason for being there was to spend time with the girls.

Louis B. Mayer knew exactly where they were because he had Eddie Mannix phone Bello with the news of Bern's death. Bello was not sorry; neither, in fact was Mannix who didn't like Bern.

'We don't want Jean involved in this,' said Mannix.

Bello agreed. 'Does anyone know why he killed himself?' Bello asked.

'He was impotent,' said Mannix. 'He couldn't make it with Jean, so he killed himself.'

Bello knew it was a lie. But he said, 'I knew from the beginning he was a queer little guy. Don't worry, Mannix, I'll see to Jean.'

Bello felt very satisfied, but he did not let Gable know his true feelings. Gable was Harlow's friend, and he felt devastated for Jean over her loss.

The news quickly spread that Bern had killed himself. But DA Buron Fitts believed he had been murdered. He even thought that Harlow might have killed him. He also suspected Marino Bello, who certainly had reason to want Bern out of the way. Following his death, Harlow's financial affairs reverted to Bello's control. Fitts thought that Bello had hired a hit man.

It seemed very convenient that Bello had 'gone fishing' with Clark Gable and didn't plan to be home that night. As he was leaving Mama Jean alone until morning, a prospect that mortified her, Bern had a good reason to insist that Harlow spend the night with her mother. It was a tight alibi.

As far as Louis B. Mayer was concerned, any suggestion of a murder could destroy Jean's career for good. A meeting of all major MGM executives was called at which they were informed that a suicide note had been found. It read,

Dearest Dear
Unfortunately, this is the only way to make good the frightful wrong I have done you, and to wipe out my abject humiliation.
I love you.
Paul.
You understand that last night was only a comedy

However, this note was not by the body when the police arrived on the scene. According to Howard Strickling, Louis B. Mayer had been called to the house by the butler before the police were informed, and Mayer had discovered the note and put it in his pocket. It was at Strickling's insistence that Mayer had put the note back where he found it. That was Strickling's story. It was all part of the cover-up.

The postscript on the suicide note suggested that Bern's humiliation had become complete in an effort to make love to Harlow. Years later, a handwriting expert confirmed that the note had indeed been written by Bern. But it was also shown that it was just part of a longer note written on a pad that was incomplete. Exactly what the message on the sheet of paper actually referred to has never been discovered. Nevertheless, the note seemed to confirm that Bern had killed himself.

Irving Thalberg met with the studio executives before Mayer arrived, and told them, 'LB is writing the script for the inquest. He and Howard Strickling are deciding who'll get the starring roles. They don't want Jean to appear, so they're figuring how to ask Marino Bello to be her stand-in.'

Somebody asked what made Paul kill himself. Thalberg, disgusted by the cover-up, replied, 'Ask L.B. He'll tell you. He's got it all figured out. Impotence! Paul couldn't make it with Jean...so he ended all his worries about it.'

'Bullshit!' shouted Al Lewin. 'I know three women at least who'll tell you that Paul was one hell of a lover.'

Mayer came in and made a seemingly sincere speech about how Paul should have been honest with Jean about his impotence before they were married and that he did the 'right thing when he picked up the gun'. He said that the public would understand, and Jean would be a bigger star than ever.

Eddie Mannix, who had already been briefed, announced that Harlow was to say nothing to anybody. 'I just talked to Marino Bello. He'll handle her. He knows the score. He didn't like Paul any more than I did. We both pegged him right, a wishy-washy queer posing as the little father-confessor.'

Mayer put everything on the line when he said, 'If you don't stand by me now, you will destroy MGM and yourselves with it.'

None of this was ever publicly known until screenplaywright Sam Marx revealed the complete cover-up in his book *Deadly Illusions*, in which he also confirmed the theory many had long believed – that Bern had been murdered by his secret and mentally sick common-law wife, Dorothy Milette.

Following the meeting, Mayer summoned Marino Bello to his office.

'I hear the DA thinks Bern was murdered,' said Bello.

'Don't worry about Buron Fitts. I've already had the Culver City police chief call him. Fitts has been promised a satisfactory reward in return for our full co-operation. No, Bello, you tell Jean I don't want her to say a word to anybody. Let her play the bereaved widow. That's it, nothing more.'

For the first time, Mayer and Bello were united, agreeing on every aspect of the cover-up. Bello saw to it that others, apart from Jean, kept their mouths shut. He even called Bern's gardener, Clifton Davis, and told him, 'You are talking too much. Move your wife and children over to the garage and keep your damned mouth shut.'

When police came to question Jean, Bello, with the help of doctors and lawyers, negotiated a deal with the police not to ask incriminating questions and to confine their questions only to Bern's possible motive for his 'suicide'. In every respect, Marino Bello was suddenly like a small-scale Godfather, and he relished it.

Jean was excused from appearing at the inquest, leaving Bello, Thalberg and the servants to testify. Taking the stand as the first witness was a thrill for Bello, and in the newspaper photographs he appeared arrogant and confident.

Coroner Frank A. Nance asked Bello to state his profession.

'Mining,' said Bello.

'Mr Bello, have you seen the remains of the deceased in the adjoining room?'

'Yes, sir.'

'What was the date of his death, so far as you know.'

'I don't know the date. It was Sunday or Monday.' He went on to affirm that he didn't know the time of Bern's death, and he said he was not present at the time of death.

Questioned further, he said that he had telephoned his wife to say he was going to be late home because the 'boat had stalled in the middle of the channel'. After his wife told him that Bern was dead, he rushed home. He didn't mention that Gable and two girls were with him and that he was actually in the Mojave Desert.

To Mayer's delight, the official verdict was given as 'Death by gunshot wound of the head, self-inflicted by the deceased with suicidal intent. Motive undetermined.'

In an attempt to stop Dorothy Milette from contradicting the suicide verdict, studio investigators pursued her and discovered that she had caught the *Delta King* ferry from San Francisco to Sacramento. But she never arrived in Sacramento. Her body was found floating in the river.

Fifty years after the event, Sam Marx wrote that Sheriff Cox had suspected Milette might have been murdered. 'I felt Dorothy Milette could have been murdered but none of the important questions were ever asked,' said Cox. 'Her diaries and letters disappeared and must have been destroyed. If she wanted to drown herself, why do it in the Sacramento River? Plenty of water in San Francisco. I was prevented from doing my job.'

Much later, a crime reporter, Hank Messick, wrote of his own theory in a book, *The Beauties and the Beasts*. He believed that Longie Zwillman had been involved, and asserted that Zwillman had collected Milette and driven her to Paul Bern's house where she shot Bern dead. Zwillman erased all evidence and drove Milette to San Francisco to catch the ferry.

Messick placed Harlow into this scene, claiming that she arrived at the house with Zwillman and Milette. Presumably then, Zwillman had taken Milette to meet Harlow who was horrified to discover Bern had a common-law wife. Harlow 'watched in horror' as Milette shot Bern. Zwillman then dropped Jean off at her mother's before driving Milette to San Francisco.

Messick raised some interesting points that have been flatly refuted by most others, including Sam Marx. But it was true that Marino Bello was friendly with Zwillman, and Bello certainly had his reasons for wanting Bern out of the picture. So, did Bello hire Zwillman to find the emotionally and mentally disturbed Dorothy Milette, bring her to meet Harlow, take them both to the house, allow Milette to do the deed and then ensure that she never lived to tell the tale?

If so, there was no one willing, or able, to testify. Witnesses, namely Jean Harlow and Mama Jean, were under Bello's influence, and remained silent. All Harlow ever said to the police, who themselves were forbidden to ask her direct questions, was, 'I can't understand why this terrible thing had to happen. As for the note left by Paul, I have no idea what it means. This "frightful wrong" he apparently believed he had done me is all a mystery. I can't imagine what it means.'

Despite those at MGM who insisted that Paul Bern was alone that night, *three* used glasses were discovered at the house, suggesting that more than two people had been there. And according to the columnist, Adela Rogers St John, Harlow was hardly heartbroken by Bern's death.

Said Adela Rogers St John, 'I told Harlow that Paul Bern had once tried to kill himself by thrusting his head down a toilet. Jean said, "He must have looked pretty silly." I said, "I wish they'd let him drown," and Jean said, "So do I".'

Nobody entered more wholeheartedly and with such enthusiasm into the cover-up than Marino Bello. Maybe he was merely acting on Mayer's orders for the sole good of Harlow. Maybe he was acting out of a sense of self-preservation.

Thelma Todd's marriage to Lucky Luciano's LA front man was in trouble from the beginning, not least because of Luciano himself. He had not met Thelma, but he knew of the actress they called the Ice-cream Blonde; he had a penchant for blondes.

But the main trouble was that Thelma would often return home to their ranch-style home in Brentwood to find DiCicco gone without so much as a note of explanation. The first time, when he eventually returned home, she was so frantic with worry that she virtually flew at him.

'Where have you been?' she cried.

'I had business in New York,' he said curtly.

'For God's sake, couldn't you have left a note or phoned or something?'

He couldn't bear this questioning and, unable to see how frightened she'd been, he slapped her hard. After a while, when they'd both calmed down, he said to her, 'Next time I have to go away, I'll phone.'

'Can't you let me know before you go?'

'It's not always possible, Thel. Sometimes, something comes up that is too urgent to stop and write notes. Sometimes I'm somewhere else when I get a call to leave.'

'A call? From who? Where?'

She was asking too many questions again and his anger was boiling up once more. 'Just stop questioning me,' he shouted, and she wisely dropped the subject.

The next time he went away, he found time to call her. 'I'm in New York, Thel, but I won't be here long,' he said. 'I got some business here.' And that was all she got out of him.

Thelma began to wonder if DiCicco still loved her. After four months of marriage there was an empty space in their lives. DiCicco's dealings in New York were destroying his marriage. Yet it was also his inability to deal with the situation. His problem was largely due to the fact that, although much of his time in New York was spent on legitimate business with theatres on Broadway, he was also meeting with Luciano. And he was unable to tell Thelma what his association with Luciano was all about.

He had put her in a dangerous position by marrying her, for she was now tied unwittingly to the underworld. He had also put her within Luciano's reach, should Luciano wish to reach her. DiCicco was aware of how vulnerable Thelma was. He should have divorced her immediately, but he was, like so many involved in nefarious business, selfish and greedy, and he was, despite his actions, deeply in love with her. He wanted her for himself and he kept her hanging on a line, knowing she would be there for him when he got home.

This was the belief of a vain man, for he must have believed that, although he was using her so blatantly, she would not turn elsewhere for solace. To an extent he was right, for she drowned her sorrows with booze and diet pills. Her alcoholism and drug addiction in one sense kept her faithful to DiCicco because she spent her lonely evenings getting totally stoned, yet it also tore them apart by instilling in her a violent temper to match DiCicco's so that their reunions were stormy to say the least.

In November 1932, Thelma became ill with appendicitis and was immediately operated on. DiCicco had been scared for her and his fright brought out his love. When he brought her home, he stayed by her side during the weeks of recuperation and helped her off the booze and pills. That Christmas was a happy time for them both. She was fit and well and off the pills, and he was at home.

Then, in February, he left for New York with no warning, no note, not even a phone call. The days wore on and Thelma, alone in the house, became more miserable. In search of a few laughs, she called Roland West and suggested they meet for dinner. He gladly accepted and they met that night at the Brown Derby.

He had married actress Jewel Carmen but they were now separated, although still on good terms. They had even worked out a business venture together, which West revealed to Thelma that evening.

They planned to buy a property and turn it into a restaurant. Thelma became intrigued with the idea and was in the process of telling West so, when into the restaurant came Pat DiCicco and a man she didn't recognize. She suddenly fell silent, stood up and walked over to DiCicco's table.

DiCicco did not seem fazed to see her standing above him, saying not a word. He remained calm and, as ever, the gentleman. He said, 'Thel, this is my good friend, Charlie Luciano.'

Luciano rose and took her hand. 'I have seen you in many films,' he said softly, 'and you are even more beautiful than on the screen.' He kissed her hand and said, 'Please, sit by me.'

She was overwhelmed by this charming, coldly dangerous man, and even though she had not even taken a drop to drink since her operation, she had trouble refusing the glass of champagne he poured for her. She finally gave in and sipped her champagne. Then she knocked it back, enchanted by Luciano's flattering attention towards her. He refilled her glass.

'I really should be going,' she said. 'I have worked all day and am very tired.'

'You would not insult me by refusin' a drink,' he said, holding her with his eyes. She relented and smiled, and continued drinking.

DiCicco watched her, glanced at Luciano and the way his cold eyes were fixed on her, and he knew that Luciano wanted her. Before long she was drunkenly relaxed and her old bubbly self. Luciano was enjoying her company; DiCicco sat by, silent and helpless.

'Luciano was soon coming to Los Angeles every other week,' said Mr Volonte. 'He was spreading his drugs ring, and a lot of my friends and relatives were paid very well for peddling his drugs for him. The big fish were the film stars and my cousins were soon finding the right people to contact.'

As Luciano's trips to Los Angeles increased, so did DiCicco's visits to New York during 1934. His dealings with mobsters such as Lepke and Benny Siegel became more time-consuming than his Broadway-based activities.

The fact that Luciano always seemed to be on the West Coast at the same time as DiCicco was on the East was not all coincidence. Patsy Kelly, who would soon replace ZaSu Pitts as Thelma's screen partner, said, 'Thelma was my pal and although we were good friends, I don't think we were as close as Thelma was with ZaSu. Hal Roach teamed me up with Thelma because ZaSu wanted more money. Roach had been very shrewd with Thelma and ZaSu, as well as with Laurel and Hardy, in having them sign their initial contracts at different times, so ZaSu's contract expired before Thelma's preventing them from making a united stand for more money. Finally ZaSu decided she'd had enough, and Roach brought me in and gave me the same kind of deal.

'I think Thelma resented losing her friend but she was still warm to me. I knew that she had been drinking heavily and was supposed to be having trouble with drugs, and there were days when she just couldn't get it together. That's when she told me about Lucky Luciano – she was having an affair with him.'

Marino Bello was delighted when Jean Harlow returned to the family home. Jean hoped for happiness but was deeply unhappy to find herself back in the same position she was in before she married Bern, and became even more desperate to escape from Bello's greedy clutches. She couldn't bring herself to just walk away from him because she was so devoted to Mama Jean, who in turn was blindly devoted to Bello, and Mama Jean wanted her Baby to live with them. Jean felt that her mother needed her.

Then, quite suddenly, in 1933, Harlow married cinematographer Hal Rosson whom she met on the set of *Bombshell* in which she played, ironically, a film star with a parasitic family. Rosson had also been her cameraman on *Red-Headed Woman*. He was sixteen years older than she and, like Paul Bern, hardly a handsome man.

'Bello was incredulous that his Baby should marry again and took great exception when Jean and Rosson moved into a tiny apartment on Sunset Boulevard, because Rosson couldn't bear to live with Mama Jean and Marino Bello,' said Jesse Lasky Jr. 'Jean began fixing up the apartment and loved doing it. Then she became ill and her mother, who by this time had become a Christian Scientist, insisted Rosson allow Jean to be treated by a Christian Science practitioner. Jean became unconscious and Rosson called a doctor. For the first and last time Rosson and Bello were in agreement and worked together in ignoring Mama Jean's protests and got her into hospital.

'When she was well, she refused to go back to work, insisting MGM give her a raise. She was suspended without pay. But she didn't care because she and Rosson were coping on Rosson's salary alone. Bello was concerned that he and Mama Jean were running low on funds; they depended on Jean's income to keep them in luxury. Marino Bello was getting desperate, and objected when Jean and Rosson went to San Francisco for a much missed honeymoon instead of getting back to work. Eventually, MGM gave her the raise she wanted and Marino Bello was happy again.'

Bello couldn't risk his stepdaughter rebelling against the studio again. He and Mama Jean knew that they had to get Jean back into the family home and out of that marriage. This didn't prove too difficult. As Jesse Lasky Jr said, 'Why did Jean marry Rosson? Well, he wasn't the most exciting man in the world – he was really rather dull and ordinary, but she saw him as a means of escape from Marino Bello. And Bello didn't like this. He didn't like Rosson, and neither did Mama Jean, and they did their best to drive him away.'

They succeeded. He just wasn't strong enough to stand up to Marino Bello and Jean lost him. It was her last chance to get right away from her stepfather.

10

Shakedown

Along one side of Fulton Street in Chicago most of the stores were run by Jews. The other side was dominated by Gentiles. Shop owners on the Jewish side were under the protection of one Willie Bioff. The protection he offered was not to get bombed or burned out for a regular fee. Bioff was a man of his word; the Jewish storekeepers chose not to cross him, and they duly paid up.

They were wise to do so, for Bioff was a ruthless small-time hood who had started his crooked career by pimping at the age of just nine, when he uséd to sidle up to men and announce, 'Mom has gone out and my little sister's at home. She's really cute.'

Then he would lead his customers to a side-street apartment where they were greeted by a group of whores who were not related to him, and not necessarily cute.

When he married he didn't give up the game but made his equally unscrupulous wife a partner in the recruitment of runaway girls who needed a roof over their heads and a regular wage. Mr and Mrs Bioff set these girls up in their Southside brothel, ensuring that the girls remained in their employ by locking them in the whorehouse so that it became a virtual prison for them. To discourage them from attempting to escape, Bioff threatened to throw acid in their faces. Some did make the attempt – he twisted their nipples with a pair of pliers. To keep the police off his back, Bioff paid off officers.

One girl who received a beating from Bioff eventually

managed to escape. She ran to the nearest police head-quarters and was lucky enough to find an officer who was not being paid off. Bioff was duly arrested and indicted for aggravated assault and battery.

He was sent to prison for six months but he greased a few influential palms and was released on parole after just one day. Then he took to shaking down the Jewish side of Fulton Street. He also worked as a 'slugger' for the Teamsters' Union, collecting dues and 'persuading' men to join the union.

It was while he was doing his Fulton Street round one day that he came across George Browne. Like Bioff, Browne was shaking down the shop owners, but on the Gentile side. He and Bioff were physically alike – both were short and fat with slicked-back hair – and perhaps that is why they took a liking to each other instead of trying to kill each other. Browne was, however, not quite so ruthless as Bioff.

As well as his protection racket, Browne was a business agent for the Chicago Stagehands Local No. 2, which was affiliated to the International Alliance of Theatrical Stage Employees. IATSE encompassed some thousand local unions in America and Canada representing property craftsmen, art directors, cameramen, sound and lab technicians, make-up artists, script supervisors, set painters and members in every branch of film production, as well as employers in film distribution and exhibition.

Bioff quickly decided that he could profit from Browne's union, and before long the dubious duo had agreed to a partnership. One of their first actions was to raise the Stagehands' Union dues by $5 a week. They also set up the B&B Soup Kitchens as a front – places where men out of work could get a bowl of soup and some bread each day. They got the idea from the soup kitchens that Al Capone had set up which gave him the appearance of a charitable man, but also proved an effective way of laundering money.

Later, over a dinner, Bioff and Browne concocted their master plan to shake down Chicago's movie theatres. They began by paying Barney Balaban a visit. Balaban and his

partner Sam Katz ran a chain of leading movie theatres in
Chicago. They had begun in 1908 with a single movie theatre
and, as the film industry grew, so did their venture; and it had
become vastly prosperous. Their theatres were the first to
have ice-cold refrigeration, a primitive air-conditioning.

Bioff and Browne turned up at Balaban's office with the
intention of threatening a stagehands' strike if he didn't pay
them what they asked for. But they were visibly nervous
and Balaban had no hesitation in chasing them out of his
office.

It was important for them to impress and intimidate
Balaban; he was the biggest of the theatre owners, and when
he fell, the rest would follow. So they returned to his office,
pushing their way in and behaving like screen gangsters.
Balaban was vaguely amused. 'OK, you got my attention,' he
said.

'Good,' said Browne. 'Now here's what we want. You give
us twenty thousand dollars in lieu of a pay rise for our union
members. The money will go into a fund set up for our members to be used in times of emergency and need, such as when
men are out of work, or need loans, get sick.'

'And if I don't?'

'Then we'll have no choice but to call a strike.'

Balaban understood perfectly that he was being bribed. 'I
see. You know, I don't like your plan and I want you both to
get out of here.'

'You'll be sorry, Balaban,' warned Bioff as he and Browne
left.

Balaban had shown fearless defiance, but he was nevertheless concerned. He had, however, noted that of the two men
Browne had seemed the less aggressive and possibly the one
he could reason with. When he heard that Browne was in
hospital with an ulcer, he went to see him. Browne was in a
private room; the two men could talk openly.

'Listen, Browne,' said Balaban, 'Tommy Maloy has been
shaking us down for years, yet he is happy to take a hundred
and fifty dollars a week from us. Now, if you could consider

having the same arrangement between us, I think we could get along just fine.'

Browne thought it over. 'OK,' he said.

Browne thought they had done as well as they could hope for. Balaban was a happy and relieved man. But Bioff was furious when he heard.

'You agreed to a measly hundred and fifty bucks a week?' Bioff ranted. 'I'll bet he's laughing at us right now. But he won't be laughing for long.'

Bioff went to see Balaban and told him, 'On behalf of Mr Browne, I'm afraid we can't accept your offer of a hundred and fifty dollars a week.'

'What's the meaning of this?' demanded Balaban who smelled a bigger shakedown about to happen.

'What's happening,' Bioff told him, 'is that you're gonna pay the union fifty thousand dollars.'

'You're crazy,' said Balaban. 'We don't have that kind of money.'

'I suggest you get it,' threatened Bioff.

'You can whistle for it,' said Balaban defiantly.

'You'll be sorry,' warned Bioff.

He was as good as his word. The word went out to a number of projectionists working for Balaban and Katz, and a series of mishaps occurred. At the Oriental, a film was run backwards. At the Uptown, *One Night of Love*, a Grace Moore musical, was shown without sound. And at the Tivoli the image was blacked out during the motel scene of *It Happened One Night*. Theatre cashiers were besieged by furious patrons demanding their money back.

Balaban was now a worried man, and he and Katz held a hurried meeting. Balaban hadn't expected Browne and Bioff to prove so ruthless in their dealings. He and Katz now felt they had no choice but to make the payoff. They wrote a cheque, payable to the B&B Soup Kitchen, and Balaban's attorney, Leo Spitz, personally handed the cheque over to Browne and Bioff, insisting they pay him $1,000 for 'carrying charges'. They agreed.

It had all worked like a dream and had been easier than either of them had thought. To celebrate, they went off to Club 100, a place owned by Nick Cirella, better known in underworld circles as Nicky Dean. They drank plenty of bootleg liquor which encouraged them to boast about their independent new racket in which they were going to make a fortune.

Nick Cirella listened closely to the story, carried on smiling like the welcoming host and poured them more champagne as well as beer and bourbon. Then he gave them two of his best girls who took them upstairs for a good time while he got on the phone to Frank Nitti.

To all intents Nitti was the new boss of Chicago, although he was actually answerable to Paul Ricca. It was the media who named Nitti as Capone's successor, and Ricca was happy to go along with that illusion, which allowed him more freedom to work in the shadows with Murray Humphreys. So while Nitti acted as front man, Ricca and Humphreys spent their time paying off police and government officials. Jake Guzik took care of the money, and taking care of executions was Sam 'Mooney' Giancana.

The next day, Nitti sent 'Cherry Nose' Gioe and a number of thugs to Browne's office to announce, 'Frank Nitti is cutting the Syndicate in for half the takings.'

This isn't Syndicate business,' Browne told him.

'Frank wants to see you at the Lexington Hotel. I suggest you turn up,' said Gioe.

Browne and Bioff figured they had no choice but to do as Gioe suggested and turned up to meet with the new crime lord of Chicago.

'We're taking over the Stagehands' Local while you two do the collecting,' Nitti told them.

'How much do you get?' asked Bioff.

'Half, I think that's fair, especially since I'm guaranteeing that you don't die. And you won't get bothered by no one else. What's more, Georgie, we're gonna get you elected as

Benny 'Bugsy' Siegel mingled with the stars and ran the Hollywood rackets on behalf of the New York Mob. *(Camera Press)*

Virginia Hill was the authentic 'gangster's moll' who became a Hollywood actress thanks to her lover Benny Siegel. *(Popperfoto)*

The screen image of George Raf[t]
seen here (left) in *Scarface*, wa[s]
just a reflection of his life a[s]
a member of Owney Madden['s]
Gopher Gang.

James Cagney actively oppose[d]
the Mafia in Hollywood an[d]
nearly paid with his life for i[t]
(Popperfoto)

president of IATSE. Then we're gonna shake down the entire movie business right across the country.'

'You figure that's possible?' asked Browne, hugely impressed.

'If you two dopes could manage it here, I'm sure we can do the same throughout the country.'

'But how are you gonna get me elected?'

With the help of friends – like Charlie Luciano and Lepke. I think we can persuade the entire union membership to vote for you.'

True to his word, Nitti called on Luciano and other crime lords from across the country to attend a special conference in Chicago. But Luciano wasn't to be as co-operative as Nitti had hoped. According to Mr Volonte, 'Luciano hated Al Capone, and he hated Frank Nitti because Nitti was Luciano's rival in Los Angeles where they were fighting for control of the drugs racket and restaurant business.'

Luciano deliberately turned up at the conference ten minutes late. The intended insult was not lost upon Nitti. Johnny Roselli, Nitti's West Coast representative, got up and began explaining how the unions were set up in Hollywood, how many men were employed by which studio, and that he estimated they would rake in more than a million dollars.

Nitti rose. 'As you can see, there is plenty of money to be made, provided we all work together, with me at the head.'

That brought the first response from Luciano. 'Nitti, you are not boss. I am *the* Boss.'

Nitti remained calm. He had the Boss of all Bosses to contend with and if he had the chance, he would be the next Boss of all Bosses. Like Luciano, he was Sicilian and wanted the Mafia under his control. 'This is good business for us all,' he said. 'There's plenty to go round. We're equal partners in this.'

'We are not equal. You cannot do this without me. But I don't need you. OK, Nitti, let's say I give my help in this – there is something I want.'

Nitti knew what Luciano was gunning for. 'Name it, Charlie.'

'You have been moving in on my drugs business in Los Angeles. Stay out. One more thing, you own a lot of nightclubs and restaurants. I want a share.'

Luciano was correct that Nitti need him, and Nitti knew it. But he had no intention of giving in to both of Luciano's demands. 'As far as the nightclubs are concerned, you're in, Charlie. The other matter is more complicated and I think we should leave that to another time to discuss.'

'I'll give you my answer later,' said Luciano, and he turned and walked out.

A week later Nitti received a telegram from Luciano. It read: 'MI INCLUDI'.

Nitti had to deal next with Tommy Maloy. The election was due in 1934, and Maloy wanted the position that George Browne was going for. Maloy made a grave error. He didn't know that Nitti and the entire underworld were about to put Browne at the head of IATSE, and he came, cap in hand, to ask Nitti to help him in his election bid. He also wanted Nitti to use his influence in certain quarters to help ease the pressure on him from the Treasury Department who wanted him for income-tax evasion. In so doing, he stepped right into Nitti's hands.

'I will see to it,' said Nitti, 'that you only get six months inside.'

'I'd be very grateful,' said Maloy.

'And while you're inside I will see to it that your union business is taken care of. Just let me have all the names and addresses of the members, and, of course, those to whom you make special payments to keep the law off your back. When you come out of prison, the international union will be yours.'

While Maloy was away, Nitti installed George Browne in his position in a 'caretaker capacity'.

Luciano, meanwhile, was taking advantage of Nitti's guarantee that he would not interfere in Charlie's investment in Los Angeles restaurants. But Nitti had made no such guarantees concerning the drugs business.

'Frank Nitti sent out his goon squads, raiding Luciano's warehouses and beating up – sometimes killing – peddlers on Luciano's payroll. Luciano knew Nitti was behind it all. He began coming to Los Angeles more often,' said Mr Volonte.

A bloodbath on the streets of Los Angeles seemed inevitable.

When he was in Hollywood, Thelma Todd became a pleasant diversion for Luciano. She was a prisoner to his magnetism, charm and power. It was, for her, like living a fantasy. Luciano was a man who easily won friends, as Mr Volonte told me;

'I only met Luciano the once. He was charming, full of generosity – they called him magnanimous. But somewhere in there was a criminal and cunning mind. He took boys off the streets and clothed them and fed them and gave them money. But he also gave them work in his syndicate. He turned them into criminals. Yet still he had soul because he would help a widow or a shop owner and he did not always ask for favours in return. He gave me money, told me to buy food for my family, and I could have become a big shot in his army. But I said I wanted to be a stunt man and he wished me luck. He left me alone, never bothered me, but he had many in my family working for him. I will never tell all they did for him. But I know how he expanded his drugs operation. Only Frank Nitti stood in his way. I think he would have killed Nitti because Nitti would have killed him. When Luciano killed, he did not do it totally *senza pieta* – without pity. He did it to survive, and he killed only those who threatened him. Those who would kill him or would not keep silent. Not that that excuses the man's crimes. But he did not kill the old widow, or the kid on the street corner. This was the way the man lived, the way he survived.'

This was the man under whose spell Thelma Todd fell, and went with him often and willingly in his chauffeur-driven car for long drives along the coast.

'I told Thelma to leave Luciano,' said Patsy Kelly. 'I told her he was dangerous. But that's what seemed to obsess her. But I felt also that she was dependent on drugs that he gave to her. She never spoke of it to me again, but while she tried to keep it secret, there were many who knew. I'm sure Hal Roach knew. Dear Stan Laurel and Oliver Hardy, whom she worked with in several films, had no idea. Roland West knew.'

West certainly did know, but not necessarily before March 1934, when Thelma divorced DiCicco on the grounds of mental cruelty and shortly after made a deal with Roland West to join him in his restaurant venture. It was a perfect agreement for her since she was not required to make any financial investment; just her presence and her name. West's estranged wife, Jewel Carmen, was to put up all the money while West took care of the general day-to-day business. Thelma was to encourage her film star friends to come and eat at what came to be called Thelma Todd's Roadside Café.

It was a three-storey building situated on the Pacific Highway. The ground floor was for the restaurant as well as a drug store. On the first floor was a bar and offices. The second floor was unused. Thelma Todd's Roadside Café opened in August and before long was a popular haunt for stars of the calibre of Gable and Spencer Tracy.

Charlie Luciano, however, never entered the place. He went to some lengths of keep his affair with Thelma Todd secret but he did have plans for the Roadside Café which he didn't share with her for the time being. Then one day he told her, 'I won't be around for a while. I got business in Florida.'

As usual, he didn't elucidate, and she didn't dare ask.

Plans to rig the next union election at the IATSE convention in Louisville were concocted in a series of conferences between Nitti and notorious underworld figures, including Lepke Buchalter. It was agreed that Bioff should continue as the power behind the throne. Bioff took his own precautions to ensure a win for Browne by securing a squadron of henchmen from Chicago to attend election rallies throughout the country.

In June 1934, George Browne officially became the president of the union. While the underworld's business affairs gradually progressed, the country's law enforcers received a welcome shot in the arm. Thomas Dewey was appointed Special Prosecutor for New York City.

Dewey had hardly graduated from Columbia Law School a few years earlier when he went to work as chief assistant to a New York Federal Prosecutor. At twenty-eight, he was the youngest person ever to hold the post of Chief Assistant US Attorney in New York, and as such he quickly won tax convictions against assassin John 'Legs' Diamond, and followed with a conviction against Waxey Gordon.

Now, as Special Prosecutor, his next target was Dutch Schultz who went into hiding, assisted by Luciano and Anastasia. There began a round-up of known gangsters and police raids on such establishments as slot-machine parlours. New York's Mayor La Guardia called Luciano 'a no-good bum', and named him as the real Public Enemy Number One.

The heat was on. Luciano decided to get out of the kitchen for a while, and towards the end of 1934 headed for Florida, as he had told Thelma Todd, taking refuge in the Palm Island Casino, run by Bill Dwyer and owned by Luciano. There, one night he watched the floor show performed by Gay Orlova.

On Broadway, she was called 'Gay All Over'. Blue-eyed and blonde, she was said to be so sexy that she could have come on stage in ball and chain and still caused a sensation.

She had been born Galen Arlova in pre-Soviet Russia and had fled the Bolsheviks as a child. With her mother, she went to Constantinople where she learned to dance. Around 1932, she landed in New York and went to work on Broadway as one of Earl Carroll's lovelies. Carroll referred to the teenage Russian beauty as 'the sexiest thrush who ever hoofed for me'.

Her big problem was that she had a permit to allow her to remain in the United States for six months only. After she opened in *Murder in the Vanities* at the Majestic, she eloped with an usher from the theatre's orchestra floor. When Carroll heard the news, he sent Gay a cable: 'YOU MIGHT AT LEAST HAVE PICKED AN USHER FROM THE FIRST BALCONY.'

Two days later, the unconsummated marriage was annulled, but Gay was now eligible to remain in the country. She wasn't lonely for long. A famed magazine cartoonist was a constant companion, and she was pursued by an ardent and wealthy stockbroker who continually proposed marriage. He followed her all the way to Florida for that Christmas of 1934 with a further proposal. She enjoyed keeping him hanging on a piece of string.

Then, one night at the Palm Island Casino she gave her usual sultry performance and was watched with great interest by blonde-loving Charlie Luciano. When she finished her act he invited her to join him at his table. Later, she joined him in bed.

Luciano spent Christmas basking in the Florida sun, enjoying Gay's sexual expertise and forgetting all about Thelma Todd. He was also able to forget, for a few weeks, about his problems with Frank Nitti over the Hollywood shakedown. Years later, Orlova said, 'Charlie was just lovely to me. I even gave up my broker friend for him.'

Christmas passed, the holiday ended, and Luciano felt ready to return to New York to figure out how to deal with Nitti and Thomas Dewey. He took Gay with him, installing her in an expensive suite on exclusive East 57th Street.

Tommy Maloy was devastated to find he had been betrayed and that George Browne had been installed in what he saw as his exclusive job as president of IATSE. Frank Nitti made plans to deal with Maloy at a party during the Christmas of 1934. 'Maloy isn't a man to stand for anyone taking over his union,' Nitti told Browne and Bioff. 'But soon he won't be a problem.'

Several weeks later, in February, Maloy drew up on Lake Shore Drive in his Cadillac. Another car hurtled down the street and screeched to a halt alongside Maloy's and from it came a burst of machine-gun fire. The Cadillac rocked under the onslaught. The gunfire finally stopped and the other car sped away. Inside the Cadillac, pumped full of holes, Tommy Maloy's lifeless and riddled body lay slumped.

It was now time to move in on the rest of Chicago's movie theatres. Bioff's first target was the Warner Bros. chain, and he called on zone manager James Coston.

Bioff talked in a businesslike and non-threatening manner, trying to sound helpful to Coston. 'The union are wanting to put two projectionists into every theatre in the city.'

'That would double the amount we pay our projectionists,' Coston exclaimed.

'That's right. But I can arrange it so that everything stays just as it is, but it will cost you.'

Coston grew suspicious. 'How much?'

'A hundred thousand will do it. But not all from you. If every theatre chain paid up, we should be able to raise that much. All you have to pay is thirty thousand bucks.'

Indignantly, Coston said, 'You're not going to squeeze me. I won't pay and you can get out right now.'

Bioff leaned forward across the desk and said, 'It's up to you. But if I can't get the money together, I can't stop the union's plan going ahead, and it will cost you far more to double the salaries than it will to come up with a mere thirty thousand dollars.'

Coston knew he had been well and truly stitched up. He said, 'I'll have to talk to my superiors in New York.'

'Go right ahead,' said Bioff. 'And just to lend support, you're going to have company.'

The support came in the shape of Browne, Bioff and Nicky Cirella, who went with Coston to New York, and waited in the hall while Coston met with his bosses. When the meeting was over, Coston emerged to explain that it had been agreed to make the payment.

Bioff, Browne and Cirella returned to Chicago with $30,000 in cash. Frank Nitti took half, leaving the rest to the trio to divide among themselves. Cirella used his share to invest in a new nightclub and casino, the profits of which Nitti shared in.

Bioff and Browne next invited John Balaban, brother of Barney, to lunch, over which Bioff gave him the same story he'd given to James Coston. Except that they demanded $120,000 from Balaban, who had no idea that Coston had only been required to pay $30,000. The lunch came to a sudden and premature end when Balaban said, 'I'll talk it over with my brother,' and left.

The Balaban brothers knew they were powerless to fight Bioff and Browne, and they made an offer to pay $60,000 instead. It was accepted, and again Nitti took half the amount. By the time all the Chicago theatre chains had been shaken down, Bioff, Browne and Nitti had collected $332,000.

The next stage was to take on the New York theatres. The first victim was RKO, run by Leslie Thompson. A meeting was set up at which Cirella, Bioff and Browne threatened Thompson with a strike by all stagehands and projectionists unless he gave union members a rise. In the background stood Lepke, silent and intimidating, while Bioff did all the talking.

As things began to look bad for Thompson, Browne offered what appeared to be a peaceful settlement. Browne was always able to convey a more sympathetic approach, while Bioff specialized in striking terror in victims' hearts. For just $150,000, Browne said, he would ensure that work was not disrupted and the call for a rise dropped. Thompson haggled until Brown agreed on a fee of $87,000.

Nitti soon had the New York theatres under his 'protection'. The next location would be Hollywood itself.

When word reached Luciano that the New York theatres were being shaken down without his prior knowledge, and that Hollywood was being primed, he got on the phone to Nitti, asking what his cut was going to be from all this.

'Charlie, you'll get your share, I guarantee it,' said Nitti.

Luciano knew Nitti was lying. 'So far I've not seen a single dime.'

'Lepke is taking care of business on your behalf.'

'Lepke does not represent me,' Luciano raged. He hung up, knowing it was time to take steps to size up the movie business for himself. Said Mr Volonte, 'He didn't want to find himself having to make his base in California. Nitti had Bioff and Browne to take care of Hollywood business, but Luciano had Meyer Lansky and Benny Siegel, a much better team. Meyer had a shrewd and cunning business sense and could handle any business transaction. Siegel was Meyer's closest friend but ruthless and cold-blooded. He was the perfect partner for Lansky. Luciano told them to take a vacation in Los Angeles; not to get into any business, just to keep their eyes and ears open.'

Benny Siegel and Meyer Lansky landed in Hollywood to discover that Jack Dragna, a survivor from the Night of the Sicilian Vespers, had, as he put it, 'been milking the suckers' in the film industry for a long time. He gave them a warning. 'This is my racket. Keep out, or you'll be very sorry.'

Siegel was amused. 'You got us scared,' he said. He was all for taking Dragna out of circulation – permanently. But Meyer had a peaceful and more practical solution. 'When the time comes, we'll put him on the payroll.'

The Combination had been disbanded. It had depended upon the support of Mayor Frank L. Shaw, but his regime crumbled when a former police commissioner turned real estate man made public the fact that he had not been paid for services rendered during Shaw's mayoralty campaign of 1933. This precipitated a re-election in which Shaw was defeated by Fletcher Bowron who promptly broke up the Combination and forced a number of early retirements in the Police Department and the District Attorney's office.

It was clear to Meyer that there was money to be made here. But for now, they were intent on enjoying themselves, and Benny Siegel took the opportunity to reacquaint himself with George Raft. They got together and reminisced about the old days in New York. Raft introduced his old friend around to his movie star friends.

When Marino Bello heard that Siegel and Meyer were in town, he was keen to get a piece of whatever action they were there for. As bait, he used Harlow once again, trying to ingratiate himself by arranging dinner dates between Siegel and Jean. But, as Jesse Lasky Jr said, 'Jean was not going to have any kind of affair with Bugsy Siegel, and she made it clear to him that while she was happy to go out to dinner with him, it would go no further than that. He was, however, quite infatuated with her, and asked her to be godmother to the new baby his wife had had back in New York. She knew that to get involved with men like Siegel and Zwillman was dangerous. Right to the time she died she remained friendly with Bugsy, but she was never intimate with him.'

Although this was supposed to be a vacation, Lansky and Siegel investigated the possibilities open to them and discovered that the extras' union was ripe for picking. Their 'vacation' over, Siegel and Meyer returned to New York and Lansky told Luciano, 'There is money to be made that Nitti hasn't thought of. The town is almost ready for us. You've already got the drugs business sewn up, but no one controls the brothels or the wire services.'

'I got too much important business here,' said Luciano. 'I can't keep running back and forth to California. I need someone in Los Angeles. Someone I can trust.'

Lepke stepped forward. 'Send Benny,' he said.

Luciano was surprised. He'd never considered Siegel to be the kind of man to run a city. Bugsy was an efficient killer and his loyalty to Luciano and Costello was unquestionable. But he had never been a 'boss'.

'Send Benny,' Lepke said again. 'He's a natural.' Luciano thought Lepke might be right. It was probably the one time he should have ignored Lepke.

Bioff had meanwhile arrived in Hollywood, and as he

virtually took over the Syndicate's business, Browne more or less faded into the background. IATSE membership was low in Hollywood. Bioff sent to Chicago for goonsquads to suppress rival unions with threats and violence. Dissident craftsmen in the studios were 'persuaded' to join IATSE.

Bioff was soon working bi-coastal and, in New York, called on Nick Schenck, president of Lowe's Inc., which controlled MGM from New York.

'This is purely a business deal,' Bioff told Schenck. 'You pay the union a hundred thousand dollars, and we ensure that all matters that may result in crippling strikes are quelled.'

Schenck didn't miss the threat diplomatically hidden by Bioff's words. What he was really saying was, 'Pay up, or else.'

Schenck told him in plain language, 'Get the hell out.' He then called Sidney Kent, president of Twentieth Century-Fox, and they hurriedly met to discuss the situation.

'If we give in to these demands now,' they reasoned, 'we'll be under their thumb for ever. No, we won't pay.'

When Bioff heard of their decision, he made it clear to the studio heads that if they failed to make the required payoff, a wave of projectionists' strikes throughout the country would bring the film industry to a halt. Schenck miscalculated; he thought he was too powerful to be touched by a man such as Bioff.

For the next two weeks there was chaos in MGM-owned theatres across the country as film mysteriously caught fire, changes of film reels were delayed and stink bombs were thrown into theatres. The theatres quickly began losing custom.

Schenck, knowing he was beaten, called Bioff and arranged for a meeting. The following day, Kent and Schenck arrived at the Warwick Hotel where Bioff was staying. Schenck brought Bioff $50,000 in cash in a brown paper bag, and Kent brought $25,000.

Bioff regarded the amount carefully. 'This is short of what I asked for,' he said.

'It's as much as we can get together,' they said. 'It's the best we can do.'

'OK,' said Bioff. 'I'll accept this offer, but I may call on you from time to time for certain favours.'

Neither Nitti nor Paul Ricca entirely trusted Bioff to do the job they sent him there for – which was to make money for the Chicago mob, or the Outfit, as it called itself. Overseeing all that Bioff did, and more, was Johnny Roselli, who spent much of his time on the West Coast. Roselli was a smooth-talking, amiable but businesslike associate of the Outfit's who took to 'sponsoring' certain Hollywood stars. Among these were numbered the Marx Brothers, George Raft, Gary Cooper, Jean Harlow, Jimmy Durante and Cary Grant.

Under Roselli's expert eye, Bioff began tithing Hollywood. $50,000 for the major studios and $25,000 for the smaller studios. To ensure that there would be no record of any money changing hands between the studios and the Syndicate, all manner of schemes were hatched. MGM's payment of $50,000 was recorded as being paid to Bioff as commission for selling film stock on behalf of the company. The rest of the studios found other ways to cook the books. It became almost impossible for anyone to track down exactly who paid how much to Bioff. But it was inevitable that in time some irregularity would surface.

11

Without Pity

In 1935 Benny Siegel settled in Hollywood, renting the mansion of movie and Met Opera star Lawrence Tibbett. It helped Siegel enormously to know George Raft, now a huge star, and Siegel pressed his association with him. But George wasn't the only star the Jewish mobster associated with.

On 8 June, he was dancing at the Trocadero with Countess Dorothy di Frasso. They were double-dating with Cary Grant and Betty Furness. 'To know and be liked by di Frasso was a sure passport to social acceptance anywhere for Siegel,' said Jesse Lasky Jr. Through her Siegel became a close friend of Cary Grant's.

When Benny Siegel first made his home in Hollywood, few knew of his Syndicate background. Most people saw him as a sociable businessman with a keen interest in movies. He spoke openly of Raft being a great actor whose gangster characterizations were so authentic they defied explanation. Of course, the explanation was clear. Raft was flattered by the attention Siegel paid him. Much later, when he was denying any close association with Siegel, Raft explained that they had common backgrounds which gave them empathy with each other, and they spoke the same language. But Raft claimed that each knew there were questions neither should ask of the other. Possibly Siegel never did ask Raft for his help in infiltrating the extras' union, but there is no doubt that Raft helped Siegel to meet many of the right people. Between Raft, Cary Grant and Dorothy di Frasso, there was not a door that was not opened to Siegel. As for Raft never asking Siegel any questions, he never had to. He had known him personally in New York.

Raft also said that he believed one of the questions Siegel refrained from asking was how to become an actor. He said that Siegel hung around the studios to watch the process of filming, and bought his own movie cameras and projectors. He came into Raft's dressing-room once and asked Raft to take some footage which Siegel later showed his friends at his home. Raft said that he had a hunch that Siegel was a frustrated actor, 'but never had enough nerve to ask for part in one of my pictures'.

It's difficult to think of Bugsy Siegel never having the nerve to ask for anything. What Siegel wanted, he got, one way or another. Raft's friendship with him, and other mobsters, would eventually affect his life, and it became necessary for him to defend himself by defending them as being men who were basically good guys. He even claimed he didn't know they were gangsters.

'As far as I'm concerned,' Raft said, 'Benny was a wonderful guy. Everyone I knew liked him. Benny had a temper – but who doesn't? As for all those things about his past, they were probably true, but in those days in New York a lot of people were into rackets.'

That was true enough – Raft himself had been in rackets. But not everybody killed in cold blood. In trying to play down his friendship with Siegel, Raft also said, 'If he was OK with producers, directors, even royalty, and other stars, there was no reason why I shouldn't get together with him once in a while.'

The fact was, they got together often, going to the races together and having dinner. Siegel began emulating Raft's style of dressing in embroidered shirts, houndstooth-check jackets, and silk ties.

Raft maintained that the appeal of Siegel was his knowledge of Broadway and sports. 'He was accepted by everyone because he was Broadway and Hollywood and he was interesting to be with.'

Despite his ruthless streak, Siegel was on the whole an amiable personality with a charm that had appealed to Charlie Luciano from the beginning. He was also generous, paying the bill at every opportunity. But he was cunning too. He wanted to be liked by everyone.

Bioff had a different tactic. He treated the studio heads like messenger boys. On one occasion, when the gateman at Warners refused to let Bioff in without a pass, Bioff phoned Jack Warner and ordered him to come down and usher him inside personally.

Bioff had a new angle to play on Hollywood. He went to Jules Brulator, the distributor of Eastman film stock in Hollywood, and told him, 'You're no longer dealing directly with the studios. When they want to buy, they'll go through me.'

'And what do I get out of all this?' asked Brulator.

'Well, what you don't get is a bomb in your warehouse. Unless you don't want to co-operate. As for me, I get seven per cent commission on all film stock that I sell for you.'

Jules Brulator had no choice, and neither did MGM, Fox and Warners, all of whom had to buy their stock through this new and despised agent. By this means, the Syndicate raked in over $150,000 a year.

Although when he had first come across Jack Dragna, Siegel was all for killing the survivor of the 1931 Mafia purge, now he took Meyer Lansky's advice and put him on the payroll. His great strength was as the most powerful gambling power in southern California. James Ragan, who operated wire services in Chicago, said, 'Dragna is the Capone of Los Angeles.'

All that changed with the installation of Benny Siegel. To describe Siegel, who was Jewish and not Sicilian, as a Don in its fullest sense, or a Godfather, is not totally correct, for being non-Sicilian he could never be accurately described as a mafioso. According to Claire Sterling's book, *The Mafia*, Luciano, following his rise to power as Boss of all

Bosses, closed Cosa Nostra's books, which meant that no more Sicilian immigrants could be sworn in as he was not actually interested in the rituals or vendettas that characterized the Sicilian Mafia. His American Mafia allowed non-Sicilians to be integrated, but there is no evidence that they were actual mafiosi.

Vincent Teresa wrote that Meyer Lansky never ran 'the mob, was never the "High Commissioner" '. He explained that 'Lansky [worked] hand in hand with the mob, or Cosa Nostra or whatever you want to call it. It's a partnership, but he runs nothing and no one, he works with all the mob bosses.' In the same manner, Benny Siegel was in partnership with the Mob, and Jack Dragna, although Mafia, worked for Siegel.

Another of Siegel's associates, and probably his closest, was Al Smiley. Studying Willie Bioff's union racket, Siegel and Smiley set about the task of taking over the extras' union. While all extras would be forced to join and pay for the privilege, studios would also have to pay for the use of these extras. If they didn't hundreds of extras might fail to turn up when desperately needed, costing studios even more in production delays. Once this racket was under way, it netted Siegel half a million a year.

Marino Bello got involved with Siegel who admitted him into his Syndicate even though Jean Harlow had shown no romantic interest in him. Under Siegel's guidance, Bello became something of a Big Shot, or so he thought, and he began playing the field with numerous women who somehow thought the ageing gangster was as glamorous as any film star.

Siegel had long stopped pursuing Harlow and was having a fabulous time with Dorothy di Frasso. His wife, Estelle, meanwhile lived with their two daughters in a five-bedroomed, $200,000 house, complete with a bath in maroon marble. Siegel may have been openly playing the field as a glitzy playboy in $200 suits and $25 silk shirts, but he made sure that his family remained financially secure. Finally, to give Siegel the freedom he so obviously wanted, and to ultimately protect her daughters from suffering as a result of their father's dangerous dealings, Estelle divorced him.

George Raft was not so lucky. He had become involved with struggling starlet Virginia Pine and was madly in love with her. But he had, of course, made a mistake which affected his life ever after, having married in haste; he could not persuade Grayce, his wife, to divorce him. And Virginia wanted desperately to marry Raft.

He tried to console her by building her a house in Coldwater Canyon, promising her that the day would come when he would move in as her husband. But his estranged wife, Grayce, still refused to divorce him, no matter how much he bargained and pleaded with her.

Raft and Virginia lived a high life, constantly dining, wining and dancing with Lucille Ball and Mack Grey – Grey had once been an aspiring fight manager who used to open the car door for George Raft when he came to visit Owney Madden. He was now Raft's constant companion and confidant.

Raft always insisted that his move to Hollywood had nothing to do with Owney Madden, but the police knew otherwise. However, the association came to an end in the mid-thirties when Madden, by then a tremendously wealthy man, decided to retire to Hot Springs, Arkansas, a favourite retreat for former racketeers. Madden totally changed his lifestyle there and married a local girl, the Postmaster's daughter. He even joined the Chamber of Commerce and became respectable.

On occasions, Madden had loaned Raft money without question. Raft had repaid his debts, but he wanted to make one final repayment as a form of interest. He bought Madden a large Chris-Craft boat and had it delivered to Hot Springs by trailer. It had cost Raft around six grand.

Marino Bello was now busily involved in Benny Siegel's rackets, and discovering the joys of being a top hood. Among the perks were eager women, and Bello indulged himself greedily. But he may have been somewhat naive to think that nobody knew about his dalliances. Certainly Mama Jean, now a devout Christian Scientist and no longer so hot in bed, seemed ignorant of her husband's adultery. But Jean Harlow knew what was going on, and she hired a private detective to spy on Bello's sexual activities.

Armed with overwhelming evidence, Harlow convinced Mama Jean of Bello's infidelities and then set about persuading her to divorce Bello. Her concern for her mother was only half the reason for getting rid of Bello. Harlow at last saw a way of being rid of Bello, and by November, 1935, divorce papers had been filed.

Harlow thought that her mother might now at last have physical and emotional freedom. But the divorce unsettled Mama Jean and she became a bigger problem than ever. Harlow was now in love with actor William Powell, a man who again was much older than she. It only served to make Mama Jean more miserable than ever.

'You have someone and you don't care about me,' her mother complained.

'Of course I care,' Harlow told her. But nothing could persuade Mama Jean of the truth and she became increasingly neurotic. She wanted Marino Bello back in her life. She didn't care if he had been with other women. She was lonely and just wanted him home again. Bello, however, was having too much fun now that he was a success in the illegal and exciting world of Benjamin 'Bugsy' Siegel.

Thelma Todd could not understand why, during 1935, with the Roadside Café less than a year old, the enterprise was continually in the red, despite the fact that the place had a steady flow of clientele. West kept asking her for more of her own money to keep the café going, until she finally confronted him.

'You've had two thousand dollars off me every month, and I'm not even supposed to put my own money into this place. Where does all the money go, for chrissake?'

West was just as nonplussed but tried to reassure her.

'Don't worry, I'll examine the books. I'll talk to Charlie about it.'

Charlie Smith was their bookkeeper; Thelma didn't trust him. 'It wouldn't surprise me if he was at the bottom of this,' she said.

A week passed. It was late in the afternoon. Thelma was at work at the Roach studios and West, as usual, was in the café. Two men entered and approached him, saying, 'We would like to talk to you – in private.'

Surprised and suspicious, West led them upstairs to the office. The two men stated their business, keeping it short and to the point: 'You'll get a visit tomorrow from two colleagues. They will take your order for liquor and steak, but you will increase your usual order.'

'But I don't need to increase my order,' said West. 'And I have my usual suppliers who ...'

'You're going to change your laundry too, and hire bartenders of our recommendation. You will not argue over the prices.'

West was beginning to realize that he was about to become the victim of a shakedown. He began to wonder seriously if Charlie Smith was indeed on the payroll of these gangsters.

The following day two 'salesmen' came to the back of the café where they told West what he was going to order, what quantities to order, and how much it would cost.

'I told your representatives yesterday that I don't need that much food and drink,' said West.

'That's no problem,' said one of the salesmen. 'You can have a smaller quantity. But it will still cost you the same.'

West chose not to tell Thelma Todd about the shakedown as he didn't want her involved or concerned. He knew of her involvement with Luciano but didn't know if his new business associates were Luciano's men.

The shakedown on Thelma Todd's Roadside Café was no more or less secret than any of Luciano's other illegal enterprises in Los Angeles. A cousin of Mr Volonte's was somehow mixed up in all this, although not necessarily in Thelma's

café. 'I didn't know then that Luciano was going out with that
actress, Thelma Todd, but after it was all over I heard how
he had tried to take over part of her restaurant business so
he could put in a casino,' said Mr Volonte. 'One thing is
sure about Luciano: when he took a woman, it was nothing
to do with business. That only complicated things all round.
What I am saying is, he didn't take up with that actress so he
could shake her down. He only wanted her for diversion.
That's all he ever wanted from women – except the prostitutes
he owned. When he came to Los Angeles he went with the
actress – back in New York he had someone else, a Russian dancer. And probably he had others around in different
cities.

'The men were shaking down the Roadside Café so that
Luciano could use the top floor as a casino. They kept him in
touch with events when he was in New York which must have
pleased him because he had had bad news about Nitti getting
into the Los Angeles drugs racket and was also setting up his
own casinos. This made Luciano even angrier with Nitti and
everybody thought there would be a showdown.'

Luciano was much preoccupied with Frank Nitti when he
was next in Los Angeles and came to pick up Thelma in
his chauffeur-driven car. As they drove along the coast,
Luciano, probably unusually morose, let slip that he had
some problems. Thelma asked him to tell her about them.
Luciano didn't appreciate what he saw as her meddling. 'You
would do better to mind your own business,' he said, his anger
simmering beneath the surface.

Thelma should have taken note of it, but she persevered. 'I
think it would help if you shared your troubles ...'

Luciano exploded and struck her across the face. 'Shut your
mouth, you fuckin' little bitch. Who the fuck do you think you
are? You're just a piece of ass for me to fuck, you stupid bitch.
You wanna get killed, is that it?'

It took him several minutes to calm down. 'You're too
good,' he then said. 'You wanna to ease my troubles, and I
turn on you like that. Nitti is winning this way. Him and those

fuckin' goons of his – Bioff, Browne ... but don't concern yourself. This is a time for us to enjoy ourselves. Let's enjoy the time we have.'

Thelma didn't push the matter further. But she recognized the names he had let slip. She was quickly putting two and two together because the word around the studios was that the IATSE leaders were using typical strong-arm tactics to recruit members. She had also heard rumours that studio heads were paying extortion money. Over the succeeding weeks, she gathered all the information she could about the Hollywood shakedown, although she never knew for sure just how Luciano was involved even though she knew he had to be.

Once back in New York, Luciano returned to his problems. He called in Lepke.

'What is all this shit with Frank Nitti?' Luciano asked him.

Lepke remained calm. 'I thought Nitti could be trusted,' he said. 'I thought maybe we could deal with him, unlike Capone. Now I see that Nitti is screwing us both over this IATSE thing. He's screwed me as well as you.'

'I want those two bastards, Bioff and Browne. I wanna contract out on Bioff and Browne. Get 'em off the streets. Send word to Benny. He'll handle it.'

'I understand how you feel, Charlie, but for chrissakes, Browne is the head of a major union. You hit on him and it'll go all the way to the White House. Then the shit will fall on us. Listen to me, Charlie, you kill those two and you're asking for trouble.'

Luciano knew Lepke was right. He mused on the matter. 'Then there is one other who must die – Nitti.'

Lepke nodded, 'I'll get Anastasia on it right away.'

'No, I'll do this myself.'

Luciano wasted no time in heading for Chicago where he confronted Nitti in his office. The two yelled obscenities and threats at each other. Luciano wanted Nitti dead, and he wasted no time in letting him know that his time on earth was short.

'I'm gonna do to you what I should have done to the fat pig Capone years ago.'

'You won't get the chance,' Nitti retorted. 'You'll be dead before you ever give the order. Who the fuck do you think you are anyway?'

'I'm the man who gave you the New York theatres and hasn't seen a dollar for it.'

'Lepke gave me those theatres. Why should you have a cut?'

'Lepke is with me. I have him, and Schultz and Siegel and Anastasia. They reply to me, not to you, Frank Nitti.'

Nitti suddenly fell silent. He knew Luciano had strength on his side, and he changed tactics. 'Christ, Charlie, what do you want? You want money? OK, you can have money. I got your share. You can have it.'

Luciano leaned on the desk, glaring coldly at Nitti. 'You can't pay me off. I'm no politician. What I want is for some of my own men to work alongside yours in the IATSE. You give me this – and what you owe me – or I pull New York out of the union. And I want you out of my way in LA. Keep out of my business. Think it over. I want an answer tomorrow.'

The following morning he called Nitti by phone: 'Meet me for lunch – and come alone.'

They met early that afternoon at an Italian restaurant. Luciano seemed much more cordial, trying to put Nitti at his ease. But both men remained cautious and on edge.

'Did you think on what I said yesterday?' asked Luciano.

Nitti nodded. 'I've already spoken to George Browne and told him you was putting a couple of your own men on his team. But who are these men of yours?'

'I will decide that next week. Now, tell me, have you decided to be sensible and stop interferin' in my drugs business?

'Look, Charlie, there are enough junkies in Hollywood for the both of us.'

Luciano suddenly stopped eating his spaghetti and put

down his fork. His eyes grew ever colder as he glared at Nitti who felt the tension suddenly rise and said defiantly, 'You don't scare me, Charlie. I'm not givin' up anything.'

Luciano continued to glare. Then he relaxed, dropped some bills on the table and stood up. 'We are finished here,' he said.

Nitti rose and followed Luciano outside. 'I'm out of cigarettes, excuse me,' Luciano said, and stepped back inside. Nitti hardly noticed the car that pulled up a moment later, until he saw the tips of machine-guns sticking through the windows. He dived to the ground as the car's occupants opened fire, blasting the front door of the restaurant to pieces. Then the car sped away.

Nitti lay breathing heavily on the ground, covered in splintered glass. He suddenly became aware of Luciano standing over him. 'Today you were lucky, Nitti,' said Luciano. 'The next time you'll die.'

Roland West climbed into the back of Luciano's car and found himself sitting in the back seat next to the feared Sicilian crime lord. The chauffeur put the car into gear and pulled away from the kerb outside the Roadside Café.

'I think this is better for you, and for me, than meetin' in your office,' said Luciano.

'What do you want with me?' asked West nervously.

'I'm takin' over your top floor and puttin' in a casino.'

'You can't do that.'

Luciano smiled. 'What I am proposin' is strictly business. You will make money from it because I will lease the room from you.'

'Does Thelma know about this?'

'Not unless you have told her. I don't like business to get in the way of pleasure.'

Luciano made it clear that he was not giving West any options, and when the conference was over, Luciano dropped West off back at the restaurant. When Thelma returned home from work, he told her what had happened. He was angry, believing she had put him in this position. 'You must either buy me out or approve the deal with Luciano yourself,' he told her. 'I want nothing to do with it. What you do is your own business.'

'But Luciano never spoke to me about it. I didn't know what he was up to. I mean, what do you expect me to do?'

'You got involved with him. I've had enough. All you got to do is buy me out and then do what you want.'

'I don't have the money to do that. Every dollar I earn I put into this place and I don't even see a return on it.'

'Then we'll sell the place.'

'No.'

West was at his wits' end. He didn't know how to get out of this situation. 'What you're saying is that we let Luciano push his way in here, because if we don't, we get killed.'

'Look, I know a lot about him. I think I can get him to change his mind.'

'What do you know?'

'It's best you never know, Roland.'

That October, Thelma was just one of scores of movie stars and executives invited to a party thrown by Joseph Schenck. Having been aware of something going on, it became impossible for her not to notice the kind of things that most other film stars might have ignored. For example, there were various unknown men who seemed to be watching everything that went on. And there, laughing and drinking with all the studio heads present, was Willie Bioff, being treated as though he were the most important person in the room. Thelma couldn't help but consider the possibility that these powerful studio heads were acting more out of fear than friendship, and that the strange men in the room were Bioff's bodyguards.

The kind of speculative information she had on Luciano was dangerous enough. To use it was even more dangerous. To use it unwisely could be totally fatal. One evening, when Luciano insisted she accompany him to the Brown Derby, she was angry enough at being forced to see him to speak un-wisely.

He had, as usual, picked her up in his chauffeur-driven car. But this time he was intent on talking business and kept on at her, probably for the first time, about him moving his gambling business into her restaurant. She refused to give in to him and he promised her that he would have his own way. Their argument resulted in them arriving at the Brown Derby in stony silence.

Over dinner, the argument started again. 'I have offered you a fair business deal,' ranted Luciano. 'Why can't you see that? I'm not askin' you to make room for me and get nothin' for it. Why can't you see how difficult this will be for you if don't agree?'

'You think you can come swaggering into our town and take over,' said Thelma.

'Waddaya mean by that?'

'Come on, Charlie, you're not fooling me. I know what's going on.'

'And what is that?'

'Everything. I could go to the DA with what I know. But I'll make a deal with you. You forget all about moving into my restaurant with your casino, and I'll forget what I know.'

'You mean, you will say *nothin'*?' he asked. She nodded. He knew that meant that she would say *something* if she didn't get her own way. 'You must do what you think best,' he said. 'But I *will* open my casino in your place by the end of this year, I promise you.'

Thelma got up and stormed out. Luciano did not bother to chase her.

'There was no future for them when she turned him down,' said Mr Volonte. 'His survival was at stake. No matter how fond of her he may have been, he could not afford for her to go to the authorities. *Omerta* ruled, and he had to make sure that she kept to this code.'

Luciano couldn't remain in Hollywood for long. He had

pressing business back in New York: the heat was being turned up full by Thomas Dewey. Dutch Schultz had what he saw as the perfect solution – kill Dewey. Meeting with his hierarchy, Luciano decided that to kill Dewey would only bring the 'fatal heat' on them all. It was decided that if anyone had to go, it was Schultz.

Luciano wanted to call in Siegel to deal with this, which considering that Siegel had become more or less firmly entrenched in Los Angeles, illustrates the implicit faith Luciano had in Bugsy's abilities. Siegel flew to New York and met with Luciano who told him, 'Go figure out a way to get rid of the Dutchman.'

Siegel set about organizing an effective spy system to follow Schultz, and learned that he planned to have dinner at the Palace Chop House restaurant in Newark, New Jersey on the night of 23 October 1935. Siegel assigned Charlie 'The Bug' Workman and Mendy Weiss to fulfil the contract.

Right on schedule, Dutch Schultz arrived at one of his favourite restaurants, the Palace Chop House, accompanied by his bodyguards, Abe Landau and Bernard 'Lulu' Rosenkrantz, and by his financial wizard Abbadabba Berman.

Dutch sat against the wall, as he always did, watching for any sign of danger. Finally, he got up and went to the men's room. Outside, across the road, Siegel sat in a car with Harry Teitelbaum and Harry 'Big Greenie' Greenberg. They were there as a 'second line of defence', just in case things didn't go quite right. They watched as Charlie Workman and Mendy Weiss, dressed in overcoats, walked into the restaurant. Workman was holding a .38, while Weiss was armed with a sawn-off shotgun.

Rosenkrantz had no time to draw his gun before he was ripped open between this chest and abdomen by seven bullets. Berman was unarmed and fell in a pool of blood that spurted from six holes in his side. Landau managed to raise his .45 and open fire before three bullets tore into him. The door to the men's room suddenly opened and Schultz burst through, gun in hand. He was suddenly felled by a .45 bullet from Landau's own gun which he was firing wildly.

Siegel and his associates watched as Workman and Weiss ran out of the restaurant and jumped into their car. Hot on their heels was Landau, wounded but able to fire his gun, although he made no impression on the car as it careered away down the road.

Inside the restaurant, Dutch Schultz was still on his feet when the bartender re-emerged from hiding. Schultz fell into a chair and gasped, 'Get a doctor, quick.' Rosenkrantz managed to lift himself off the floor and made the call. An ambulance, and the cops, arrived. Schultz was taken to hospital where he hung on for several hours more before dying.

Luciano, Lansky and Costello congratulated Siegel, believing that Schultz's death would make Dewey think twice about going after the men who had saved his life.

On 11 December, Thelma Todd picked up the phone and dialled through to the District Attorney's office.

'I'd like to speak to Mr Fitts,' she said.

'I'm afraid Mr Fitts is in a meeting at the moment. Who is calling?'

'Thelma Todd.'

There was a pause. Then, 'Can you give me a number where Mr Fitts can reach you?'

'I'm at the Roadside Cafe.'

About an hour later, a man from Fitts's office called her back. 'Can you tell me the nature of your call, please?'

'I would rather discuss this with Mr Fitts personally.'

'I understand that, Miss Todd, but if you could just tell me the nature of your call.'

'Please, can you just get me to see Mr Fitts?'

'I will have to check with his secretary to see when he is free. I shall call back later.'

Five minutes later, he rang again. 'Please, Miss Todd, I must know the nature of your business with Mr Fitts.'

'All I can say is, he'll be very interested to hear what I have to say.'

There was another pause. Then the voice said, 'I can make an appointment for you for Tuesday the 17th at 11.30 a.m.'

'That will be fine, thank you,' said Thelma, and hung up.

In New York, a call came through to Luciano. 'She called the office,' the voice said. 'I made her an appointment for Tuesday the 17th.'

'Thank you,' said Luciano, and the man from the DA's office hung up. He called through to his secretary. 'I'll be leaving for Los Angeles Friday.'

Three days later, on Saturday, 14 December, Ida Lupino threw a party at the Trocadero at which Thelma was guest of honour. The party was in full swing when, at 12.15 a.m, Pasquale DiCicco turned up accompanied by an attractive young actress named Margaret Lindsay. He had not been invited, but when he'd heard about the party, he persuaded Ida Lupino to allow him to come.

DiCicco and Thelma spoke for a while, their voices rising and becoming more heated as she berated him for slighting her and Ida Lupino, then DiCicco and his companion retreated to a table, and finally left the party at about 1.15 a.m. Thelma soon forgot the incident and for the next few hours was the life and soul of the party.

At about two a.m., Thelma joined Sidney Grauman, who operated the Chinese Theater on Hollywood Boulevard, and three other men. According to Grauman's testimony, Thelma had asked him to call West to let him know that she had drunk too much and that West should ensure she got to bed safely. After several minutes actor Arthur Prince noted that 'when Thelma came back she was totally different. All her gaiety had evaporated. She seemed terribly depressed.'

Grauman then made a phone call. Thelma's lawyer, Ronald Button, believed that when Thelma went to speak with Grauman at the Trocadero on Saturday night, the subject of Luciano's offer to her came up. Grauman was known to number gangsters among his associates, and at least one, if not all three, of the men at his table was an associate of Luciano's. She was given a final chance to accept Luciano's offer. She turned it down. Grauman then called Roland West and warned him not to be found with Thelma that night. West therefore locked the doors, thought Button.

Shortly afterwards, the party came to an end and a hired car arrived to collect Thelma. As soon as she got into it, she told the driver, Ernie Peters, to drive to Santa Monica at top speed because, Peters said, 'she feared that she might be kidnapped or slain by gangsters'. Having no reason to doubt her and fearing for his own life, he drove at between 65 and 70 miles an hour, reaching the Roadside Café at about 3.30.

'Will you be OK?' asked Peters as she got out of the car.

'I'll be fine now, Ernie. Good-night.'

'Good-night, Miss Todd,' As Peters drove off towards Hollywood at a more sedate speed, he glanced in the rear mirror and saw that Thelma was still standing outside the restaurant.

On Monday morning, 16 December, Thelma's maid, Mae Whitehead, arrived to take Thelma's car out of the garage adjoining West's home up on the cliff above the café. She discovered Thelma slumped in the front seat. The car engine had been running and the garage was filled with fumes. The maid shook her frantically. 'C'mon, honey, wake up.' Then she saw the blood splattered over her face and evening gown. A replacement tooth was missing. The maid screamed, and ran from the garage crying, 'She's dead! She's dead!'

An inquest was held. The jury spent weeks deliberating the evidence and announced their verdict 'Death due to carbon monoxide poisoning.' The case was closed. But Ronald Button didn't believe for a minute that Thelma had killed herself. He believed he could pin the murder on Luciano. He prevailed upon the District Attorney for a second inquest at which, he claimed, he would prove his theory.

When Hal Roach heard about the second inquest, he begged the District Attorney to drop the matter. The DA agreed and persuaded Button to forget the matter. But this didn't stop people believing the very thing Button had hoped to prove.

Clark Gable had taken David Niven fishing. He told Niven, 'Thelma didn't read the small print. We all have a contract with the public. On the screen, and in our private lives, we are the standards by which they measure their own ideals of everything. They love to put us on a pedestal and worship us and write thousands of letters telling us how great we are. But they have read the small print, and most of us haven't. They expect us to pay the price for it all. We have to get it in the end. So, when we get knocked off by gangsters, like Thelma did, or get hooked because of scandals or because we just grow old, that's the payoff and the public feels satisfied.'

Although many suspected that Thelma had been murdered, very few knew the truth. Said Mr Volonte, 'The death of the actress was essential to Luciano's survival.'

It transpired that after Ernie Peters drove away, leaving Thelma standing outside the café, Luciano's car pulled up and he ordered her in. We can only guess at what they talked about, but it seemed that he plied her with champagne and assured her that he had come to say goodbye. He told her that she would never see him again.

They arrived back in Los Angeles Sunday morning, and sometime during the day arrived at the home of an important Hollywood figure who was well connected. There Luciano interrogated Thelma, knocking her about until she told him everything that she knew. 'She signed her own death warrant,' was how Mr Volonte put it. 'Luciano could take no chances. He promised her she would never see him again. "I am not lying," he told her. "I will not break this vow." She must have known, then, what was to happen to her.'

But Luciano did not relish Thelma's death. She was not his wife, but she was his woman, as he saw it, and no wife of a mafioso could hope to run and tell. According to an account given by Andy Edmonds in her book *Hot Toddy*, Luciano's Hollywood host had to calm Luciano down. Then Luciano made a phone call, saying only one word: '*Cominci*' – 'Begin'.

Then Luciano and Thelma left the house. Because she was being taken home, she began to feel that her fate might not have been sealed.

They arrived back at the West house up on the cliff. She got out of the car, Luciano again promised he would never bother her again, and then pulled away. She never saw the man who came up behind her, grabbed her and beat her into unconsciousness. Then he dragged her into the garage and dumped her on the front seat of her own car. He turned on the ignition, went outside and shut the garage door tight.

As word got around that Thelma had been 'knocked off by gangsters', there was fear in Hollywood. Who would be next? Was Los Angeles to be turned into another Chicago? Benny Siegel assured those closest to him, such as George Raft and Cary Grant, so that they could assure others, that his pal, Charlie Luciano, was not capable of killing women.

Criminal history was about to dispute that.

Perhaps if Luciano had not concerned himself so much with Thelma Todd and her Roadside Café, which he never managed to take over after all, he might have thought better about taking out Schultz in the belief it would take the heat off him for a while. All it did was make Dewey more determined than ever, and he began a purge on the prostitution rackets, finding himself with a number of witnesses – madams and whores – who had in common a single name that kept cropping up: Charlie Luciano. Dewey drew up compulsory prostitution charges against Luciano and had him arrested.

In his defence, Gay Orlova hastily called a press conference. She told the eager news reporters, 'I haven't seen him for weeks, but I can't believe what they're saying about him. I don't know why they say such mean things – he's just a dear. I don't believe any of those charges. Especially that one about compulsory something-or-other. It just doesn't sound like him at all.'

In fact, for years Luciano denied that he had ever been involved in prostitution at all. But he also denied ever having any involvement with drug trafficking. Even in his last days he said, 'There was so much dough to be made in everything else we had, why ruin it with the dangers of playin' around with junk? I tried to make 'em understand that... we was businessmen runnin' businesses and givin' people what they wanted in a way that didn't hurt nobody. People wanted to gamble, we helped 'em gamble; they needed booze, cigarettes and meat durin' the war, we took care of that.

'Sure, here and there we would squeeze some guys, but look at all the money we was puttin' in circulation just from other good businessmen buyin' our protection. I said there wasn't a politician or a cop who could hold onto none of the money we paid him off with, that they spent it as soon as they got it, and that was very good for the American economy – to put money in circulation. But it didn't mean a fuckin' thing. On the subject of narcotics, I could see I wasn't gettin' through. All the time I was talkin', most of 'em had stone in their faces.'

Yet he wasn't prepared to deny that people had died at his hands. 'Killin' – I hadda lifetime of it,' he said. Charles Siragusa, a narcotics agent, noted that while Luciano was 'nothing but a pimp and a dope peddler', he recognized that those things were the 'the two things no gangster wants to be considered'.

Luciano was brought to trial, beginning 13 May 1936, presided over by Justice Philip J McCook.

Thomas Dewey told the jury, 'Frankly, my witnesses are prostitutes, madams, heels, pimps and ex-convicts. I wish to call to your attention that these are the only witnesses we could possibly have brought here. We can't get bishops to testify in a case involving prostitution. And this combination was not run under the arc lights in Madison Square Garden. We have to use testimony of bad men to convict other bad men.'

Dewey pointed out that prostitution had always been an operation run by 'independents' until Luciano put out the word to these independents that he was taking over, installing Dave Betillo as his lieutenant in charge of the racket. The Syndicate controlled more than two hundred whorehouses in Manhattan, the Bronx, Queens and Brooklyn, and grossed over a million dollars per month.

One of the first state witnesses, a swarthy Romanian madam and operator of one of the smaller brothels in the tenement district, displayed an intense hatred for Luciano, and told how his henchmen had used strong-arm methods on her to persuade her to join his racket combine. They wrecked her house, subjecting her and her girls to rough-house treatment until they agreed to fork out monthly tributes.

A key witness was Florence Brown, nicknamed 'Cokey Flo'. She had been a prostitute and a drug addict since she was fifteen when she fell for one of Luciano's soldiers. She was now in her mid-twenties, and the operator of a plush brothel.

She had been present when Luciano said, 'We're gonna organize the cathouses like the A&P.' He wanted the madams put on commission, forcing more and more work out of the girls.

Challenging her testimony, Morton Levy, Luciano's attorney, curtly remarked to the jury, 'Drugs, of course, have impaired her memory.' At this, she flew into a rage, shouting that, regardless of the fact that she had served more than three thousand guests, the remembered all their faces, voices and other characteristics.

She had also been present when Luciano gave instructions for the torture and intimidation of girls and madams, so that they would work without complaint around the clock. 'Talking won't do no good,' she'd heard him say. 'You got to put the screws on. First you got to sit on them, then you got to step on them.' She also testified that Luciano had told her that he was taking over the racket, and that she had to pay him from that time on.

Another young witness informed the court that she had been afraid and unwilling to testify against the Luciano because there were 'plenty of girls, who talked too much, had their tongues cut, and their feet, stomachs and sex organs burned with cigarettes.'

Dewey rested his case on 29 May 1936. Luciano's attorneys, Polakoff and Levy, advised him not to testify, but he insisted and took the stand on 3 June. He was briefly questioned by his own counsel, and made a statement that he had never 'gotten a single dollar from a prostitute or from the prostitution racket'.

Dewey took over and quickly established that Luciano had been involved in nothing but criminal activity for the previous eighteen years. He also quickly established, through direct and clever questioning, that Luciano was a compulsive liar, and had at least five aliases.

Dewey asked in rapid succession, 'Do or did you know Louis Lepke Buchalter?'

'Yes.'

Dewey hardly waited for Luciano to finish his reply. 'Jacob Shapiro?'

'Yes.'

'Benjamin Siegel?'

'Yes.'

'Al Capone?'

'No.'

'Ciro Terranova?'

'No.'

Dewey then read off Luciano's telephone records from the Waldorf Towers and the Barbizon Plaza, listing calls from Luciano's phone to Ciro Terranova's unlisted number in Pelham, New York, and to Capone in Chicago. Luciano claimed that somebody must have broken into his apartment and made the calls.

Dewey read off repeated calls from Luciano to the vice ring's headquarters – Celano's Restaurant, on Manhattan's Lower East Side. Luciano blandly stated that Celano's spaghetti was good, and he liked to make reservations.

Dewey questioned him for hour after hour. Again and

again Luciano denied ever being involved 'in the prostitution racket'. I gave to them,' he said. 'I never took.'

Dewey used every scrap of information at hand to portray Luciano as a ruthless crime boss and referred to an incident when Luciano and an associate, Joseph Scalise, had been discovered possessing various firearms. Dewey asked outright, 'Were you with a man named Joseph Scalise on July 19th 1929 and did you have two revolvers, a shotgun and forty-five rounds of ammunition in your car?'

'Yes, we was huntin'.'

'And what had you been hunting?'

'Peasants,' replied Luciano, causing general hilarity in the courtroom.

'You mean pheasants?'

'That is right – *peasants.*'

'What? You mean to tell me that you were shooting pheasants out of season in July?'

Dewey brought up the subject of income tax. Luciano had never filed a report except one, a year and half before. 'Well, why did you ever file a return?' asked Dewey.

'I suddenly decided to be honest,' replied Luciano, causing another burst of laughter from the court.

Dewey had done his work well, and the jury returned a verdict, finding him guilty as charged, and he was sentenced to serve 30-50 years in Dannemore prison, known as the Siberia of New York penal institutions.

The madame and whores who'd testified breathed a sigh of relief. But Luciano had already put out the order to his men to see to them. A number of them were beaten and tortured. One girl, Jean Bell, fled to Washington, thinking she was safe. One of Luciano's men trailed her there and broke into her apartment. He threw her down on the bed, ripped off her nightgown and slashed the initials C.L. on her abdomen with a heavy banana knife. Then he turned on the gas, leaving her to die.

She was luckier than Thelma Todd. The smell of gas brought somebody to her apartment, and she survived.

12

Tough Guys

It didn't take long for Benny Siegel to consolidate his power, influence and position on the West Coast. He masterminded the gambling affairs at casinos in small resort towns like Redondo Beach, and at Agua Caliente's race track in Mexico where gambling had been outlawed in 1935, and at the Culver City dog track. He took his cut from the numbers racket and he blueprinted and engineered the dope-smuggling operations from Mexico into lower California.

But by far his most successful and valuable service for the Mafia was the war for control of the race wire business, known to those connected as 'The Service'.

The race wire was vital to bookmakers. The Service operated a broadcast of all racing information – including details on jockeys, horses, and sudden shifts in betting odds at all tracks – over its very own nationwide network on wires leased from commercial telegraph companies. Legally, the results of all races were delayed until after they were declared official. In the case of fouls or photo finishes, this could take several minutes. Bookmakers without the wire service were at the mercy of 'sharpers' who had the Service and were able to make bets on a race not yet over. As a monopoly, the Service controlled bookmakers and the Mob were able to exact enormous tributes from them.

The largest of the services was Continental, run by James Ragan, on behalf of Frank Nitti. Siegel set up a rival network in the far-western areas of Nevada, Arizona and California, and succeeded most spectacularly in bringing the Nevadan bookmakers under his control. His personal profit from Las Vegas alone was $25,000 a month.

In California, Continental held out longer than Siegel ever expected, and the war for the wire services raged on until August 1946, when James Ragan was gunned down in Chicago.

Such operations earned Siegel a favourable reputation among the East Coast bosses, particularly Frank Costello who was now caretaker Boss while Luciano was in prison. They saw Siegel as a shrewd businessman and not just a cold, efficient killer.

Thomas Dewey knew what kind of man Siegel was. But he needed the evidence. Now that he had Luciano behind bars, he turned his attention on Siegel, intent on implicating him in the murder of mobster Tony Fabrizzo. Siegel had an alibi; he'd been hospitalized at the time of the killing, he said. Unfortunately for Siegel, Dewey had blown his alibi apart and had joined forces with newly elected Brooklyn District Attorney William O'Dwyer who had won his campaign by vowing to take Murder Inc. apart.

Lepke Buchalter had, in a sense, been doing Dewey's and O'Dwyer's job for them; he had been carefully setting about closing the lips – permanently – of every witness who could testify against the hierarchy of the murder squad, effectively stopping the law enforcers in their tracks.

Safe in Hollywood, Benny Siegel set about emulating Raft and built a palatial house in Beverly Hills, not too far from George's Coldwater Canyon home which Raft had originally built for Virginia Pine. Siegel consulted Raft on every aspect of his new project, and Raft often witnessed the hot-tempered Siegel badgering the contractors, carpenters, and plumbers to make sure they were following the blueprints. Raft accepted these hot flushes that had given Siegel the nickname Bugsy, because he had a quick temper too. And as his friendship with Siegel grew, so Raft considered himself something of a Big Shot. He knew that few people would want to cross a man who had Benny Siegel as a close friend.

But Siegel was all too aware of the dangers of being a Big Shot in the Mob. He often brought Raft to his house, as it was nearing completion, after dark, touring the rooms using lighted matches or flashlights. Once, when they came to the master bedroom on the second floor, Siegel showed Raft a sliding panel controlled by a concealed button.

'What's the secret exit for?' asked Raft.

'It will come in handy one of these days when I gotta get out in a hurry,' explained Siegel.

Benny Siegel was no different from a good many of the most powerful mobsters in that, while he was cold and ruthless to his enemies, he was generous to a fault to those he was fond of – people like George Raft and Cary Grant whom he considered friends, and Jean Harlow; he had never succeeded in getting in between the sheets with her, but he was sincerely fond of her. So when the news broke on 7 June 1937 that she had died in the Good Samaritan Hospital, he was devastated. She was, after all, godmother to one of his children.

It is ironic to consider that had Marino Bello still been with Mama Jean, Harlow might not have died. She had been filming *Saratoga* with Clark Gable when, on Saturday 29 May she complained of feeling ill. She went to the neighbouring set where William Powell was working to let him know that she was going home. When Powell phoned that evening, Mama Jean told him, 'Jean is resting quietly.'

Throughout Sunday morning the phone kept ringing as people like Clark Gable and Carole Lombard called to enquire after her. At midday Jean, according to Mama Jean, suggested she take the phone off the hook. Later that day she began vomiting and complained of pains in her back and stomach. Mama Jean, a practising Christian Scientist, nursed her herself. On Monday the film's producer, Bernard Hyman, and director, Jack Conway, tried to phone Jean but could get no answer, so they sent a messenger round who returned with a message from Mama Jean saying that Harlow should return to work tomorrow. But Harlow didn't. When Gable called by, Mama Jean refused to let him in.

A few days later Harlow's agent Arthur Landau, along with Gable, actor Frank Morgan, Conway and Hyman, drove out to her house. Mama Jean opened the door but kept the safety chain on. Landau insisted that she open the door and, eventually, she allowed them in. They rushed into Jean's room.

'Doesn't she look better now than last Saturday?' asked Mama Jean.

On the bed lay Harlow, pathetically pale, only half conscious, groaning in pain, racked with fever and messy with fresh vomit. Morgan felt for her pulse and, trembling, said, 'Get a doctor.'

Despite Mama Jean's protestations, they called a doctor to the house who told them, 'This girl's got to be hospitalized and operated on immediately.'

'No,' cried Mama Jean. 'She is not leaving this house.' Gable and Morgan pleaded with her to allow them to take her to hospital, but all she agreed to was for a nurse to come to the house. No one dared override Mama Jean's demands because of the adverse publicity her church might stir up in the press.

Harlow was cleaned up and blood and urine samples were rushed to a laboratory. It became apparent that an acute infection from the gall bladder had spread throughout her body. Her kidneys were damaged and uraemic poisoning was setting in. Gable leaned over to kiss her. He later said he could smell the urine on her breath. He said it was like 'kissing a dead, rotting person'.

When it became obvious that Harlow was dying, they got Louis B. Mayer on the phone who gave them the go-ahead to ignore Mama Jean and rush Harlow to hospital. But it was too late. She died with William Powell and Mama Jean at her side.

Because of Mama Jean's Christian Science beliefs, because those who found her were scared of adverse publicity, Jean Harlow was dead. The one person who might have been able to prevent it from happening was Marino Bello who, had he still been married to Mama Jean, would undoubtedly have got

Jean medical treatment, as he had done on previous occasions.

Three days later, Marino Bello and Benny Siegel were among the mourners at her funeral at Forest Lawn, the graveyard of the stars. Dr Carpentier was there too. Two hundred people were invited and two thousand sightseers crowded round the gates to watch the funeral cortège pass by. When the coffin was closed after the traditional lying-in-state there was a single gardenia, Harlow's favourite flower, in her hand, placed there by William Powell with a note that read 'Goodnight, my dearest darling.' At nine o'clock in the morning, when the service began, a one-minute silence was observed in all the studios of Hollywood. The casket was covered by fifteen hundred lilies of the valley and five hundred gardenias, provided by Powell and Mama Jean.

That year, George Raft's mother died. The funeral in New York was attended by Owney Madden and Frenchy DeMange, Madden's former partner. Madden's presence was the act of a loyal friend, but it was the last time Raft was to see him.

Back in Los Angeles, Benny Siegel, looking out for any racket that could profit him, invested in off-shore gambling, an enterprise run by 'Admiral' Tony Cornero.

Cornero was a criminal, but he was no ruthless hood. He gradually distanced himself from violence and saw himself simply as someone who had to act outside of the law to provide people with pleasure. An immigrant from north Italy, he had worked in San Francisco as a taxi driver until 1922 when he set up a hijacking business in southern California.

By 1924 he was rumrunning and two years later he was the major source of smuggled booze in Los Angeles. He later told reporters, 'I had to keep a hundred and twenty million Americans from poisoning themselves with bathtub gin and moonshine.'

Federal agents went after him, trailing him on board a train bound for Seattle, en route to Vancouver, British Columbia. He saw them coming at him, their guns drawn, and he jumped from the train into the wilds of northern California.

He found his way to a remote airfield where he chartered a small plane to fly him to a town near Portland in Oregon. There he caught the same train he had jumped from, only to discover the Feds were still on board. He jumped again, but eventually made his way to Vancouver.

Unable to return to the States, he went to South America and Europe, but went back to California in 1927 where he surrendered to Federal agents and served two years in prison. He emerged from there with the decision to embark on a career as a gambler. He bought himself a steamship, the *Tango*, and turned it into a floating casino, operating off Venice Beach.

In 1935 he offered to buy out his three partners because, while they were prepared to take even splits, they refused to pull their weight. They turned him down but agreed when he said he would roll a dice for the ship. He lost, but had enough money to buy another ship, the *Star of Scotland*. He turned it into another floating casino, renaming it the *Rex*, which led to other such vessels which were anchored off southern California. The *Rex*, a steel-hulled British barquentine built in 1887, was the most ambitious of his casino-ships. Cornero spent $300,000 converting it into a casino, installing a 250-foot glass-covered gaming deck that offered roulette and craps. Dancing and entertainment took place on a lower deck along with 120 one-armed bandits.

It operated twenty-four hours a day, often holding up to 2,000 people on busy nights. The daily gross profit was in excess of $10,000. Security was tight and business was conducted behind steel doors. Bouncers were armed. And to ensure that they could repel any attacks such as occurred on the *Monte Carlo*, when it was boarded one foggy morning and robbed of $40,000, Cornero had machine-guns installed. The entertainment Cornero offered on board was openly advertised in newspapers, and Hollywood folk generated much of Cornero's profits.

This was a business that appealed to Benny Siegel and he came to George Raft asking, 'Lend me twenty thousand dollars so that I can buy a piece of the action, and you'll get a share of the dividends.'

'I haven't got that much cash, Ben,' said Raft.

Presumably Siegel had the money, but he preferred to risk other people's. He persisted until Raft drove forty miles to Arrowhead Springs where his agent, Myron Selznick, wrote him a cheque as an advance on a future movie. Raft returned to Los Angeles, cashed the cheque and delivered the required amount to Benny Siegel.

His reason for doing it, he said, was because 'I just hate to turn a guy down and Benny acted like he needed the money bad.'

A few months later Raft discovered that the gambling ship venture was making a huge profit, and figured it was time he had some of his investment returned. But when he asked about it, Siegel changed the subject. Raft wrote him a letter requesting that his loan be repaid.

Not long after, Raft was driving his car when Siegel came up alongside of him and flagged him down. It was a moment when Raft might have expected Siegel to live up to his name of Bugsy, but instead Siegel handed him a cheque for $2,000, 'That's on account, Georgie,' he said. 'I'll get the rest to you when I can. I'm pulling out of the ship deal.'

Siegel repaid his debt, in individual amounts of $5,000 and $1,000 in cash. He pulled out of his deal with Cornero just in time. That year, 1938, Los Angeles County Prosecutor Buron Fitts and California's Attorney-General, Earl Warren, decided to put a stop to Cornero's activities. On 13 May Fitts and a squad of policemen boarded the *Rex* and arrested Cornero and fifty of his employees on gambling charges. All were immediately freed on bond. Fitts suspended all water-taxi services between Santa Monica Pier and the *Rex*, so Cornero had his ship towed to a point off Redondo Beach where it continued operations.

In October Fitts raided the *Rex* once more, so Cornero moved further south, anchoring twelve miles off-shore in the choppy Catalina Channel. His passengers often became seasick and business suffered, so Cornero returned to Santa Monica. Earl Warren and Fitts came up with a plan to sink Cornero's activities once and for all. Police set out in water taxis and boarded Cornero's other ships, smashing the tables with axes and carting off slot machines and roulette wheels. Then they set out to board the *Rex*.

Cornero's men were ready with the hoses, and for nine hours they kept the police at bay. The law finally gave up. But in November, California's Supreme Court held that the three-mile limit should not be measured from the beach at Santa Monica, as Cornero had always maintained it should, but from the headlands marking the mouth of the bay. The *Rex* was thus operating illegally in Californian waters. To anchor further out to sea, beyond the limit, made business impossible. Cornero surrendered and the *Rex* was drafted into the US Navy.

In 1938 Siegel was easily coaxed into another seafaring venture by Marino Bello who convinced Siegel that there was treasure – $90,000 worth of pirate gold – on the Cocos Islands. Then Bello went to Cary Grant and told him that for a small investment he could throw in with Benny Siegel on a voyage for lost treasure. Grant agreed to invest but he declined to go himself. There was apparently another reason for the voyage. Siegel was to ship an illicit cargo to Lepke Buchalter who was currently 'on the lam'.

On board the *Metha Nelson*, Siegel was joined by Dorothy di Frasso, Marino Bello and his girlfriend Violette, British man-about-town Richard Gully, Harry 'Champ' Segal who was Owney Madden's old partner and now Siegel's personal trainer, and several others. They sailed along the Californian coast, doing shark-fishing en route, and arrived at the Cocos Islands to discover nothing more than some rusty nails, mouldy boots and evidence of former treasure hunters.

Siegel was furious and flew home from Guatemala. Then a typhoon struck the *Metha Nelson* in the Gulf of Tehuantepec, bringing the voyage to a dramatic conclusion. Marino Bello married Violette on the last day of the trip. The matter was recalled some time later, when a Federal Grand Jury asked Dorothy di Frasso why she had been in the company of a well-known gangster.

'On the contrary,' the Countess replied with cunning wide-eyed innocence, 'I was in the company of a *good friend*. And, anyway, Mrs Bello was there to chaperon me.'

Perhaps because he was the friend of mobsters, or simply because he had survived the tough early years in New York and in Owney Madden's gang, George Raft was one of Hollywood's genuine tough guys. To his friends he was a 'real nice guy', as James Cagney described him, but to those who crossed him, he was as belligerent as any of the gangsters he portrayed on the screen.

Despite movie success, his private life was little short of an unqualified failure. He was to forever pay the price of his hasty marriage to Grayce, and by 1939, his four-year affair with Virginia Pine was beginning to fall apart. Their relationship was punctuated by emotional tornadoes, such as the night the couple, along with Lucille Ball and Mack Grey, went dancing at the Trocadero. Everyone was happy and having a good time, but Raft said something that clearly annoyed Virginia. Later, at the Coldwater Canyon house Raft had built for Virginia, a furious row broke out between the couple. Virginia stormed into the bedroom and proceeded to smash thousands of dollars' worth of perfume which Raft had bought for her. In the lounge, Raft sat quietly, intent on remaining calm in front of his friends as they heard bottle after bottle shattering upstairs. The bedroom reeked of perfume for months after.

Raft decided to make another attempt to persuade Grayce to give him a divorce when he was in New York on a personal appearance tour. He phoned her, asking if he could come over and talk. She was hesitant but when he said that it was important, she agreed.

He arrived with a large amount of cash in his pocket and hostility welling up inside him. He felt that having agreed to give her ten per cent of all his earnings, he owed her nothing more. But now he tried to do the very thing that had kept the law off the backs of Luciano and Capone for so many years: he tried to buy her off. As he sat with her in the living room of her house, he put the cash on the table and said, 'I don't have to tell you our marriage was a big mistake. You know we really didn't even have a marriage.'

'That's your side of it,' she said.

'Look, I don't want to argue or to fight, all I want is a divorce. Here's a hundred and fifty thousand dollars in cash. All ya gotta do is divorce me.'

'George,' she said, shaking her head, 'are you trying to pay me off?'

Grayce was calm, which only served to make Raft more angry. He had never understood Grayce's fervent belief that divorce was a sin; he couldn't accept that he had made no attempt to make their marriage work, and now he was trying typical underworld-type tactics to buy a divorce. He believed that all she wanted was more money which she could only get by remaining his wife. But all Grayce was getting was a life of loneliness.

He returned to California to explain to Virginia that Grayce would still not divorce him. She went to pieces and began smashing things. Then, within weeks, she began to see other men, an outright attack on Raft's ego which inflamed his jealousy. Restless and depressed at not finding her at home, he asked Mack Grey, over and over, 'Where's Virginia? Where the hell did she go?'

He began to follow her, and one night discovered her having dinner at a restaurant with Joseph Schenck, Willie Bioff's pawn. Schenck was getting deeper into hot water, furnishing Bioff with favours that he felt helpless to refuse. One such favour was to lend Bioff 'clean' money which he needed to buy a ranch. Schenck foolishly agreed to accept $100,000 in cash from the IATSE kitty in exchange for a personal cheque from Schenck to Bioff for the same amount. This single incident was later to bring about Bioff's downfall, and land Schenck in trouble with the Federal authorities.

Raft parked across the road from the restaurant and waited; a classic stake-out. Eventually Schenck and Virginia emerged from the restaurant, got into Schenck's car and drove off, not knowing that Raft was following not far behind. They arrived at Schenck's house and went inside. Raft pulled over to the kerb, his anger mounting. Schenck should have been a wiser man than to cross Raft. As James Cagney told me, 'George was the only genuinely tough man I knew in the business.'

Raft got out of his car, walked to Schenck's front door and rang the bell. No one answered. He didn't wait to ring again. He flew at the door and broke it down. Inside he found Schenck looking terrified and Virginia just looking angry.

'Go ahead, go with Schenck,' Raft ranted at Virginia. 'He's the kind of man you should have. You know, if you drive into the studio in his limousine – everyone would turn around. That's what you really want. Someone who's a bigger shot than I am.'

Again Raft reverted to bland underworld tactics; he paid her $15,000 to go back to New York. This time it worked; she took the money and left Hollywood. Mack Grey moved in with Raft into the house on Coldwater Canyon, now nothing more than a lavish bachelor pad.

Raft's emotional wounds soon healed. He attended a party thrown by Charles Boyer for movie star Norma Shearer at the Waldorf-Astoria. Raft had never met Shearer before, but when they came face to face for the first time there was instant and mutual attraction. They tangoed in the Empire Room and that night they became lovers.

In 1939 Cagney and Raft worked together in the classic gangster picture *Each Dawn I Die*. The two Warner Bros stars, along with Edward G. Robinson, whom Raft was to work with a year later, were the three leading actors specializing in gangster roles. Cagney understood Raft. He'd come from the same kind of background and they had each known the same brand of tough characters during their childhood years. They had mutual respect and a sincere fondness for each other, yet politically they were poles apart. Raft numbered mobsters among his friends. Cagney was instrumental in flushing out underworld figures from Hollywood. As an active member of the Screen Actors Guild, which under the presidency of Robert Montgomery began a campaign to expose Bioff's studio shakedown, he became a prime target for reprisals from Willie Bioff.

In a campaign of terror against Cagney, Bioff had goons give Cagney's wife a series of phone calls, telling her that some terrible mishap had befallen him. On one occasion they told her that he'd been killed in a car crash. Containing her panic, she phoned the studio and found him to be alive and well. But it was all a build-up to the murder that Bioff had planned. He was going to ensure that she finally received a phone call saying that Cagney had been killed on the set by a falling klieg light. Only this time she would ring the studio to find it was true.

However, Bioff failed to carry out the plan, although just why isn't too clear. There are a number of conflicting stories. Cagney made it sound straightforward. He said, 'The Mob arranged for a heavy klieg studio light to be dropped on me on the set. When George [Raft] got wind of it, he made a call to the right man, and the surprise was called off. He may have saved my life.'

Raft's own version was that he saw Willie Bioff on the set looking with obvious dislike at Cagney. Then Bioff stared up at the overhead lamps and exchanged 'meaningful looks' with his boys. After the film was finished, Raft met Bioff in New York where Bioff told him, 'You did pretty good with *Each Dawn I Die*. You can thank me for that. The studio wasn't going to pay off and we were planning to take care of Cagney.

We were all set to drop a lamp on him. But I got word to lay off because you were in the picture.'

'You sonofabitch,' swore Raft. 'It's a good thing nothing happened to Jimmy. He's one of the greatest guys in Hollywood and if you had hurt him, you would've hurt me.'

Another version claims that the plan to kill Cagney was called off because Raft's friends didn't want to risk damaging his career with a murder scandal.

The truth is probably closer to Cagney's version. He knew that Raft had friends in the underworld; he even knew that Raft had worked for the Mob. It's strange, therefore, that Cagney, in his campaign to end the Mob's control over Hollywood, didn't extend it to Benny Siegel's activities. Not that Cagney would have favoured the likes of Siegel, any more than he did Bioff. So either Cagney had no idea what Benny Siegel was really up to, or he chose to turn a blind eye for the sake of his pal Raft who would undoubtedly have been implicated in an investigation into Siegel's affairs. The former suggestion seems the most likely, which would mean that Siegel was a lot smarter at covering his tracks than Bioff.

Cagney had previously starred in *Angels With Dirty Faces*, and following *Each Dawn I Die* began work on his third major gangster film within a year, *The Roaring Twenties*. The story for this film was written by Mark Hellinger, the former journalist who had been a friend of Raft's back in the New York days when they had both hung out with leading mobsters.

Not surprisingly, Hellinger was able to write the following as an introduction for *The Roaring Twenties*: 'In this film, the characters are composites of people I knew, and the situations are those that actually occurred. Bitter or sweet, most memories become precious as the years move on. This film is a memory – and I am grateful for it. Mark Hellinger.'

The Roaring Twenties featured an actor who had established himself as a major co-star in similar films, but was to go on to make a career for himself as a star of contemporary thrillers – Humphrey Bogart. Hellinger, already a friend of Raft and Siegel, became a close friend of Bogart's and when

Hellinger began producing films in 1940, Bogart was starring in them, including *It All Came True*, *Torrid Zone*, *Brother Orchid*, *High Sierra*, and *They Drive By Night* in which Bogart was teamed with George Raft.

During his days as a New York newspaperman, Hellinger had fallen for Ziegfeld Follies girl, Gladys Glad. She lived with him in an enormous house in Beverly Hills, and bore him two children. It was Warner Bros who gave him the chance to produce films, under the guidance of Hal Wallis, and he proved successful, concocting gangster pictures that had an authentic feel because he was drawing on his memories. He tended to emulate the hoods he'd known, dressing sharply, often in grey suits, grey shirts, white ties and always a grey fedora. He was an extravagant tipper, often giving $10 bills to parking attendants and $20 to waiters. He carried stacks of cash all the time and refused to allow anyone else to pay the bill. According to Lauren Bacall, he was a 'sweet, vulnerable man. A good friend, loved by all.' Hellinger, despite his background, was one of the gentler guys in Hollywood.

There were, fortunately, tough men in Hollywood who had nothing to do with the underworld. One was Arthur Ungar, editor of the trade paper *Daily Variety*. He, Robert Montgomery of the SAG and columnist Westbrook Pegler, instigated an investigation into Willie Bioff's past, hiring private detectives who uncovered Bioff's conviction for running a brothel. Pegler wrote of these findings, defying all threats from Bioff.

Another tough Hollywood figure, one of the toughest, was Cecil B. De Mille. Bioff even tried his strong-arm tactics on him, arguably the most patriarchal and fearless of Hollywood's directors.

Gangsters had tried to get rid of him before, during the pioneer days of movies when an illegal trust fought, literally, to keep independent film-makers under their control in New York. De Mille was one of the first to move West, and according to legend discovered Hollywood when he went there to make *The Squaw Man* in 1913. The Trust sent gangsters from

New York to California to force De Mille and others like him back East.

Said Jesse Lasky Jr, 'My father told me that De Mille had a revolver on when he arrived in Hollywood because after stopping off at Flagstaff he and my father had found themselves in the middle of a war between the cattlemen and sheepmen, and De Mille wasn't taking any chances. As well as the revolver, he also kept a wolf, which he had acquired for the film, and it made for an excellent guard dog.

'One day De Mille arrived at his studio and found that gangsters from the Trust had already got there and had destroyed the negative. Fortunately, De Mille had another copy or he would have had to start filming *The Squaw Man* all over again.

'Next they started sending him letters saying, "Get out of town" or words to that effect, threatening him with death if he continued making films. What he did was to buy himself a bigger and more powerful revolver. Then while he was coming home one evening through a place called Cahuenga Pass, he was shot at by someone, hired obviously by the Trust, and he felt the bullet whizz just past his head. He was lucky not to have been killed.'

The Trust was eventually defeated and Los Angeles, and particularly its suburb Hollywood, became the centre of the American film industry, thanks to the courage of men like De Mille. It seemed a folly, therefore, when Bioff, perhaps feeling his hold over the studio heads slipping by 1939, tried his luck at threatening De Mille who was directing *Union Pacific* at Paramount Studios.

'De Mille was working frantically and collapsed from overwork and a troubled prostate gland,' Lasky Jr told me. 'He underwent an emergency operation and was ordered to bed for two weeks. But being Cecil B. De Mille, he continued to direct the the film on his back from his stretcher.

'A gangster running the technicians' union came to him and said that unless he paid however much money, De Mille might find himself the victim of an accident. I wasn't there to see this, but I understand that De Mille rose up like the Pillar of Fire from *The Ten Commandments* from his bed and said, "I've been shot at more than I'd care to remember, and threatened with death. When I first came out to Hollywood the Trust sent small-time gangsters like you to kill me, but as you see, I'm still alive. Do you know why I'm still alive?"

"'No," said the gangsters.

"'Because" said De Mille, "I've got God on my side." Now, De Mille was a greater actor than many of the actors he hired, and he must have been in great pain but he remained standing and he said, "I was told I would never stand again. But as you can see, God has made me stand. Do you honestly think you can succeed where all others have failed? I defy you to cause an 'accident'. God defies you. Now get out of here."

'And they got out of there and nothing happened to De Mille.'

13

The Bug

By the spring of 1939, Big Harry 'Greenie' Greenberg was in Canada, where he had fled when Dewey launched his investigation into Murder Inc. Short of enough money to maintain his apartment in Montreal, he wrote to Frank Costello and Meyer Lansky, unwisely, threatening to blow the whistle on the entire Murder Inc. mob if they didn't send him $5,000 immediately.

Mendy Weiss, now the boss of Murder Inc., sent his trusted lieutenant, Allie 'Tick Tock' Tannenbaum to Canada to dispose of Greenie. Tannenbaum arrived in Montreal only to find his quarry had fled to California.

Tannenbaum returned to New York to report what had happened.

'OK,' said Weiss, 'we'll let Benny handle it. Call him in Los Angeles.'

Allie Tannenbaum made the call. 'Big Harry Greenberg's about to name names. He's got to be silenced.'

'Has this got the OK from Frank?' asked Siegel.

'It's got the OK of everyone at the top. And they want you to handle it. This is too important to leave to anyone else, Benny. We'll send some extra help.'

On the night of 22 November 1939, Big Harry 'Greenie' Greenberg picked up a newspaper from the corner newsstand and climbed back into his car where he began reading the paper. A car pulled up alongside. Inside sat Allie Tannenbaum, Frankie Carbo, Harry 'The Champ' Segal and Benny Siegel. Siegel reached through the open window, a gun in his hand, and shot Greenberg five times. The car sped away as Greenberg staggered out of his car and dropped dead in the gutter.

The Los Angeles Police Department recognized that they had a Syndicate killing on their hands and made some efforts to investigate, but got nowhere. Siegel knew he was safe – that is, until March, the following year.

He turned on the morning radio and was shocked to hear the news that New York DA O'Dwyer had caught Abe 'Kid Twist' Reles, who was preparing to sing like a canary. Reles had been picked up for questioning about the murder of a longshoreman that had occurred the previous year, and was persuaded by his wife to co-operate with the New York District Attorney. Mrs Reles herself interceded for him by bargaining with the DA to give her husband immunity in return for information about Murder Inc.

Siegel got on the phone to his brother-in-law, Whitey Krakower. 'What the hell is going on?'

'The shit is flying everywhere here,' said Krakower. 'The DA's got not only Reles, but Tick Tock, and a couple of others. I think they're singing. There's no one running the shop. They've all gone to ground.'

Siegel slammed down the phone and got himself on a flight to New York. He had to try to restore order and calm all the nerves until the heat was off. Concurrently, Isidore Bernstein from Detroit's Purple Gang was also on his way for the same reason. The DA had his spies everywhere, and they knew it the moment both Siegel and Bernstein set foot in New York.

Cooped up in a room on the sixth floor of the Half Moon Hotel on Coney Island, four canaries – Reles, Tannenbaum, Myer Sycoff and Sholem Bernstein – were, as Krakower had said, singing. Reles told O'Dwyer what he knew of Tony Fabrizzo's murder by Siegel. Unfortunately for the DA, Reles's knowledge was second-hand; corroborating witnesses were unavailable. But when it came to the murder of Greenberg, O'Dwyer had Tannenbaum.

Tick Tock agreed to tell the DA how he trailed Greenie to Montreal and then out to Hollywood, but insisted that it was Siegel who actually pulled the trigger. He was also prepared to testify against others, including Whitey Krakower.

O'Dwyer got on the phone and called his counterpart in Los Angeles, Buron Fitts. 'I've got somebody here who's prepared to testify that Benny Siegel killed Greenberg in your town,' said O'Dwyer. 'I'm sending him by plane.'

The most secret and elaborate precautions were taken in flying Tannenbaum out to Los Angeles. On 16 August the Los Angeles County Grand Jury heard Tannenbaum's testimony and promptly returned an indictment against Siegel, Frank Carbo and Harry Segal. The indictment would have included Whitey Krakower, but he had been shot dead a month earlier.

Benny Siegel was at his Bel Air house when the police turned up. Over a loudspeaker, he was ordered to come out. When he failed to do so, the police broke in and swarmed through the place. For some reason, Siegel had failed to use his special escape route from the master bedroom, but instead hid out in the attic and that's where the police found him. They also found a .38 revolver and a .38 Colt automatic in a strongbox. He was charged with the murder of Harry Greenberg and interned in the county jail in Los Angeles.

Life in Los Angeles County Jail wasn't too bad for Siegel who made payments to Fitts's office and received permission to 'visit the dentist'. Accompanied by a guard and handcuffed, Siegel was led out to a waiting car and driven to Lindy's Wilshire Boulevard Café. They made their way to the men's rest room where the guard unlocked the cuffs. In a room upstairs his girlfriend, British actress Wendy Barrie, waited for him. While the guard waited downstairs, having been sufficiently paid to be patient, Siegel was upstairs screwing Wendy Barrie. Some hours later, Siegel emerged, had the cuffs slapped back on, and was led back to jail.

Inside again, he wondered about his 'pal', George Raft. He wasn't known as 'The Bug' for nothing, and his temper flared up as he wondered who else might have been involved in putting him behind bars. For some reason, he concluded that George Raft must be a part of the conspiracy, and he swore he would get even when he got out.

Norma Shearer's son, Irving Thalberg Jr, was excited at the thought of George Raft as stepfather because 'he's supposed to be a gangster'. Shearer firmly explained to her son that George only *played* gangsters in movies.

The prospect of Raft becoming Irving Junior's stepfather, however, was distant. He was still married and once more he tried to persuade Grayce to divorce him. According to Gavin Lambert, Norma Shearer's biographer, the publicity surrounding Raft's affair with Shearer 'made Mulrooney up the ante', suggesting that Grayce was by this time prepared to divorce Raft, but for a huge price.

Raft began meeting with Grayce's lawyers, trying to negotiate a divorce settlement he could afford. Grayce demanded $500,000 plus a percentage of his earnings. Raft could not, or would not, meet the asking price, and Grayce remained his wife which, probably, was the outcome she had intended. Shearer was devastated. She could not accept a permanent love without marriage.

In 1940 Mark Hellinger cast George Raft with Eddie G. Robinson in *Manpower*, presumably believing that Raft would get along as well with Robinson as he did with Cagney. But Robinson was different creature from Raft or Cagney. He came from a comfortable middle-class family and had gone to Columbia University. There was nothing rough about Robinson, despite his screen image. He had cut his acting teeth on the stage and, whereas Raft portrayed his screen characters by instinct, Robinson used technique. Robinson had suffered a drop in popularity but had risen to the top again at Warners with the success of *The Sea Wolf*. But George Raft had been slipping and his gambling got him into financial trouble. He still figured he was a Big Shot, but it was thanks mainly to Mark Hellinger that Raft was still an important actor at Warners.

There was a total clash of personalities between Raft and Robinson, not helped by their rivalry for the attentions of their leading lady, Marlene Dietrich. Raft had always had a yen for Dietrich, and was jealous when she invited Robinson to her house to get acquainted before filming began. They sipped wine and chatted, finding they both loved Impressionist paintings. She also invited Raft to her house. According to Gavin Lambert, he made 'serious headway' with her while Norma Shearer kept a dignified distance.

The competition between Robinson and Raft for Dietrich fuelled their mutual dislike. Cagney recalled, 'George dropped one on Eddie Robinson's chin one time and knocked him assways. As I remember the story, Robinson had the reputation of taking over on the set. He'd say, "You stand here and do this, and then move over here." As he was doing this with George, he grabbed his arm and kind of ushered him. Raft said, "Don't grab my arm." Eddie didn't heed the warning and the next time he grabbed Raft – bang! Robinson was on the floor.'

The story was a little more complex than the way Cagney told it. There were arguments on the first day of filming. Robinson was essentially an actor; George Raft was cut from a different cloth. The script called for Raft to hold Robinson's arm to prevent him from falling from a height to his death, eventually losing his grip in the pouring rain. Raft objected to being made to look weak on screen. After heated arguments, the scene was changed to have Robinson grasping a rope which breaks.

Another scene called for them to climb a pole in a downpour to repair a high-tension wire. Robinson wanted to include some dialogue before they started climbing. Raft argued, 'I don't want to say anything down here.'

'I think we've got to say something,' said Robinson.

'Why?' asked Raft. 'To me, silence is golden.'

As the argument got louder and more furious, Raft threw a punch at Robinson, and a fight ensued. A photographer was on hand to snap a picture of the fight and it made the front pages of newspapers the next day. Raft stayed home for the next few days, claiming he was ill. Robinson retaliated by staying home, insisting he had hurt his knee. It was Robinson that studio echelons fussed around, which only further enraged Raft.

When they got back to filming, Raft told director Raoul Walsh that he thought a particular line of Robinson's was wrong for his character. Robinson said, 'Look, George, you may think the line does not make any sense, but I have to speak it and it is all right with me.'

Raft yelled obscenities that shocked cast and crew, and Robinson stormed off the set. The day's filming was lost, but the two men's egos were placated and they reappeared on the set next day.

About a week later, on a Saturday, they filmed a scene in which Raft had to keep Robinson from getting into a fight in a bar. Robinson said to Raft, 'Let me struggle a little bit. Let me fight back.'

But Walsh said, 'Just pick him up, George, and carry him out without a struggle.'

But Raft decided to ignore the director and went over the top with Robinson, rough-housing him and pushing him around the set. He ignored Walsh's command to cut, continuing to shake Robinson furiously.

'What the hell is all this?' yelled Robinson, and Raft began swearing at him again. 'George, you're a fool for carrying on in such an unprofessional manner,' said Robinson. 'I came here to work, not indulge in anything of this nature. It seems impossible for me to continue.'

At that Raft punched Robinson. Fellow actors Ward Bond and Alan Hale jumped in to break up the fight, but it took Walsh's added strength to calm them down. Robinson, with tears in his eyes, walked off set and production halted until Monday morning.

When filming finished, Dietrich finished with Raft and he took to seeing Betty Grable.

Walsh, with Robinson's approval, filed charges against Raft with the SAG. The $16,000 budget had soared to $825,000. After the film was released in 1941, the studio, with Robinson's permission, dropped the charges. Robinson and Raft did not speak to each other for fifteen years.

This was almost the last straw for Warners as far as Raft was concerned. He refused to do *The Maltese Falcon* and *High Sierra*, the last-named produced by Mark Hellinger, and he also turned down *Casablanca*. Humphrey Bogart replaced him in all three pictures and became a huge star. Warner Bros had had enough and when his contract with them came up for renewal in 1943, they dropped him. Raft considered that Jack Warner had betrayed him. George Raft, the Big Shot, was growing smaller.

While Siegel was in jail awaiting trial, John Dockweiler became the new Los Angeles DA. In New York, O'Dwyer was busily engaged in the prosecution of other members of Murder Inc., including Lepke Buchalter. O'Dwyer became reluctant to send Reles to Los Angeles to testify against Siegel, reckoning that Reles was too vital to the homicide cases he was prosecuting in New York against Lepke. He was sure that, despite all the law's precautions, the Syndicate would do everything to shut Reles up permanently. Tannenbaum was also back in New York, and O'Dwyer considered him to be just as essential to the case against Lepke, and just as vulnerable to assassins.

Lepke had actually turned himself in, later claiming that Frank Costello had told him to give himself up 'or else'. J. Edgar Hoover of the FBI had, apparently, let Frank Costello know that unless Lepke surrendered, every known hood of Italian or Sicilian extraction would be deported. Lepke was told by Costello that he'd made a deal with the Feds to charge Lepke only with dealing in narcotics, and not for murder. But Tom Dewey wanted Lepke, who had been snatched away by the Federal Government, and a bitter wrangle broke out between the State and Federal authorities. Dewey finally got his way and was allowed to try Lepke for murder. With the valuable testimony of Reles, Dewey convicted Lepke, who remained in prison until he was sent to the electric chair in 1944. Buchalter was the only mob leader to be executed.

In Los Angeles, on 11 December 1940, Assistant DA Vernon Ferguson moved for the dismissal of the indictment against Benny Siegel as Reles and Tannenbaum were not allowed to testify. John Dockweiler, the newly elected DA of Los Angeles, supported the motion. Shortly after, journalist Florabel Muir alleged in her syndicated column that Siegel had contributed $30,000 to the Dockweiler campaign. When Dockweiler read this, he got straight onto his campaign manager and demanded that the said amount be immediately returned to Siegel.

Siegel had sworn vengeance upon George Raft. The Bug was in a murderous mood as he collected a gun and drove to George Raft's house. Raft was understandably alarmed when Siegel burst in on him, threatening to kill him for informing on him.

'Why would I want to do that?' Raft asked, trying to keep calm. Siegel accused him of being interested in Wendy Barrie. Raft knew of Siegel's reputation for exploding into violent anger but had never seen it first hand. But he had known him for years and knew how to calm him down; he began calling him 'Baby Blue Eyes'. It was peculiar, somewhat pathetic ploy but it had a strangely calming influence over Siegel. Before long, Raft was able to convince Siegel that his suspicions were groundless and without reason.

Siegel's Hollywood friends didn't pay much attention to the murder allegations. Cary Grant invited him to various parties, and Siegel and Dorothy di Frasso, who had no idea Siegel was two-timing her, were seen as often at Barbara Hutton's mansion or Grant's beach house as they were at George Raft's home. He was often to be seen in Raft's special box at the racetrack with Raft. The headlines about his exploits somehow enhanced his prestige in social circles.

Cary Grant had associated himself closely with Dorothy di Frasso who often stated she was an enemy of Mussolini. In 1939, following his engagement to Phyllis Brooks, the couple took off for Italy and stayed with di Frasso at her Villa Madama near Rome, where she entertained them with stories of how Field-Marshal Goering had wallowed in her famous gold bath while Mussolini gobbled food at her table. The house had been built during the time of the Borgias, and the Countess kept Phyllis terrified with tales of hauntings. All this delighted Cary Grant who seemed oblivious to her ulterior motive for being based in Los Angeles.

She and Benny Siegel were financing the development of an explosive device which they hoped to sell to the Italian Government. Hollywood served as a very useful point of departure for Mexico where the device was being developed. Some have suggested that Grant was actually some kind of government agent and was spying on di Frasso and Siegel. If so, he neglected to have them turned in.

On 18 November 1940 the Countess threw a lavish birthday party for Barbara Hutton, which Grant co-hosted. Nine days later the Associated Press reported that Mussolini had paid the Countess two million dollars for the purchase of the Villa Madama. Di Frasso refuted the reports and claimed that the Italian Government had expropriated the mansion.

An enigma the Countess may have been, but Cary Grant remained her close friend, as well as Siegel's. In December 1941 he was guest of the Countess at a party she gave for King Carol of Romania. That month a Foreign Activities Correlation report described the Countess as 'very anti-American, being both pro-Nazi and pro-Facist'. It stated that in September 1941 she was 'in close contact with the Italian minister, Marchetti, and the German minister, von Collenberg'. A naval information file was circulated in official circles citing that the Countess had made around fifteen trips to Italy over the past five years and was well acquainted with Benito Mussolini, his daughter Edda and her husband Galeazzo Ciano, that she was an aunt of the Italian Consul at Pittsburgh, Alessandro di Bugnano, and was also an intimate friend of Prince Boncompagni who was in custodial detention at Ellis Island, suspected of being an Axis agent.

While many of those in Hollywood society were falling over themselves to be courteous to Benny Siegel, the tide had turned against Willie Bioff and George Browne. Bioff attempted to bribe Arthur Ungar, the scrupulously honest editor of the *Daily Variety*, and when Ungar proved that he couldn't be bought, Bioff made threats. But Ungar didn't knuckle under, as had many of the studio heads. Instead, Ungar continued to campaign for the removal of Bioff and Browne from the IATSE. In fact, he called for their complete expulsion from Hollywood.

Robert Montgomery, president of the Screen Actors' Guild, was fighting Bioff's futile attempts to make inroads into the SAG. While Westbrook Pegler continued to syndicate articles about Bioff, Ungar used the pages of the *Daily Variety* also to expose Bioff's true background and nature.

The Federal government had been waiting for an opportunity to pounce and became alerted through tax inspectors to the cheque from Schenck made out to Bioff. The Feds moved in and began asking questions. Joseph Schenck told them that he had given Bioff the money as a loan. But other studio heads, breathing huge sighs of relief at this first sign of deliverance from the hands of racketeers, came forward to confess their own creative book-keeping in order to bribe IATSE's representative.

In May 1941, Bioff and Browne were charged before a Federal Grand Jury in New York of extorting huge sums from Fox, Warner Bros, Paramount and MGM. Schenck made the terrible mistake of testifying that the cheque had been just a loan. He was persuaded to co-operate with the government. What the Feds probably didn't know then was that Schenck, according to Sam Giancana, had funnelled more than half a million dollars to Roosevelt's presidential campaign on behalf of the Syndicate. According to Sam Giancana, Roosevelt had a 'a lot of favours to pay back'. Joe Kennedy was said to be another who fed millions to the campaign on the Syndicate's orders.

The jury had no hesitation in finding Bioff and Browne guilty of extortion. Bioff was sentenced to ten years in prison; Browne got eight. Chicago's Hollywood interests were left in the hands of Johnny Roselli. Chicago wasn't about to give up the movie business so easily, not with people like Louis B. Mayer of Metro, Harry Cohn of Columbia and Harry Warner of Warner Bros in Roselli's pocket.

Joseph Schenck was given a year for tax evasion. A. Scott Berg suggested in his biography of Samuel Goldwyn that Schenck, the only Hollywood mogul without children, volunteered to take the rap for the rest of the industry. To Schenck's horror, the judge ordered that his citizenship be revoked. He was suddenly a Russian again.

Goldwyn dined with Schenck on the eve of his prison sentence in May 1942, and thereafter wrote him regularly. When Schenck came up for parole, Goldwyn wasted no time in writing to the Department of Justice. He stated 'with the utmost sincerity that I have never known a finer man than Mr Schenk'. In September Schenck was released and was the guest of honour at a dinner hosted by Goldwyn.

In 1941, Siegel heard that the Feds wanted him to testify before a grand jury that he had harboured Lepke at one time. No subpoena had been issued and Siegel kept his cool. On 17 April a squad of Federal agents turned up at his home and slapped handcuffs on him.

'What's this all about?' asked Siegel. 'I paid my taxes.'

'You're being arrested for hiding a fugitive from justice.'

'What fugitive?'

'Louis Lepke Buchalter. You upset a lot of people in government by hiding him before he got caught. Now it's your turn to satisfy justice.'

They took him before United States Commissioner David Head in Los Angeles. 'How do you plead?' asked Head.

'I don't know nothin' about hidin' nobody.'

'Just tell me how you plead for crissakes.'

'Not guilty.'

'I'm granting bail for twenty-five thousand dollars.'

The bail was immediately posted and Siegel went home.

On 29 May Siegel was back in court for extradition proceedings to New York. Siegel was happy to be sent to New York to escape the heat put on him by Dockweiler, who hadn't forgotten how Siegel had tried to stitch him up by making that $30,000 investment in his election campaign.

It began to look as though Siegel's trial wouldn't occur much before Christmas or the New Year, so Siegel had to remain in Los Angeles for the time being. Then he heard that he was to be indicted again for the murder of Greenberg, based on the testimony of Reles. He began to wonder how he was going to wriggle out of this one. His spirits lightened when Al Smiley came to visit him with a message from Frank Costello that everything would soon be sorted out.

In New York, Abe Reles was under the protection of the police by order of William O'Dwyer. In his sixth-floor suite of the Half Moon Hotel, Reles was having difficulty sleeping. He looked through the door to the living room, where his police guard was supposed to be sitting, to discover that he was not there.

Suddenly two policemen, neither of whom had he seen before, came into the room.

'What's up?' Reles asked them. The cops tried to grab him but he fell back on the bed. They pinned him down and, as he struck and kicked out at them, they covered his face with a chloroformed cloth. He began to black out.

The cops went into the front room where one of them tied two sheets together. The other attached a wire to the radiator, tied the wire to the sheets, and then cut the wire in two with a razor. Watching all this in a semi-conscious state was Reles. One of the cops spotted him. 'Christ, he's awake,' he said.

His partner had already drawn his gun. 'Easy does it, Abe. We're going to give you a break.'

They picked him up and half carried him to the window. One of them said, 'We're going to let you escape, with the sheets.'

Abe had seen them cut the wire. He tried to swing at the cop nearest him but missed. Then they grabbed him around the chest and legs, and lifted him to the window. Reles screamed in terror as he was thrown forward and sent hurtling towards the cement below. He died instantly.

Looking down at the body lying six floors below them, one of the cops said to the other, 'You idiot. You threw him too far! He's supposed to *fall* from the building, not *fly*.'

With the chief witness against Siegel now dead, the charges against Siegel were dropped. A year later, William O'Dwyer, the man who had installed Reles in that hotel under police protection, called on Frank Costello to get his approval to run for Mayor of New York City.

14

Sugar Hill

By 1939, there was a new face, a beautiful face, among the hardened faces of the underworld in New York. It belonged to 'Sugar' Virginia Hill, a much admired and desired woman who made Joe Adonis a happy man when she ended her reign in Chicago as the top underworld moll by going with Adonis to New York to become 'Queen of the Mafia'.

She had arrived in Chicago in 1932 when she was only fifteen. Even at such a tender age she had the body of a mature woman, and it was a body bound to attract attention from men. She'd mysteriously left home in Bessemer, Alabama, where she'd been born and bred – one of ten children – and set off for Chicago with a much older man. Her irate and alcoholic father called the police and told them that his daughter had been hustled off to the Windy City by a married man.

Police in Chicago were alerted that a man had taken a minor across the state line for immoral purposes, and traced Virginia and her male companion to their hotel room. As the police burst in, charging the startled man with violating the Mann Act, Virginia leapt to his defence, saying that he was simply her bodyguard, there to ensure she kept out of trouble. She explained that she had come to Chicago to try and make some money for her poor family. She was one of ten children, and her father barely made an adequate living for them all as a marble polisher.

With no evidence to the contrary, the police brought no

charges and Mr Hill, back in Bessemer in Alabama, had to accept that his daughter wasn't coming home.

Virginia's Southern accent made her stick out like a sore thumb in Chicago. She set about finding a job and for a short time she was a hash slinger. Oozing sex appeal with her wide eyes, chestnut hair and buxom figure, she made her first public appearance on the Midway of Chicago's World Fair where she performed in a show billed as the *Elephant and the Fleas*. Shortly after, Virginia began frequenting places that no proper young lady should be seen in, making friends of dubious character, and working hard to adorn herself in the kind of finery that gave her the appearance of being a classy lady.

After seven years of working her way into and up the first few rungs of the underworld, mingling with pimps and thugs with no more class than Marino Bello, she met Joe Epstein, a big-time bookie and operator of a plush gambling salon. She was slinging hash in a café when Epstein discovered her. He was in charge of Capone's bookmaking operations; he had plenty of money, and that's exactly what she wanted.

Epstein nicknamed Virginia the Flamingo because of her long legs and reddish hair. He was balding and unattractive, but he was crazy about her and she allowed him to shower her with fine clothes, furs and jewels. But it wasn't enough for her. She figured there was a gold mine out there in the world she was being exposed to as she acted as a messenger between Epstein and his associates in the Syndicate. She was only twenty-two years old but full of ambition to become a millionairess. She knew she could make good use of her considerable charm and humour, which made her a desirable date for bigger fish than Epstein.

She was generally faithful to Joe Epstein who seemed prepared to move heaven and earth to help her achieve her ambition. But Joe Epstein was small potatoes compared to Charlie Fischetti.

Fischetti was Al Capone's cousin. He'd poured much of the

fortune he'd amassed through criminal activity into a fifteen-room duplex penthouse on North Sheridan Road. The house was full of antiques and modern art. Fischetti's lifestyle was impressive to Virginia.

One of his more important functions in Chicago's Mafia operations was to muscle in on the city's labour unions. He'd assigned his front men, Paul Ricca and Louis Campagna, the task of forcing unions to take in large numbers of his own men as regular union members, and to elect three mobsters to executive posts. When the union turned Ricca and Campagna down, it was up to Charlie Fischetti to step in. He had to do little more than give the union leaders one of his cold, calculated, piercing stares, and the deal was set.

In association with Jake Guzik and Tony Accardo, he also ran the gangland gambling arena. He made Virginia welcome into his life and she promptly dumped Epstein. She did for Fischetti pretty much what she'd done for Epstein, acting as a go-between, and in return Fischetti kept her cosy with jewels, clothes and anything she wanted. But what she really wanted was to make her way up in the underworld where it really counted – in New York. She had her sights on Frank Costello.

Through Fischetti she met all the Big Shots of Chicago, but none of them led to the likes of Costello. Then, one day, she met Joe Adonis while he was on a visit to Chicago and she wasted no time in making herself available to him. Real name Joseph Doto, he was a big shot in the mob. It's said that he was the one gangster who looked like the movie version of a major mobster. His hair was greying at the temples and there always seemed to be a dangerous glint in his eye. After Humphrey Bogart saw him, he said, 'That's the guy I'd like to play in a movie.'

With Lepke, Reles and Anastasia, Adonis signed death warrants of at least sixty-three persons during the existence of Murder Inc. He also smuggled heroin and cocaine, and he controlled the Longshoremen's Union, victimizing its members while his loan sharks extorted usurious rates. He bought a $32,500 mansion in Brooklyn's sedate Shore Road. The walls were bullet-proof and bomb-proof and the cellar converted into a bar-room.

To Fischetti's chagrin, when Adonis left for New York and his swank Sedate Road mansion, Virginia went with him.

Benny Siegel efficiently divided his complicated love life between Dorothy di Frasso and Wendy Barrie, successfully ensuring that neither woman knew about the other. George Raft knew what was going on and because he liked Wendy Barrie, he took it upon himself to warn her that she was 'playing with fire'.

Wendy was not of the same cloth as the Countess who led a dangerous life with Siegel, and was excited by it. Wendy Barrie was a sweet girl; the well-brought-up daughter of a British lawyer. She had been born in Hong Kong and educated in England and Switzerland before making her London stage début at the age of twenty-six in 1930. In 1933 she played the sluttish Jane Seymour in Alexander Korda's hugely successful *The Private Life of Henry VIII*, and consequently came to Hollywood. But Raft, in doing for Wendy what he saw as a favour, had made what was very nearly his last mistake.

During one of her Saturday night encounters with Siegel, Wendy happened to mention Raft's warning to her.

The following morning, Siegel, packing a gun and in one of his murderous tempers, drove to Raft's. Mack Grey came out to meet him.

'Where the hell is he?' Siegel bellowed at Grey.

'Take it easy, Benny. George had a big night and he's still sleeping.'

'Sleeping, huh? I'll make sure he's sleeping – *for ever.*'

There was nothing Grey could do to stop Siegel, who ran up the stairs and, gun in hand, burst into Raft's bedroom. Grey was right behind but powerless to do anything. Raft woke up suddenly to find himself looking down the barrel of Siegel's gun.

'You dirty son of a bitch,' yelled Siegel. 'I thought you were my friend, but you told Wendy all that crap about me. I'm going to wipe you out.'

Raft, knowing he could be dead any moment, kept his cool. 'OK, pal, just settle down. You're liable to do something neither of us would like. We've been friends a long time, Baby Blue Eyes ...' and he went on for the next ten minutes, talking about their friendship and the good times they'd had. 'So come on, let's forget it, Baby Blue Eyes.'

The magic worked and Siegel calmed down. Smiling, he told Raft, 'It's OK this time, Georgie. But you shouldn't have told all that stuff to her.'

'You know you're not doing her any good. Right?' asked Raft.

'Maybe you're right, Georgie.' Then they shook hands and went downstairs for breakfast.

George Raft co-owned a swank Broadway restaurant called the Hurricane. It captured Virginia Hill's imagination. She saw it as a way to stardom; she had become intent on a career as an entertainer since coming to New York as the Mob's most glamorous party hostess. In a way she was already famous, partly as Joe Adonis's girlfriend, but also as an ardent rumba dancer, and through Adonis, she landed a number of engagements in nightclubs as a dancer. To ensure her success as a popular new entertainer, she spent more than $1,000 on people she 'invited' to come to watch her.

She told Adonis, 'Joe, what I really need now to make me a star attraction is my own place – somewhere where people already love to come. I was thinking of the Hurricane restaurant.'

'I like the idea,' said Adonis who set about making the restaurant's owners an offer to buy the place. Virginia was the resident entertainer, and became known as 'The Alabama Hurricane', but it was to be a short-time engagement. A two-night engagement to be exact, due to Frank Costello who, as acting Boss of all Bosses with Luciano in prison, wasn't impressed by the glamour-hungry moll whom he thought would eventually bring trouble within the ranks of the Syndicate.

When Frank Rizzo, a close friend of his, told him that he had been offered a job at the Hurricane, Costello said, 'No, you're not going to work there. The Hurricane can't last long. Virginia Hill is a big *bitch* and if she remains here she'll call many dogs in New York to her. There'll be big trouble. I want her out of New York.'

His word was law and after just two nights at the Hurricane, Virginia Hill headed west. She turned up in Los Angeles, loaded with money, jewels, furs, and a yen to become a movie star.

She wasted no time in making herself known to talent scouts, casting directors and producers. Her only advantage over the thousands of other would-be stars hustling around Hollywood was her considerable wealth. Carl Laemmle Jr, whose father had founded the Universal film company, discovered Virginia during her rounds of the studios in 1941, and began to pursue her with a passion that she failed to return.

He had found himself in charge of production at Universal at the astonishingly young age of twenty-one while his father placed seventy other relatives on his payroll. Junior had initiated a new policy of producing high-budget quality films, such as *All Quiet On the Western Front*, and he also instigated the hugely successful cycle of horror films beginning with *Dracula* and *Frankenstein* in 1931. But in 1935, Laemmle Senior was forced to sell the studio due to his own extravagances during the Depression. Junior was a casualty of the sell-out and went into independent production. But by the time he began chasing Virginia Hill all over Hollywood in 1941, his fortune of more than thirty million dollars allowed him the luxury of early retirement, and this was of no use to Virginia.

She succeeded in getting enough attention from studios to take a series of screen tests; they were all flops. However, her fame increased as she threw huge parties, spending money on these shindigs with abandon, and entertaining fun-seekers with her rumbaing at Falcon's Lair, the house she bought which had been owned at one time by Rudolph Valentino. She became highly recognizable as she sped about Hollywood in her bright red Cadillac convertible.

She didn't skimp on jewels and furs either, spending over $400,000 a year on adorning herself. She owned a hundred pairs of shoes, a dozen mink coats and several wardrobes' worth of assorted other furs. Not even the war succeeded in rationing her intake of new clothes. She had sportswear flown in by some mysterious influence from London. She claimed to be an heiress and that the vast fortune she lavished on her parties, her clothes and her jewels was the inheritance left by her late husband, George Rogers. But there had been no husband, no George Rogers, no inheritance. Her fortune quite simply came from the Mob; her share of the profits creamed from prostitution, drugs and gambling.

When word reached Benny Siegel that Virginia Hill, whom he had met previously in New York, was trying to break into movies, he called her.

'I got a few contacts,' he told her. 'Why don't you come over to my place and we'll talk things over.'

'What about the Countess?' she asked. 'I hear she's a very possessive lady.'

'Dorothy's in Mexico at the moment. She's got a few business matters to deal with there and won't be back for a few days.'

Since the attack on Pearl Harbor by the Japanese on 7 December 1941, changes had taken place, not just in the normal world as America entered the war, but also in the criminal world. Dorothy di Frasso was in Mexico consulting with a Dr Bonotto – who had formerly been authorized by the Italian government to supply it with the new and secret explosive device financed by di Frasso and Siegel – about trying to sell the same explosive to the US War Department. This had little to do with any kind of allegiance. The Countess was, after all, a friend of Mussolini. It was just that it became easier to sell to a customer closer to home. Besides, were they all caught trying to sell to Italy, they might well been executed as spies.

So, with Dorothy away, Virginia drove over to Siegel's house, and they didn't waste too much time over the next few days discussing her future in films.

George Raft was alone and feeling rather depressed. His career was on the wane since his troubles with Eddie Robinson, and his love life was a disaster. No woman wanted a serious relationship with a man who was not free to marry. His only consolation was that he was still able to afford the company of whores, sometimes two in one night. On this particular evening, as he pondered on his troubles, he was paid a surprise visit by Dorothy di Frasso. She was distraught and had been crying.

'I'm fed up hearing about Benny running around with other girls,' she wailed. 'And, you – I thought you were my friend, George. You know I'm crazy about Benny – and you also know he's running around with other girls. Why didn't you tell me?'

'Take it easy, Dorothy,' said Raft, trying to console her. 'I'll talk to Benny about it, OK?'

'You tell him if I catch him with anyone else, I don't care who she is, I'll kill her.'

Raft watched her drive away in her Rolls-Royce and wondered, 'Here's this wealthy, attractive woman who has everything money could buy wasting her tears on a guy like Benny, who couldn't care less.' One thing was sure. He wasn't going to interfere with Siegel's love life again.

Benny and Virginia were fast becoming a Hollywood item, making a glamorous, charismatic and exciting couple. He fell head over heels for her. Unlike all his other girlfriends, Virginia understood him – she knew his lifestyle and outlook, and she was willing to have him share it with her. Their circle of friends included Cary Grant and his new wife, heiress Barbara Hutton, George Raft, Mark Hellinger – and Stephen Crane.

Crane's real name was Joseph Stephenson Crane. He had

gone to Hollywood, like countless others, to seek fame and fortune. But while he toyed briefly with the idea of being an actor, he chose instead to open his own restaurant. It was a way of making big money and meeting women – his main goals in life were to have money and women. From his beginnings in Hollywood, he carefully cultivated friendships with club owners, restaurateurs and famous hosts and hostesses. He became a successful host himself, running Sunday afternoon card parties at his apartment. Among his guests were numerous gangsters, some more notorious than Benny Siegel. With him on occasion came 'Sugar' Virginia Hill, and she and Crane became good friends.

Crane found her engaging and whenever Siegel had to leave town for reasons Crane never enquired about, he escorted her to the Colony Club and the Clover Club, both of which had underworld ties. Columnists even reported their outings but everyone knew that their relationship was purely platonic. Crane, whom everybody liked, was trusted by Siegel with his girl, and Crane would do nothing to betray that trust. Especially when her boyfriend was the notorious 'Bug'.

When Crane came to Hollywood, he was in the process of making a whole new life for himself, and that included making a new face. He wanted to have cosmetic surgery, not to change his face radically, but merely to improve his looks, and it was Virginia Hill who lent him the money for the operation that lengthened his jaw by grafting bone from his right thigh.

On 17 July 1942, Stephen Crane eloped with an actress to Las Vegas. She was Lana Turner. She loved going with Crane to Virginia's parties where the guest list included film stars and gangsters. She was to remember that Benny Siegel was 'a great dancer', and she found Sugar Hill to be 'a fun gal'.

Lana Turner's studio, MGM, forbade her to mix with underworld figures. But she ignored them. Louis B. Mayer refrained from chastising her in any way for her disobedience; he had his own discreet list of Mob phone numbers. Lana's marriage to Crane wouldn't last, but it did produce a daughter, Cheryl, who would be unwittingly drawn into a tragic confrontation in years to come, due to her mother's passion for a violent small-time gangster who would spring from the Bugsy Siegel stable.

Despite Benny Siegel's killer instinct, he was a soft-centred, old-fashioned lover with Virginia, writing her love poems addressed 'To My Sweetheart'. The couple adopted Mildred Cram's book *Forever*, which was a modern version of *Romeo and Juliet*, as their very own. They read the book together, identifying with the leading characters, Julie and Colin, who, unable to be together in this life, promise they will find a way to consummate their love in death. For Siegel and Virginia, as for Julie and Colin in the book, their love was for ever. That's what they believed; they were like two teenagers in love for the first time.

But for just now, there were certain practicalities that needed to be arranged, and, on Siegel's advice, Virginia sold Falcon's Lair and moved in with him. He was the owner of a number of properties, including a $200,000 35-room hacienda, complete with marble bathroom and swimming pool, in Holmsby Hills, where his uncomplaining wife and two daughters were now tucked away out of sight.

Virginia finally landed her first screen role in Samuel Goldwyn's production, *Ball of Fire*, directed by Al Capone's friend Howard Hawks, and starring Gary Cooper and Barbara Stanwyck. Virginia had only a small role, no doubt arranged by Benny Siegel, and he was there with her at the glittering gala première and party, behaving as though he were a movie star himself.

By late 1942, the war had begun to impose on the underworld. Naval Intelligence was worried about sabotage and espionage along the sprawling New York waterfront. The great French liner, *Normandie*, converted to a troop ship capable of carrying an entire division, had been burned and sunk at her Manhattan pier in a mysterious disaster. And German submarines seemed to be supplied with uncannily accurate information about sailing dates of convoys bound for England.

Naval Intelligence felt a counterforce was needed along the waterfront and it was suggested that Charlie Luciano should be asked for his co-operation. Operation Underworld Counter Espionage was set up and the District Attorney assigned Murray Gurfein, then in charge of his rackets bureau, to work with the Navy. With Gurfein's help an approach was made to Luciano.

Even before the official approach was made, word reached Luciano's ears of what was to happen, and he subtly announced that he would be found to be patriotic but was unhappy in Dannemora Prison; he would be more malleable if he were comfortable in Great Meadow Prison, known as the 'country club' of New York State penal institutions. His transfer was promptly arranged, and Luciano's attorney, Michael Polakoff, made the first trip from New York to the prison, just north of Albany, to officially explain the Navy's proposition to Charlie.

Luciano is reported to have appeared surprised, as though this was news to him, but agreed to do whatever he could to help. There began a series of visits by various underworld figures to Great Meadow Prison; these conferences with the still recognized Boss of all Bosses were organized and allowed by the authorities for the direct purpose of discussing the Navy's defence problems. No doubt, there was also much discussion about the Mafia's more regular business. Nevertheless, throughout the rest of the war, there were no particularly damaging acts of sabotage in the vital port of New York.

While George Raft was busy during the war years with his 'Cavalcade of Sports', and touring Europe with the USO, Siegel saw little of him, and consequently spent more of his social time with Cary Grant. But he missed Raft who was his own soul mate, so when Raft returned in June 1944, Siegel immediately called him. 'Hey, Georgie, it's been almost a year since I saw you, so how about it if you come over to Al Smiley's place?'

Raft went over to Smiley's apartment at Sunset Towers, and discovered a number of others there who were studying racing sheets and making bets on the phone on horses running at Churchill Downs in Kentucky. Raft studied the form and picked a few likely winners, and then sat with Siegel and reminisced about 'the good old days in New York'.

Siegel was on the phone placing a bet when the apartment door burst open and in stormed members of the Los Angeles Sheriff's Vice Squad, led by Captain William Deal who told Siegel and Smiley that they were under arrest for bookmaking.

Raft told Deal, 'Look, if you're arresting them, you better arrest me too.'

'Are you bookmaking?' asked Deal.

'No, and neither are they.'

'That's not how it looks to me.' The captain clapped the cuffs on Siegel and Smiley, and led them off to jail.

The studio Raft was working at told him to stay away from the ensuing trial, warning him that if he admitted publicly that he was a friend of Siegel, his career could be over. He might have agreed with them but he was subpoenaed and had to turn up in court.

The trial was held before Justice Cecil Holland, and Siegel and Smiley were represented by Isaac Pacht, a former Superior Court Judge and member of the State Parole Board. There were stormy scenes in the courtroom that morning when Raft was called to the witness stand to testify. Never a respecter of decorum, he deliberately baited Captain Deal, and he testified that neither Siegel nor Smiley had been booking bets.

Then Raft told the court, 'I've known Mr Siegel for twenty years. We have been friends a long, long time.' There was no way the newspaper reporters were going to keep that statement from the public and they rushed to the nearest phones to ensure the next editions carried the story that George Raft was a personal friend of Benjamin 'Bugsy' Siegel.

While being questioned, Raft became so abusive to the prosecutor and vehement in his defence of Siegel that Judge Holland cautioned him several times that he was in contempt of court, and could face charges.

Mark Hellinger also came to court. The press were delighted that another prominent Hollywood figure was there in defence of Siegel. They ate it all up, describing the dapper Hellinger in his 'uniform of a dark blue shirt and white necktie', saying under oath that Bugsy was 'a man of good moral character'.

Raft and Hellinger helped to break the case, and the prosecutor offered to drop the felony charges if Siegel and Smiley pleaded guilty on one bookmaking count. They agreed and were fined $250.

That Christmas Benny Siegel and Al Smiley were among Mark Hellinger's guests for dinner. Also there were Humphrey Bogart and Lauren Bacall. At that time Bogart was still married to Mayo Methot, but her alcoholism had driven him into Bacall's arms. Unlike Raft, Bogart didn't court friendship with gangsters, but he was a close friend of Hellinger's.

This was Lauren Bacall's first and only encounter with the Mob. She said, 'Mark always invited his closest friends for dinner at Thanksgiving and Christmas. Bogie and I had our first Christmas at his enormous house where he lived with Gladys. Sitting round the table were Bugsy Siegel, Al Smiley and their girlfriends. They seemed very polite and soft-spoken. I didn't know who they were until Bogie told me they had connections with the Mafia.'

15

Flamingo

One day in 1945 Siegel and Virginia caught a plane for Las Vegas Airport where they picked up a car and drove the three miles into the town's centre. It was a sleepy, underdeveloped town, not unlike a real-life Western town with its small gambling saloons that had sprung up since the state of Nevada had legalized gambling in 1931.

But for the most part it was a piece of desert which Siegel showed Virginia as they drove back to the airport, telling her, 'This is it. This is where I'm gonna build the biggest hotel and casino in the country. It'll make Monte Carlo look like peanuts. It'll be just the beginning. All along this strip, all the way to the airport, there'll be hotels and casinos, all luxurious and legal.'

Virginia leaned over and kissed Benny. 'It's going to be great, Ben,' she said.

But it was also going to be costly. Siegel needed *big* money, and he knew that the Syndicate would invest if he could convince them of its potential. He knew it wouldn't be as easy as it had been to convince Virginia. So the next day he kissed Virginia goodbye and boarded a plane bound for New York where he met with Frank Costello, Meyer Lansky and numerous Mafia leaders. He succeeded in persuading them to invest heavily towards the initial estimate of around one and a half million dollars.

He returned to Las Vegas and bought a tacky hotel and its accompanying land from a bankrupt widow. Under his personal supervision, an army of architects, builders and decorators moved in to begin erecting the Flamingo Hotel in December 1945. At some point Siegel attracted the attention of Howard Hughes whose interest in making films was waning while his obsession with designing and flying aeroplanes was becoming legendary.

While Siegel was busy bringing about the beginning of his gambling empire, George Raft's association with the underworld was becoming increasingly public. When he returned from his 1945 USA tour, he made a personal appearance at the New York première of *Follow the Boys*, after which he took some friends to the home of Leo Durocher, manager of the Brooklyn Dodgers and a close friend of Raft's since their early days in New York when they had both hustled in the poolrooms. Raft loved baseball, and, when film commitments allowed him, during the baseball season he often moved in with Durocher who was also close to Joe Adonis. Likewise, when Durocher was in California, he stayed with Raft.

On this occasion Durocher was not at home, being at the Dodgers' camp in Bear Mountain, so Raft let himself and his friends in. A game of cards began, money was exchanged, and then someone suggested a dice game. They played until the early hours and Raft walked away the supreme winner.

Seven months later, New York's DA, Frank Hogan, received a complaint from a man called Martin Shurin who had lost a lot of money to Raft at Durocher's home; he accused Raft of using loaded dice to win $18,500 from him in thirteen straight passes. The charge was leaked to the press and Westbrook Pegler, who had been instrumental in the campaign against Willie Bioff and George Browne, wrote in his column:

Martin Shurin, the chump of the evening, a young man with illusions about celebrities, particularly movie actors, is disenchanted now. He lost $18,500 to Raft in a few minutes.

Shurin recalls that in the scramble for position at the crap table, he found himself alongside Raft. He would have preferred a place where he could retrieve the dice and count the spots as Raft ran up his 13 passes, all fours and tens, most of them the hard way.

However, a spot next to the great man was a place of honour, so he did not scuffle and began to lay the conventional price against fours and tens. He says he gave Raft $1,500 in currency and a cheque for $1,000 that night and sent him ten $1,000 bills a few days later.

In answer to the charge, Raft insisted he had not used loaded dice and had only won $8,000, mainly in cheques. Unable to make the charge stick, the DA dismissed the case, but Pegler had another story to print in October 1946.

Durocher's choice of companions has been a matter of deep concern to Branch Rickey, the business manager of the Dodgers. The old practice of 'whispering out' players and even managers 'for the good of the game' could be retrieved....

If the moving picture business knows that one of its stars prefers the underworld and doesn't care, that is one matter. For a time, and for a profit, Hollywood joined the newspapers and the Department of Justice in discrediting the Adonises and Little Augies, friends of George Raft. All that time, however, Hollywood was developing an underworld of her own, as evil and bold as the prohibition and union rackets, and without repudiation by the industry.

Nobody would bet on the outcome of a picture, but a few killings on fixed ball games would degrade something that the public, perhaps without realizing as much, has come to regard as an American ideal or treasure.

The moral 'climate' of Durocher's circle and Raft's is ominously similar to that in which the corruption of 1919 occurred.

When Branch Rickey, a sports authority, read this, he

immediately phoned the airport where Durocher was about to board a plane for Italy, and ordered him not to allow Raft to use his apartment again. But even with Durocher's reluctant promise, the matter didn't end there. The baseball commissioner, Happy Chandler, held a secret meeting with Durocher at the Claremont Country Club during one of Durocher's stays with Raft in California, and told the manager to leave Raft's home. He told Durocher that if he ever saw either Siegel or Joe Adonis again, he would be asked to resign from the game completely.

Durocher had to return to Raft's home to collect his belongings. When Raft saw the consternation in his friend's face, he asked, 'Go ahead, Leo, tell me what's up.'

Durocher explained what had happened and how he had to dissociate himself from Raft, who, all the while, raised no protest, knowing Durocher had no choice if he was to save his career.

It was becoming clear to everyone, even in the underworld itself, the Raft's associations with them was damaging his career. Even Joe Adonis, who at a dinner in New York told Raft, 'George, I like you, so I'm going to give you some good advice. We like each other, but it's no good for you to be seen with me.'

But George Raft wouldn't heed even the advice of the Mob itself.

Meanwhile, other things were happening in regard to the underworld's connection with Hollywood that had nothing to do with Raft. In prison, Willie Bioff made a deal to spill beans every which way in return for an early parole. He pinpointed Frank Nitti as the man who put him into Hollywood. Nitti couldn't bear the thought of another spell in prison, and he shot himself in the head. Paul Ricca went to prison for ten years.

Chicago was now in the hands of Anthony J. Accardo, Jake Guzik and brothers Charlie and Rocco Fischetti. Sam Giancana saw his opportunity for promotion. He began rubbing shoulders with senators, Federal judges and legislators and, with Johnny Roselli in prison, taking control of the Outfit's interests in Hollywood. He even took his wife, Ange, on a tour of the studios. She recalled how they were treated 'better than the stars by the heads of all the studios', and that the stars they met 'acted like Mooney was their best friend'. By 1946 Giancana was Tony Accardo's underboss.

There was little aggression now between Chicago and New York for the Los Angeles territory, for Giancana and Frank Costello had long been friends, and they now joined forces to distribute smuggled gems throughout the Midwest and West.

More important for the whole underworld, Charlie Luciano was living up to his name of 'Lucky', and had obtained a pardon of sorts from the American government for his co-operation during the war. He was released from prison but deported back to Sicily.

On a freezing February evening in 1946, he was driven to the port of New York, which he had helped to protect, and escorted to the SS *Laura Keene* which had made many Atlantic crossings during the war, transporting troops. Docked next to her were the *Ile de France* and the *Queen Mary* to which anyone would have normally expected the press would flock as Clark Gable, Cary Grant and Jack Benny were boarding the French ship, while John Wayne was among a host of dignitaries boarding the *Queen Mary*. But on this day the press were interested only in taking snaps of and getting quotes from Lucky Luciano. There to send him off were Frank Costello, Meyer Lansky, Albert Anastasia and Vito Genovese.

Frank Costello was still taking care of the Mafia and its connections, but in all respects, Lucky Luciano was still the Boss of all Bosses, and in time would re-establish his rule over the Mob, and handle the disturbing developments pertaining to the Hollywood connection.

As construction on the Flamingo progressed, the costs began to skyrocket. Siegel insisted on nothing but the best, and kept the contractor, the Del E. Webb Construction Company of Phoenix, under pressure and on their toes. He demanded materials in short supply or unavailable during those post-war years, and he procured steel, copper, tiles and everything else through the black market. All the wood was imported, and Charlie Luciano smuggled several tons of Carrara marble to him. The plumbing bill alone finally reached $1 million.

The hotel was still incomplete when the first million and a half ran out. Siegel contacted Meyer Lansky, asking for more money. Lansky, whose position in the mob was to invest their money *wisely*, reluctantly went to Costello and other Mob leaders on his behalf – but he envisaged a tragic end to all this. One of the chief investors denounced Siegel as 'a psycho wasting money', and Lansky was told to keep a sharp eye on the Bug.

Costello sent his slot-machine partner Phil Kastel to Las Vegas with a million dollars in cash in two suitcases. Upon its delivery, Siegel said, 'It isn't enough. I need a million more.' Kastel returned to New York and reported to Frank Costello that Siegel needed another million.

Costello was a worried man. Many of the investors had gone along on the deal at his urging because of his reputation as a straight-talking businessman, relatively speaking. He began to wonder if the hotel would ever be completed, and feared that if it were, the venture would probably be so deep in the red, it would go bankrupt.

There was further trouble in August 1946. Following the death of James Ragan, who had run the Continental wire service, Siegel turned the profits from the Nevada and Arizona service over to the Mob, but decided to keep all profits from the California service for himself. Jack Dragna remained loyal to him, running the wire service on his behalf, until two characters landed in Los Angeles and informed him that Siegel was getting into hot water with the Mob. Dragna suddenly turned neutral.

In the autumn of 1946, Siegel and Virginia quietly slipped

off to Mexico where they were secretly married. This was a secret that Virginia Hill kept for years after Siegel's death, and among the very few who knew about their marriage were Raft, Cary and Barbara Grant, and Dorothy di Frasso.

Howard Hughes probably knew also since he was a partner with Siegel in the Flamingo. Hughes had been closely watched by the FBI since J. Edgar Hoover first suspected that Hughes had obtained large quantities of raw film stock on the black market for *The Outlaw*. Now the FBI were more interested than ever and began investigating Hughes's partnership with Siegel. They also investigated another partner in the Flamingo, William R. Wilkerson who was a friend of Cary Grant's. An FBI agent, Richard Hood, questioned Cary Grant about the Las Vegas activities, giving him severe cause for concern about his friendship with Siegel.

Believing that the Flamingo would make a quick profit and solve all his problems, Siegel decided to open the hotel-casino earlier than planned, on 26 December 1946. The hotel facilities were incomplete, but the casino was ready. He showered Hollywood with invitations to the grand opening, but few bothered to reply. What he didn't know was that William Randolph Hearst, the powerful newspaper tycoon, had made it known to the front offices in Hollywood that he was against the Mob-run gambling operation being set up, and that he would not hesitate to name every star who patronized the Flamingo.

Having received so few replies, Siegel called George Raft. 'I'm in a spot, pal. Can't you get some of your friends up to the opening? What about Joan Crawford and Greer Garson? And Spencer Tracy and Gary Cooper?'

'I don't like to tell you this, Ben,' said Raft, 'but William Randolph Hearst has put the word around the studios that he's opposed to the whole idea. So the studios told everybody to stay away.'

Siegel exploded. Raft tried to console him. 'You know you can count on me being there, and I know that Charlie Coburn and George Jessel are coming. I'm sure we can get some others to be there.'

On the day of the opening, a cold rain drenched Los Angeles and fog rolled in from the Pacific. The aircraft chartered by Siegel to carry a crowd of celebrities out to Las Vegas was grounded. As it became clear that the weather wasn't going to improve, the disgruntled passengers began returning to their cars to drive home.

Benny Siegel, in a swallow-tail coat and a white tie, heard this disastrous news over the phone, and again he exploded. He was desperate for a successful opening. He'd planned everything down to the tiniest detail. Virginia Hill, looking stunning in a special gown she'd ordered for the occasion, joined him as they waited for the countdown to open the doors.

George Raft, intent on not letting his friend down, drove all the way to Las Vegas in appalling conditions. Another car carried George Sanders, Sonny Tufts and George Jessel. Charles Coburn, at the age of seventy, wisely took the train. An assortment of Nevadans turned up, hoping to see a glittering array of film stars, and waited eagerly outside for the doors to open. Finally, when it became clear that things weren't going to improve, Benny and Virginia opened the doors and welcomed the small crowd inside.

There were few gamblers among them willing to part with their money, and, disappointed to see so few stars, it wasn't long before they began drifting home. Only half the tables were seeing action. George Raft, having arrived exhausted from the hazardous drive, tried his luck at chemin-de-fer, and lost $65,000 in cash. Entertainment was provided by Jimmy Durante, Eddie Jackson, Baby Rosemarie, the Tunetoppers and Xavier Cugat, but they played to a small crowd.

In New York, a phone call came through to Meyer Lansky, who informed Frank Costello, 'It's a washout.'

As news spread through the underworld the Flamingo had gone $500,000 in the red within two weeks of opening, investors started wondering where the blame lay. The men who had encouraged them to invest were Meyer Lansky and Frank Costello.

Unable to risk losing any more money, Benny Siegel closed the Flamingo and thought about what to do next. The building costs had risen to $4 million and still it wasn't complete. Dorothy di Frasso, for the sake of old times, turned up at Siegel's and offered him help. But by this time she had spent much of her vast fortune and didn't have enough money to bail him out.

He even considered taking whatever money he had left and escaping to Europe with Virginia. But he decided he would prefer to find a way to get the Flamingo in the black, make a profit and retire in Europe without the constant fear that he might be tracked down by the Mafia and murdered.

He turned to George Raft for help. 'I gotta have $100,000, not just to save the Casino, but to save my life as well.'

'I want to help,' said Raft, 'but I just don't have that kind of dough, especially now. Things are really tight.'

'Yeah, I know. But you can raise it. I know you can. You've never let me down. You won't let me down now.'

Raft set about borrowing the money on a substantial annuity fund he had maintained. Siegel put up no collateral, but took Raft's money, along with borrowings from other Hollywood people, and made plans to reopen the Flamingo. It was a last-ditch effort to save his dream, and his life. He phoned Meyer Lansky and told him the plan. Lansky wasted no time catching a plane to Las Vegas to impress upon Siegel that even if he approved the plan, no one else would. There was a bitter quarrel as Siegel refused to take any advice from his childhood friend.

Siegel was no longer a powerful and influential figure. He was now a failure, both as a businessman and a mob leader. He no longer commanded respect from the Mafia, and he began to fear the consequences. But there were some who still revered him. Thirty-one-year-old bobbysox idol Frank Sinatra and thirty-four-year-old comedy actor Phil Silvers were one day having dinner at Chasen's when Benny Siegel

came by. Sinatra and Silvers stood as he passed and, wide-
eyed and with reverence in their voices, said, 'Hello, Mr
Siegel. How are you?'

Sinatra and Silvers were enthralled by Siegel, and they en-
thusiastically discussed Siegel's achievements and wondered
how many people he'd killed, and which were his preferred
methods of killing. Silver's wife, Jo-Carroll, always remembered 'the awe Frank had in his voice when he talked about
[Siegel]. He wanted to emulate Bugsy.'

And he did. He dressed sharply 'but in a vulgar, showy
way', and, 'like gangsters, he gave great big crude showy
presents'.

In 1943, Sinatra had moved, with his wife Nancy, to
Hasbrouck Heights, New Jersey, where Willie Moretti
operated. On Friday nights, Sinatra frequented Madison
Square Garden to watch the fights and mix with Frank
Costello and, particularly, Willie Moretti, who lived close to
him. Sinatra's associations with the Mafia have long been the
subject of conjecture, and while there is no question of his
friendship with mobsters, some stories have grown from
rumours and become legend. One such story is that Willie
Moretti had gone to Tommy Dorsey, who held Sinatra's
contract, and forced him at the point of a gun to release
Sinatra over to MCA. Sinatra's friend, Nick Sevano, insisted
that the story was 'crap. It was a simple buy-out by MCA.
Frank was involved with the racket boys later but not on the
Dorsey deal.'

Meyer Lansky's slot-machine associate, Joseph 'Doc'
Stacher, said that the Mob 'told me they had spent a lot of
money helping him in his career, ever since he was with
Tommy Dorsey's band'.

According to Kitty Kelley's biography of Sinatra, *His Way*,
in January 1947 Sinatra received a phone call from Joe
Fischetti, the youngest and least powerful of the Fischetti
brothers. Sinatra and Fischetti had been friends since 1938.
Joe told him that Charlie Luciano had installed himself in
Cuba and that many of the Syndicate leaders were making a

pilgrimage there to pay their respects to the still enthroned Boss of all Bosses. Sinatra was invited to join Joe and his brothers in Miami for a few days and then to fly to Havana to meet Luciano in February.

In Miami, Sinatra and the Fischettis stayed in Luciano's mansion on Allison Island and, the night before flying to Cuba, Sinatra put on a free show at the Colonial Inn in Hallendale, a casino owned by Joe Adonis and Meyer Lansky.

The next day, 11 February, Sinatra and the Fischettis flew to Havana, watched closely by FBI agents who noticed that Rocco Fischetti and Sinatra both carried attaché cases which the agents suspected held $2 million in cash as tribute for Luciano. They booked into the Hotel Nacional where Luciano had a luxurious penthouse suite and where thirty-six suites had been reserved for the visiting mobsters.

Sinatra spent four days in Havana where men like Albert Anastasia, Vito Genovese, Willie Moretti, Meyer Lansky, Joe Adonis and Frank Costello delivered packages of cash as tribute to Luciano. Sinatra, whose singing Luciano admired enormously, entertained, and having played his part flew on to Mexico to be with Nancy.

Meanwhile, Luciano and Costello had business to discuss, concerning Benny Siegel and the Flamingo. Costello had had his attorney, George Wolf, approach former friends in an effort to borrow several million dollars to pay back the irate investors in the Flamingo. Costello and Luciano talked over old times, of their days as young hoods, and of the young boy with the dark curly hair, baby-blue eyes and flashing teeth who came to be known as 'Bugsy' because of his flash-flood temper. And they talked of the trouble Bugsy had caused them all over his crazy gamble in Las Vegas.

Luciano had been pressed by other Mob leaders to pronounce judgement on Siegel, Lansky and Costello, the three responsible for losing their money. Luciano convinced them that Meyer Lansky was worth his weight in gold and should be allowed to continue. It was rare for Lansky to make any mistakes, and Luciano was sure he would more than

make up for the loss incurred by the Flamingo. As for
Costello, he said, 'He'll get you your money back. Just give
him time.'

He warned Costello, 'You got to get the money somehow,
Frank. Otherwise I can't hold them back.'

'I'll get it.'

'Meanwhile, you retire as head of the commission.
Genovese takes over. But I told the boys that as soon as you
get them their money back, you take over again. I want you
there, not Vito.'

'And what happens to Benny?' asked Frank.

'Him I can't help.'

Al Capone had been out of prison since November 1939,
having been previously moved from Alcatraz to Terminal Island Federal Correctional Institution, near Los Angeles in
January 1939. But the once all-powerful boss of Chicago, now
riddled with syphilis, was a frail shadow of his former self. He
spent the rest of his life as a paralytic in seclusion, fearful that
he would be assassinated by mobsters.

The end for Al Capone came on 25 January 1947 when he
died from a brain haemorrhage. The funeral, in Chicago's
Mount Olive Cemetery, was small, and minus the full
Catholic rites because of his criminal life.

In February 1947, Howard Hughes invited numerous
friends and colleagues to join him on the inaugural flight to
New York of his masterpiece, the *Hercules*, a huge seaplane
and the largest aircraft to date ever to fly. It was supposed to
be his contribution to the war effort, but it took five years to
build and had cost the taxpayers of America 18 million.

Many declined the invitation because they knew that
Hughes was in trouble with Washington who were intent on
investigating why he had spent so much money on what they
considered a white elephant. Benny Siegel declined because
he was too tied up with his own worries. Among those who
accepted were Cary Grant, Eddie G. Robinson, Alfred
Hitchcock, Linda Darnell, William Powell, Celeste Holm and

Paulette Goddard, all of whom made the flight with Hughes on 14 February.

In New York, Cary Grant and James Stewart threw a huge party at the Clover Club for Hughes and his aide (and pimp) Johnny Meyer. The guests were put up in a hotel where they were eventually joined by Benny Siegel. Also there, in the hotel lobby, were FBI agents who were keeping tabs on Hughes and Meyer.

Around this time an article appeared, written by columnist Robert Ruark who had been in Havana during the under-world convention, in which he declared:

> If Mr Sinatra wants to mob up with the likes of Lucky Luciano, the chastened panderer and permanent deportee from the United States, that seems to be a matter for Mr Sinatra to thrash out with the millions of kids who live by his every bleat...
>
> This curious desire to cavort among the scum is possibly permissible among citizens who are not peddling sermons to the nation's youth and may even be allowed to a mealy-mouthed celebrity if he is smart enough to confine his social tolerance to a hotel room...
>
> But Mr Sinatra, the self-confessed savior of the country's small fry, by virtue of his lectures on clean living and love-thy-neighbor, his movie shorts on tolerance, and his frequent dabblings into the do-good department of politics, seems to be setting a most peculiar example for his hordes of pimply, shrieking slaves, who are alleged to regard him with the same awe as a practicing Mohammedan for the Prophet.

Frank Sinatra refuted the article's claims, saying, 'Any report that I fraternized with goons and racketeers is a vicious lie. I was brought up to shake a man's hand when I am introduced to him without first investigating his past.'

Another columnist, Drew Pearson, also wrote articles about the goings-on in Havana. But Ruark wrote with such aggression, especially in regard to his opinions of Tom Dewey for releasing Luciano from prison in the first place, that the US government tried to hide their embarrassment by insisting that Cuban authorities throw Luciano out. But Cuba was unwilling to rid itself of Luciano.

In March 1947, the Flamingo was reopened with a number of rooms and suites ready for occupation. By May it began to show a profit. This should have been good news for all concerned. But Meyer Lansky had heard disturbing news and called a meeting at the Waldorf-Astoria. There he told the stockholders that his spies had informed him that Virginia Hill had flown to Paris and Siegel had put together a bankroll of $600,000 from hotel funds and was planning to join her. Lansky admitted that he now agreed that Siegel could no longer be tolerated.

Albert Anastasia said bluntly, 'Kill him!'

Lansky's report that Virginia had flown to Paris to await Siegel may have been true, but some sources agree that in fact Virginia had grown tired of living in constant fear, and she also hated living in dusty Nevada. She had wanted to return to Los Angeles, and had walked out on Siegel. He later turned up at the house and found Virginia packing her things, announcing that she was going to Paris 'to think things over'. Other reports claim that Virginia had found out that Siegel was secretly meeting with a flamboyant French actress, Marie MacDonald, nicknamed 'the Body', and that she had asked him to apologize to Luciano for the trouble he'd caused. He begged her not to go, and she told him, 'You don't own me, Ben Siegel.'

In Paris she took up with Nicholas Feuillate, the son of a socially prominent French family.

Whatever the truth, while Virginia was in France, Siegel was in a state of nerves back in Los Angeles. Even Cary Grant steered clear of him now, made nervous by further questioning from the FBI.

On the morning of 21 June 1947, Siegel arrived at Raft's

house during breakfast.

'Having something to eat, Ben,' said Raft. 'You look awful.'

'I haven't slept in days, Georgie. I'm in trouble. Big trouble from the boys in New York. Look, Georgie, why don't you come over to Jack's tonight for dinner?'

'I got a meeting planned with Sam Bischoff.'

'Cancel.'

'I can't. We're putting together a three-picture deal, and you know how much I need something like that.'

'OK, Georgie. I'm going to be at the house later on, so why don't you come by when you've finished. We can talk there without interruptions.'

As Siegel left, Raft had the impression that 'he had something to tell me'.

That evening, Al Smiley went with Siegel to Jack's Restaurant where they had dinner and talked over whatever plans Siegel had. Later, as they were leaving the restaurant, Siegel picked up a free copy of the *Los Angeles Times*. Clipped to the front page was a card that read, 'Good-night. Sleep well with the compliments of Jack's.'

They got in the car and drove back to the mansion where Virginia's brother, Chick, was entertaining his girlfriend upstairs in a bedroom. It was about ten o'clock. Benny and Al sat down on the chintz-covered sofa, their backs to a large window that looked out on the garden. They talked for a while and then Siegel began reading the newspaper.

Suddenly, it seemed to Smiley that the whole room was exploding, as a series of gunshots shattered the window. He dived towards the fireplace, watching as Siegel's body jerked and glass flew around the room. Nine times the killer fired. The first blast smashed into Siegel's skull, blowing out his right eye. The second went through his neck and then burned into Al Smiley's sleeve. The third blasted his neck again and then ripped into a painting of an English duchess. Another slug crashed into a nude figure of Bacchus that stood on the piano. The remaining five shots peppered the room.

Chick and his girlfriend came running from their room, naked. The girl saw the carnage and the blood and began to scream hysterically. Smiley cowered by the fireplace, shaking violently and uncontrollably. He was still shaking an hour later after the police had arrived to find Siegel sprawled on the sofa, half his head gone, the remains of his face covered in a mask of blood.

The significance of Siegel's death in regard to Raft's life was not lost on the gangster star. When police questioned him, he said, 'I don't know who killed Benny. But I tell you this, when they killed him, they killed me too.'

When news reached Virginia in Paris, she fainted from fear for her own life, and shock at her husband's death. She went into hiding in Monaco and tried to end her own life several days later with an overdose of pills. When asked to give her account of the events surrounding Siegel's death, and giving no real clearer idea as to what transpired between her and Siegel prior to his death, she said, 'The last time I saw Ben was three weeks ago at his brand-new casino in Las Vegas. He was working hard, and I told him he could not come to dinner with all those nice people we were going to eat with in a dirty white sports-shirt. And he barked at me that I should mind my own business. I am not taking that from anyone. So I packed my bags and left. I phoned goodbye from Chicago last week and said I was going to Europe. He said goodbye. I never heard from him again.'

Siegel's brother-in-law Chick Hill said, 'Maybe he did kill people. Maybe he had to. But he was like a father to me, and the best friend I ever had.'

Columnist Walter Winchell believed Siegel 'was a brainy guy who might have made it big on the right side of the law'.

Benny Siegel was buried in Beth Olam Cemetery. The gangster, who so often turned up at the funerals of movie stars that he had liked and admired, was not mourned publicly by a single star. Not even George Raft came to see him put away in the ground for good.

16

Aftermath

No one in the Mafia displayed grief at the news of Bugsy's death. Frank Costello said that Siegel had broken every rule in the book, and Costello had himself paid heavily for Siegel's mistakes. But he also claimed that he didn't know who killed Siegel. It is generally accepted that Lucky Luciano had agreed to Siegel's extermination, and if so it seems likely that Frank Costello would certainly have known about it. Frank Rizzo had another theory. He claimed that Siegel may well have been killed by, or on the orders of, Joe Adonis, who, according to Rizzo, was Siegel's rival for Virginia's affections.

Rizzo said that when Virginia took up with Siegel, Adonis 'got mad and a war started between the two of them. It was finished with the death of Siegel.'

It is significant, though, that waiting to take over the Flamingo, on behalf of the Eastern stockholders and on the very night Siegel was killed, was Gus Greenbaum who went on to manage the hotel-casino for the next seven years very successfully. Costello also had his own plans to build a hotel in Las Vegas, conceived in cahoots with Phil Kastel before the demise of Bugsy Siegel.

This gangland-style Hollywood murder indicated to the public that organized crime was now nationwide, that such killings were no longer confined to the streets of New York and Chicago, and it was the last straw in a series of headline-making incidents – beginning with Frank Sinatra's appearance at the Mafia conference in Havana – for the American government. In an effort to put a stop to organized crime once and for all, they had to take action that resulted in the

Kefauver Committee being set up to investigate organized crime. But before that Charlie Luciano, who ran the whole show, had to be moved from Cuba.

Consequently, the US State Department brought to bear all the pressure they could on Cuba, threatening to immediately cut off all shipments of legal drugs to that country. Harry J. Anslinger, the Federal Narcotics Commissioner, announced that the ban would continue as long as Luciano remained in Cuba.

The following day Cuban police turned up at the Hotel Nacional and arrested Luciano. He was thrown into a prison camp and shortly after deported to Italy. But the Mafia were better organized than that. Costello had paid off the investors and had been reinstated. With Luciano no longer on the pulse of the American underworld, Frank Costello became the Boss of all Bosses.

Nobody actually superseded Bugsy Siegel. The Flamingo was taken care of in Las Vegas. In Los Angeles, the Mafia's grip on the film industry loosened. Only Siegel's gambling empire in Los Angeles survived under the leadership of his cohort, Mickey Cohen. If anybody was Siegel's heir and successor, it was Cohen.

He set up headquarters at an exclusive haberdashery, complete with a backroom bookie shop. He rarely sold anything as he didn't want to be bothered with having to reorder stock, although he was generous in handing out ties and handkerchiefs to visitors.

He now began to try and fill the void left by Seigel as a public figure, and he courted newspaper space. He appeared in the papers so much that the *New York Daily News* called a series of stories about Cohen the 'LA Vicecapades'.

Since Siegel's death, the Los Angeles Police Department had dubbed Cohen the 'Number One Hoodlum of Los Angeles', and anyone associating with him became a 'Mickey Cohen henchman'.

Cohen tossed off such descriptions: 'If I see a guy a couple of times or go out socially with him, all of a sudden he becomes my "henchman". What the hell is a henchman, anyway?'

One of these henchmen was Johnny Stompanato, a seemingly inconsequential small-time gangster. Unlike the usual type of hoods off the streets, Stompanato was not a thug as a child but, following a marriage and divorce, he went to Hollywood where he worked as a greeter-bouncer in one of Cohen's clubs. Before long he was promoted by Cohen to be one of his bodyguards for $300 a week. For the next few years Stompanato ran Mob errands and became skilled in the arts of petty fraud and extortion. As a cover, he ran a variety of small businesses selling cars, pets, flowers, furniture and even lovebirds which he bred himself in his private aviary.

In 1949 he married actress Helen Gilbert who had appeared in the Andy Hardy pictures. Checking into the honeymoon suite at Bugsy Siegel's Flamingo Hotel, he signed himself Johnny Valentine. They divorced three months later. He had a number of other aliases – John Holliday, Jay Hubbard, John Truppa among them. But to Mickey Cohen he was Johnny Stompanato.

Frank Costello agreed that Cohen could be left alone to run the LA rackets providing he didn't, like Benny, forget to cut in the Boss of all Bosses. Just to make sure, Costello ordered Jack Dragna to ensure Cohen toed the line. Cohen resisted and Dragna put a price on his head.

On 18 August 1948, Cohen was visited by Jimmy 'the Weasel' Frattiano, his wife and son. In the shop were Cohen's henchmen Slick Snyder, sitting at a desk, and Jimmy Rist. As usual Cohen found something for each of them to take as a memento of their courtesy call. Then the Frattianos left.

Cohen got up to go to the bathroom to wash his hands. Just as he left the shop a man walked in off the street, a gun in his hand. He lurched forward, firing at Snyder who was hit in the arm and ducked behind his desk. Rist wrestled with the gunman but was shot in the ear. Still he held onto the gunman and managed to grab the gun. The gunman broke loose and, as Rist fired at him, ran out.

Inside the bathroom, Cohen, who was unharmed and had
no idea who was shooting whom, lay flat on the floor with his
feet bracing the door, effectively barricading himself in.

Before Rist and Snyder knew what was happening, a
second gunman had come in, carrying a shotgun. One of
Cohen's men, Hooky Rothman, had heard the first shots fired
as he was approaching the shop, and came rushing in. The
gunman turned on him and fired at point-blank range, blowing his face away. Then the gunman fled.

The police arrived and arrested Cohen, Snyder and Rist for
Rothman's murder, but later dropped the charges. Cohen
said afterwards that he knew who had ordered the hit, but he
would settle the score personally.

Some months later someone – probably Dragna, or at the
very least someone acting on his orders – placed a bomb under
the picture window of Cohen's Brentwood home. It was discovered by one of his henchmen who defused it. Following
this, Cohen had a radar security system installed.

One evening in May 1949 Cohen arrived home in his Cadillac, and as he drew up, a man in a parked car across the
street opened fire with a shotgun. Cohen ducked down behind the dashboard and pushed down on the accelerator. The
car roared off down the street, careering about, as Cohen was
unable to see where he was going, finally running up against
the kerb and coming to a halt. Cohen had made such a racket
that it was enough to scare the gunman off.

On the night of 18 July, Cohen drove to a Sunset Strip
nightclub, Sherry's, with his chief lieutenant Neddie Herbert,
his bodyguard Johnny Stompanato, and Harry Cooper, an
investigator from the Attorney-General's office, there to
protect Cohen who had been ordered to give testimony'
concerning police corruption.

On a stairwell behind a vacant lot across the road stood
two men with shotguns. They ate sardine sandwiches as they
waited for the Cohen party to re-emerge.

It was 4 a.m. when Cohen and his friends left the nightclub.
The two men came out of the shadows and opened up on

them, firing police-style. Cohen was hit in the shoulder. Needie Herbert went down, hit in the back. Cohen's girl-friend, actress Dee David, was peppered. Harry Cooper was hit in the belly.

Cohen, despite his wound and the hail of bullets, managed to lift Cooper and place him in his Cadillac. Dee David, blood pouring from her wounds, staggered to the car and climbed in. Then Cohen drove them to the hospital, saving Cooper's life. Dee David also recovered, as did Cohen. But Neddie Herbert died eight days later.

In 1985 veteran newsman Jake Jacoby wrote that the killers were mobsters out to get Neddie Herbert who was suspected of being a stool pigeon. But the most likely motive for the shooting came from Sergeant Stoke of the LAPD who years after the event revealed the extent of police corruption, and wrote that the 'murderous attack [on Cohen] had been made by members of the LAPD whose motive was to seal Cohen's lips'.

On the morning of 6 February 1950, at about three o'clock, Cohen's radar system sounded. He fled from the house and not long after there was an enormous explosion under his bedroom window. About thirty sticks of dynamite had been placed in front of a heavy concrete floor safe which had deflected the blast, although the explosion blew out every window in the house and blasted a 10-foot section of his bedroom closet wall.

Reporters flocked to the scene to get an interview from Mickey Cohen in his monogrammed silk pyjamas. 'I wish I knew who the sons of bitches are who are doing this to me,' he told them. Then pointing at the damage he added, 'I don't think I'm going to be able to rent this room now.'

It seemed that Mickey Cohen led a charmed life. Neither Jack Dragna nor the LAPD seemed able to send him the way of his mentor, Benny Siegel.

Johnny Roselli had been released from prison in 1947 and had gone straight back to work. Sam Giancana had been keeping business simmering in Hollywood, and although he was treated like royalty by movie stars, Mooney had contempt for a lot of people in show business. He found Hollywood a place where everybody was 'waiting to be used'. He told his brother Chuck, 'All anybody out there cares about is whether they're gonna be a star or not. We help 'em along and we own 'em.' He was particularly contemptuous of the women. 'The broads, Chuck,' he said, 'beautiful and dumb.' As far as he was concerned movie stars were 'worthless bums and whores'.

He was happy to see Roselli back in harness. 'He's perfect for Hollywood,' said Mooney. 'Out there you gotta have class. And Roselli's smooth as fuckin' silk.'

In fact, Roselli integrated himself so well he even managed to produce a few films and was a member of the prestigious Friar's Club. Yet despite his legitimate movie-making enterprises, he remained on the lookout for those desperate to become stars and didn't object to being given a helping hand from those who were well connected. Those whom the Chicago Outfit helped become stars were made to understand that they would forever remain in the Outfit's debt.

Among those helped in this way, according to Chuck and Sam Giancana (the younger) in their book *Double Cross*, were Ed Sullivan and Ronald Reagan. Another was a blonde starlet – the former Miss Norma Jean Baker who had been working in Los Angeles as a model and had developed aspirations to become an actress. Her photograph appeared in numerous magazines and she posed nude for a calendar. In 1946 she came to the attention of Ben Lyon, head of casting at Twentieth Century-Fox. He offered her a contract and changed her name to Marilyn Monroe.

Word quickly spread that Lyon had a new beautiful blonde under his wing, and he received one call after another from producers. 'That new blonde you've got,' they'd say. 'What's her name, Monroe – I may be able to offer her something. Send her to my office at six o'clock.'

Lyon knew that any such meeting at six o'clock had little to do with film offers, and Marilyn knew it too. Ben Lyon always insisted that as far as he knew she never accepted any of these invitations. But one offer she did take up came from John Roselli.

Hollywood tradition has it that seventy-year-old Joseph Schenck, then working as an executive producer at Fox, took an interest in her and, when Fox dropped her after only a year and small roles in two films, he persuaded Harry Cohn of Columbia to put her under contract.

In fact, it seems now that Roselli got to know Marilyn through Joseph Schenck, and although Monroe always insisted that her friendship with Schenck had been purely platonic, Sam Giancana, who would later get to know Marilyn well, claimed that she allowed Schenk sexual favours in return for his assistance.

Then Roselli, with the Outfit's backing, persuaded Harry Cohn to put her to work at his studio. In return, she also granted him certain sexual favours. She would repay her debt to Chicago later.

In December 1950, the nation sat glued to their TVs as Meyer Lansky, Frank Costello, Willie Moretti, Albert Anastasia and countless other members of the Mafia and its associated mobs appeared in a series of hearings that lasted until March 1951. The hearings were based on the evidence collected by the committee set up by Senator Estes Kefauver who told TV viewers:

The Mafia is a shadowy international organization that lurks behind much of America's organized criminal activity. It is an organization about which none of its members, on fear of death, will talk. In fact, some of the witnesses called before us, who we had good reason to believe could tell us about the Mafia, sought to dismiss it as a sort of fairy tale or legend that children hear in Sicily, where the Mafia originated. The Mafia, however, is no fairy tale. It is ominously real, and it has scarred the face of America with almost every conceivable type of criminal violence, including murder, traffic in narcotics, smuggling, extortion, white slavery, kidnapping, and labor racketeering.

The hearings made compulsive television viewing for thirty million Americans. Robert Montgomery, former president of the SAG who was instrumental in getting Willie Bioff out of Hollywood's hair, took a deep interest in the proceedings and managed to get himself a job at the hearings as a radio reporter, giving a running commentary on the hearings.

One of the main aims of the hearings was to link witness after witness to Frank Costello who was now the Boss of all Bosses. Willie Moretti couldn't deny any link with Costello; they were cousins. But Moretti cleverly evaded every question intended to link him directly to the Mafia. 'You go to the racetrack and you go to Florida and you meet them,' he answered in response to a question about his ability to meet so many people from all over the country. 'And a man that is well known meets everybody; you know that.'

'Are these the people you are thinking of when you are talking about the Mob?' asked Rudolph Halley for the Kefauver committee.

'Well, the newspapers call them the Mob. I don't know whether they are right or wrong. If they would be right, *everybody* would be in jail; is that right?'

Halley tried again. 'Is that what you mean when you say the Mob?'

'People are mobs that make six per cent more on the dollar than anybody else,' answered Moretti, causing laughter. Moretti succeeded in entertaining the viewing public with his knack for comedy.

When Costello took the spotlight, Halley asked him what the term 'boss' meant. Costello answered, 'Well, there is an error there somewhere. I was never a boss – never had any interest.'

When Mickey Cohen took the stand he was asked by

Senator Charles Tobey, 'Is it not a fact that you live extravagantly, surrounded by violence?'

'Whadda ya mean, "surrounded by violence"?' Cohen retorted. 'People are shooting at *me*.'

One of the highlights of the hearings was the appearance of Virginia Hill (now remarried and called Virginia Hauser), adorned in a silver-blue mink stole, and giving a performance that must have had Hollywood bosses wondering if, perhaps, she might have made a great actress after all. She had the senators, and the nation, goggle-eyed as she talked about the life she led and the money she spent. She talked a lot, but revealed nothing. She played the demure, dumb broad, but was sure to cross her legs for all to see, with her tight skirt up to her dimpled knees, when she knew that action would speak louder than words. Her much-admired knees, occasional side remarks, and a dumb look when things became tense, worked well, even if few actually believed what she said.

Before they had got down to any intense questioning, Virginia stirred up a real hornets' nest by objecting to the press taking her pictures. 'Make then stop doing that,' she told the senators.

'All right,' Kefauver told the photographers, 'let's not flash any more bulbs.'

As they continued, Virginia said, 'I'll throw something at them in a minute. I hate those things.'

'All right,' repeated Kefauver, 'let's not flash any more bulbs.' The bulbs stopped flashing and Kefauver said, 'All right, Mr Halley.'

'Now, Mrs Hauser,' began Halley, 'most witnesses have had their pictures taken and the photographers have stopped as soon as they started to testify.'

'I know,' said Virginia tearfully, 'but most of them never went through with those bums what I did.'

During questioning, she didn't deny her close friendship with Phil Kastel, Meyer Lansky, Charlie Fischetti, Frank Costello and Joe Adonis. But she swore that she knew nothing – almost nothing – about racketeering. She said that Joe Epstein was her 'accountant'. She was a 'very bad figurer', knowing little about how to keep accounts, which got her into trouble with the IRS.

Costello, she said, never gave her a red cent, and Adonis, a dear friend who was married with children, took her out occasionally but 'quite on the up and up ... no mushing, no tomfoolery!' Nor did Fischetti or Lansky give her any money. All her wealth was won at the race tracks.

It was, she said, Benny Siegel who gave her presents, and when Halley referred to him as Bugsy, she snapped, '*Ben*. His name was Ben.'

She went on to explain: 'He bought me everything. He gave me money too, bought me a house in Florida.' Despite his penchant for showering her with lavish presents, she insisted, 'I was never very friendly with Ben. There was no mistress business involved.'

'Now, you left the United States shortly before Siegel was killed,' Halley said to her. 'Would you tell us the circumstances that led to your leaving the United States?'

'I was planning to leave the United States long before that. I had gone to San Francisco. I got my passport, and I knew these people in France, and I was supposed to go there and visit them. But then a friend of mine wrote me a letter and said about all the people we were going to see, and I told her not to do that; that if Ben ever saw the letter, he would get mad. So he got the letter and read it and saw all these things I had planned to see in Europe and these people, and he didn't like this boy that I knew in France. So then he told me I couldn't go. So then, later on, I had a big fight with him because I hit a girl in the Flamingo, and he told me I wasn't a lady. We got into a big fight. I had been drinking, and I left, and I went to Paris when I was mad.'

She neglected ever to mention that she and Siegel were married.

When Halley asked if her position in the Mob was to throw parties as an aid to certain people in their business, she exploded in righteous indignation and replied in a state of tongue-tripping emotion, 'That isn't true. That isn't true at all. Because people I have known – they told me that is the worst thing to do – you know, the people you were talking about – supposed to be racketeers – they always said that's the worst possible thing I could do, that people talk too much.'

'And the parties that were attributed to you were really run by other people?' said Halley. 'Is that the point?'

'The fellow I went with – if you want to have a good time, have a party, all right ...'

Upon leaving the hearings, she came face to face with reporters on the elevator, and remembering the adverse newspaper stories about her, she exploded. Marjorie Farnsworth, a slim, attractive reporter, found herself on the receiving end of Virginia's neatly laid punch. Then she yelled at the others, 'You dirty, lousy bastards, get out of here, you sons of bitches.'

Intent on escaping her past, and the tax men trying to get their hands on her money, Virginia settled in the hills of Austria with her husband, skiing instructor Hans Hauser, and a son, Peter, for what she hoped would be a life of peace and respectability. But the emotionally charged former gangster's moll never got over the loss of Ben Siegel, and made a few attempts to take her own life.

Senator Estes Kefauver had come into possession of eight glossy photographs. In one, Sinatra was on the balcony of the Hotel Nacional with his arm around Lucky Luciano. In another, he was sitting with Luciano at a nightclub. Another showed him getting off the plane carrying an attaché case. He was with the Fischettis in a couple of other pictures. Kefauver handed lawyer Joseph L. Nellis the pictures and said, 'I want you to arrange a meeting with Frank Sinatra.'

Kefauver needed to decide whether or not Sinatra should be called before the hearings. Nellis contacted Sinatra's attorney, Sol Gelb, and a secret meeting was arranged. The last thing Sinatra needed was to actually appear on the televised hearings as it would almost certainly be the end of his career.

According to Kitty Kelley, Nellis met with Sinatra and Gelb at four in the morning of 1 March 1951, on the top floor of the Rockefeller Center. Nellis began by asking him about the contents of the case he took with him to Havana when he met Luciano. Sinatra said that he was carrying an attaché case filled with razors and crayons.

Nellis suggested that the case was full of money 'in excess of $100,000'. Sinatra denied it, and said he gave no money to Luciano. When Nellis asked him if he knew what business Luciano was in, he said he didn't. He insisted he knew Costello, Lansky, Zwillman, Siegel and Adonis enough only to say hello and goodbye.

He complained that Nellis was going to put him on TV just because he knew a lot of people, and so ruin his career. Nellis told him, 'Nobody wants to ruin you, Mr Sinatra,' and asked him if he knew Willie Moretti. Sinatra said that Moretti had arranged for some band dates when he first got started, but insisted, 'I have never had any business dealings with any of those men.'

The secret session lasted two hours, at the end of which Nellis had learned nothing that would allow him to subpoena Sinatra to appear at the official hearings. Thus Frank Sinatra escaped a premature end to his career. Investigations into his connections, however, continued with five subsequent Grand Jury subpoenas, two Inland Revenue Service investigations, a congressional summons, and a subpoena from the New Jersey State Crime Commission.

Further references to the Mafia's Hollywood connection came with the testimony of Bill O'Dwyer, the former New York District Attorney, former New York Mayor and then current Ambassador to Mexico. Part of his testimony concerned the death of Abe 'Kid Twist' Reles which had resulted in murder charges against Benny Siegel being dropped. In the event, O'Dwyer ran off so much rope that he hanged himself.

The questioning began with the subject of Jim Moran, a

known friend of Costello whom O'Dwyer admitted was his closest political adviser and whom he had appointed as Commissioner of Water Supply, a lifetime job. He also appointed Willie Moretti's brother-in-law, Philip Zichello, as Deputy Commissioner of Hospitals, and Joseph V. Loscalzo as a Special Sessions Justice as a favour to Frank Costello. He also admitted appointing another of Costello's friends, Abe Rosenthal, as Assistant Corporation Counsel, and one of Adonis's friends, Frank J. Quayle, as Fire Commisioner. When asked why he appointed such men, O'Dwyer replied, 'There are things you have to do politically if you want co-operation.'

O'Dwyer had been involved in the investigation of Murder Inc. and had placed Abe Reles under police protection. Without Reles's testimony, there was no case against a number of implicated mobsters, particularly Siegel who should have answered for the killing of Harry Greenberg in Los Angeles. According to former Deputy Police Commissioner Frank Bals, who'd testified before O'Dwyer, six policemen had guarded Reles and had all gone to sleep. Reles had decided to simply play a joke on them by tying sheets together and pretending to escape. Unfortunately, the joke went wrong and Reles fell to his death.

But O'Dwyer said that Bals's story was nonsense. He said that Reles had in fact been trying to escape. When asked why the police had failed to stop him, O'Dwyer replied, 'A simple case of negligence.'

Halley immediately asked, 'Weren't you reported in the newspapers as having appeared at the police trial to defend those same policemen?'

'Well, not to defend the particular act of carelessness,' O'Dwyer answered vaguely.

Halley persisted. 'Did you feel justified in publicly stating that you were going to the defence of these policemen?'

O'Dwyer was still vague. 'Why not?'

Then the committee revealed that Bals had in fact been the

man in charge of Reles's guards, and that O'Dwyer had sub-sequently promoted him.

Senator Tobey brought up the subject of a meeting in Cos-tello's office in 1942 at which were present the men O'Dwyer had appointed who were linked with Costello and Adonis. O'Dwyer had said that the meeting was to investigate clothing contracts for the air force. Tobey asked if O'Dwyer would agree that the presence of leading and professional politicians in Costello's apartment said a lot 'about the influence of this man Costello on political affairs in New York'. Then Tobey said, 'A funny thing what magnetism that man had. How can you analyse it? You look him over, you wouldn't mark him except pretty near minus zero. But what is there? What has he got? What kind of appeal does he have?' He stared O'Dwyer in the face and added with finality, 'What is it?'

O'Dwyer was stunned into silence, and after a few mo-ments said, 'It doesn't matter whether it is a banker, a businessman, or a gangster – his pocket book is always attractive.'

That statement, one of the most famous to emerge from the hearings, implied what was already suspected but not proven, that corruption in high places was rife. O'Dwyer went into exile in Mexico.

As for the rest of the underworld, the hearings had some effect. They exposed organized crime as a reality and, having put the likes of Costello in the spotlight, the old-order mem-bers were unable to continue to function efficiently, and many of them would be toppled from power, or killed. The first to go was Willie Moretti, on 4 October 1951, when he was lured into a restaurant and held back in a chair while bullets were pumped into him.

For walking out on the congressional committee, and tax evasion charges, Frank Costello spent the next five years in and out of prison. Mickey Cohen, at the age of thirty-seven, was indicted in 1951 for tax evasion. He served four years in prison and later opened an ice-cream parlour – with a back-room bookie racket.

17

Mooney on the Rise

Sam 'Mooney' Giancana often claimed he had the stars in his pocket, and he set out to prove it in May 1951, with his support for an extravagant event, Night of Stars. It was sponsored by the Italian Welfare Council, a genuine charity supported by Giancana and his wife Ange, with the proceeds going straight to poor children of the neighbourhood. Mooney Giancana enlisted the services of entertainers such as Frank Sinatra, Dean Martin, Jerry Lewis, Jimmy Durante and Bob Hope.

Despite its good intentions, members of the Outfit were despatched to pursuade customers to buy tickets. After three years, however, Giancana's good intentions faded away and he withdrew his support for the extravaganza.

That year of 1951 was the year he saw for himself where the Outfit's investment in Marilyn Monroe was leading to. Columbia had dropped her in 1948 and she had freelanced for a while, until 1951 when Darryl F. Zanuck of Twentieth Century-Fox put her back on the contractual payroll. He decreed that she be put into any picture that required a sexy young blonde, and she drifted from picture to picture as pure decoration while the studio continued to show no enthusiasm for turning her into a star.

That is when her past caught up with her. *Playboy* magazine published the famous nude calendar picture of her, causing a sensation. Not the least impressed was Sam Giancana when he saw her spread across the pages of the first issue of *Playboy*. Chicago's investment looked very promis-

ing. More than that, Giancana made a prediction, a promise
– or maybe it was merely a boast. He told his pals Needles and
Willie Potatoes, 'Yeah, I'll fuck her.'

Tony Accardo and Paul Ricca were still running the Outfit,
and Giancana remained one of their most trusted under-
bosses. He had risen fast in the esteem of his associates and
even the elders of the Outfit, such as Ricca, deferred to
him.

His power grew in 1952 when Johnny Roselli secured the
co-operation of Howard Hughes.

'He's rich and he knows how to play the game,' Roselli told
Giancana. 'He's got Vice-President Nixon eating out of his
hand. I tell you, Sam, this guy's got Washington paid off.'

Piece by piece, Giancana was buying America. Roselli had
connections with the CIA in Asia, while Howard Hughes and
Murray Humphreys were well in with the FBI (Hughes presumably having come to some arrangement with them following their investigation of him). The way was open for Giancana and the Outfit to work with the FBI within the States,
and the CIA outside of it.

While Sam Giancana's star rose, many of those associated
with Bugsy Siegel and the Hollywood shakedown were
fading. On 15 August 1953, Marino Bello died.

In the wake of Benny Siegel's death, Countess Dorothy
di Frasso's health declined. She had never really recovered
from the shock of the murder, and she was further troubled
following a brief reunion with Gary Cooper. Her heart was
gradually giving out and she was ordered by doctors to give up
alcohol, cut down on her eating and even give up her passion
for younger, virile men. She no longer had the strength even
to walk up a flight of stairs and complained to Cary Grant that
she was forced to live like 'a turnip'. Nevertheless, she continued to party night after night. Grant begged her to take
things easy.

When she insisted on going to Las Vegas to see Marlene
Dietrich in cabaret in 1954, he went with her, behaving like a

mother hen. They stayed, along with Clifton Webb and other friends, at the home of a Las Vegas producer, Tom Douglas. There they had a huge party, followed by another the next night at the Sands Hotel. There, while leaving the ladies' room, the Countess collapsed.

She told Grant, 'You know, darling, I am going to die.'

Grant insisted she return to Los Angeles to see her doctor. He drove her, accompanied by Clifton Webb, to the station. She climbed on board the train, hugging her mink coat about her, complaining of feeling unnaturally cold.

She slept in her compartment. In the morning, Webb came in to wake her up. He found her dead.

On the night before the funeral, Cary Grant, his wife Betsy and friends stayed up all night paying tribute to the Countess through laughter and tears with the coffin in the house with them. Grant told the *Hollywood Reporter*, 'We did it because we remembered how much Dorothy hated being alone.'

George Raft was right about Siegel's assassin killing him too. He was shortly to lose everything, including the $100,000 he 'invested' in the Flamingo, causing a shortage of money from which he could never recover. The best part of his career was behind him, his reputation tarnished by his underworld connections, and no major studio wanted to risk him in their important pictures.

By 1953, George Raft had been relegated to B movies. One evening he went over to the Beverly Hills Hotel to pick up a friend of Jimmy Durante's, Lou Cohn. When he arrived he found John Capone, a brother of Al's, in the room, and a character called Joe Laino. John was more of a gambler than anything else and was so embarrased about his family connection that he often called himself John Martin.

Raft had hardly stepped in the door when two cops burst in. 'They walked in like *Dragnet* characters,' said Raft. They promptly arrested Capone and Laino on suspicion of robbery and took them to the precinct. Raft wasted no time in calling his attorney, Cyril Moss, to intercede. The police, who had no evidence whatsoever against the two men, released them.

The next day, 30 September 1953, the *Los Angeles Times* proclaimed in a headline: RAFT FREES CAPONE. It went on to say

> Actor George Raft today helped his 'old pal'. John Capone, 49, brother of the late mobster 'Scarface' Al Capone, get out of jail here.
>
> The coin-flipping film star was in Capone's Beverly Hills Hotel room last night when the police burst in to arrest the Chicagoan and a friend, Joe Laino, 42, on suspicion of robbery, the customary 'roust' booking.
>
> Capone, who had $5,362 in cash with him, said he was in Los Angeles 'to collect some dough I loaned a guy – and then drop a little in Las Vegas on the way home'.
>
> Today, Raft interceded, asking Police Chief C.H. Anderson to release the pair and guaranteeing they would 'take the first plane out of here'.

The article summed up the image that people had of Raft – that of a friend of the Mob. And Raft was never going to live it down. While Hollywood may have deserted him, the Mafia hadn't. Although it now had little influence in the movie business, it had a more lucrative and more easily controlled industry, thanks to Bugsy Siegel: Las Vegas was becoming the gambling capital of the world.

'The only man who wins in the casino,' said Meyer Lansky, 'is the guy who owns the place.'

Raft was given a job at the Sands Hotel, run by Joseph 'Doc' Stacher, a member of the New Jersey mob. Raft's job was simply to be a star attraction.

Frank Sinatra was also brought in to draw the crowds, and in the process became an investor in the place, buying two per cent of it for $54,000. Stacher was very fond of Sinatra, as were a good many members of the Mob. But he wasn't popular with every mafioso. According to Vincent Teresa, the Boston mob couldn't stand Sinatra.

He had been dropped by CBS TV, his agents MCA, and

Columbia Records just prior to being brought into the Sands deal, and was, said Teresa, begging for night spots to sing at. In reponse, the Palladinos – Joseph Palladino Senior, known as Joe Beans, Joseph Jr, known as Little Beans, and Rocco Palladino, brother of Joe Beans – allowed him to sing at their Copa in Boston.

'He did all right,' said Teresa, 'not sensational, but all right. Then he went to Joe Beans and asked if he could borrow money.'

Sinatra offered to pay back the money straight from his fee from his next performance at the Copa. His come-back movie, *From Here to Eternity*, was due out in a month and he would be back to perform after that. Joe Beans happily lent him the money. When the film came out, it was a smash hit and Sinatra was on top again. He paid back the money he owed, but, said Teresa, never came back to play at the Copa. The Palladinos, and Teresa who was Joseph Jr's partner, never forgave him.

However, Sinatra was favoured by Sam Giancana. 'Frank thought Giancana was the king,' Peter Lawford told me in 1974. 'I don't want to say too much about it, but it was because of his association with Giancana that Frank and I fell out, and I don't want to say too much about that either. But I'll tell you this; when Frank sang *My Kind of Town Chicago Is*, it was his tribute to Giancana.' Lawford said he detested Giancana and described him as 'an awful guy with a gargoyle face and weasel nose. I couldn't stand him, but Frank idolized him.'

When Sinatra won the coveted role of Maggio in Fred Zimmermann's 1953 hit picture *From Here to Eternity*, it was rumoured that the Mafia had pursuaded Columbia Studio boss, Harry Cohn, to cast him. Following a slump in his career, the film brought Sinatra not only renewed success but also an Oscar as Best Supporting Actor. The legend was enlarged by Mario Puzo's novel *The Godfather*, in which a fictitious Italian singer lands a plum film role to put him back to the top through the nefarious efforts of a Mafia don.

The rumour suggested that Frank Costello had approached

Johnny Roselli, who then presided over the Mob's dealings in Las Vegas and Los Angeles and was, according to the Justice Department, the key 'to keeping the peace in the movie industry in Hollywood'. Costello wanted Roselli to talk to Harry Cohn, who reputedly wore a friendship ring given to him by Roselli. Other sources theorize that Costello simply contacted George Wood of the William Morris agency, who now took care of Sinatra's deals, and some movie executives who couldn't refuse to repay favours received from Costello in the past.

Sinatra has always denied the story and successfully sued the BBC for saying he got the role through his underworld connections. The film's director, Fred Zinnemann, also refuted the claims saying, 'If *I* hadn't wanted Sinatra, he wouldn't have done it.'

George Raft's career as a star of casinos began to overtake his career as a star of movies. When the Flamingo was sold in 1955, Raft was hired by the new owners as a part-time entertainment consultant, and he set about booking, among others, Pearl Bailey, Frank Sinatra and Dean Martin. Then Raft was offered the chance to buy two per cent of the Flamingo for $65,000. The fact that he'd previously put a hundred thousand in made no difference to the owners. He had to sell his Coldwater Canyon house, giving half his profits to Grayce, and file for an application with the Nevada State Gaming Control Board.

The application was turned down because of his associations with gangsters. A number of influential and respected personalities interceded on his behalf and the commission spent six months appraising his background. They finally concluded there was no reason to deny him a licence. By this time, however, he was in urgent need of cash and he sold his two per cent of the Flamingo with considerable loss on his investment.

That year, the IRS began taking a great interest in Tony Accardo and Paul Ricca. Nervous of ending up the same way as Capone, the two men stepped aside and a convention was held at the Tam O'Shanter Country Club in Chicago to crown their successor. They named Sam Giancana as the Outfit's new Boss.

In November one of Giancana's Las Vegas cronies, Marshall Caifano, called Giancana. 'You'll never guess who Greenbaum's got working at the Riviera,' said Caifano. The Riviera in Vegas was now under Gus Greenbaum's management. 'Willie Bioff,' Caifano continued. 'He's calling himself William Nelson.'

'What the hell is Greenbaum doing giving that son of a bitch a job?' asked Giancana.

'You want me to deal with Greenbaum?'

'Later. First there's Bioff. No one squeals – that's our first rule. I want Bioff dead.'

Bioff was now living in Phoenix, Arizona. Since his release from prison, he had become a reformed character and had formed a friendship with Senator Barry Goldwater, supporting the senator in his campaigns and travelling around the country in Goldwater's private plane. He'd been working at the Riviera since 1952.

On 4 November Willie Bioff, alias William Nelson, got into his truck to drive to the Phoenix brokerage to check up on his stocks. The Mafia and all its dealings were far from his mind. But the Mafia had not forgotten – nor forgiven him for 'singing' to the Feds.

He turned the key in the ignition, and the truck exploded into little pieces.

Around this time a call came through to Giancana. It was Sammy Davis Jr, asking for a 'Dr Goldberg'. That was the name he, and other entertainers, called Giancana when they needed his help.

Some years before Davis had taken a loan of $23,000 from Giancana. Mooney's brother Chuck recalled in his book *Double Cross* how George Unger and Chuck had once gone backstage at an Atlantic City nightclub to collect on the debt. Neither Chuck nor Unger had had to muscle Davis. He was so terrified by the sight of them that he paid up.

Now Davis was a very nervous man having read in a newspaper, 'Sammy Davis Jr has been warned by top Chicago gangsters that if he ever sees that blonde movie star again, both of his legs will be broken and torn off from the knee.'

Davis had been seeing blonde Kim Novak who was under contract to Columbia. That studio's boss, Harry Cohn, was known to have important connections with organized crime. And Cohn hated the thought of his blonde star getting involved with a black man.

Another paper said, 'The boss of a certain [moving] pitcha company has a photo of Sammy Davis Jr on his office walls. Flings darts at it.'

With 'Dr Goldberg' on the phone, Davis asked outright, 'Am I in trouble with your guys?'

'No, and if you were, you know I'd handle it for you.'

It was reassuring to hear. Yet, not daring to take any chances, Davis decided to stop seeing Novak. He hoped that any threat from the underworld was now past.

But then a friend of Davis's – a friend whom Davis said was 'well connected' but declined to name – came to his Las Vegas dressing-room one day and said. 'Sam, you've got a problem with the guys.'

'No, it's OK,' said Davis. 'I talked to Sam in Chicago. That was just phoney shit in the columns.'

'I'm not talking Chicago. I'm talking Los Angeles. Harry Cohn's mad and he's got a contract out to have your legs broken. Be careful, Sam, those guys enjoy hurting people. Fortunately, we can protect you while you're here in Las Vegas, or in Chicago, Miami, New York – we can protect you there. But don't go to LA unless you straighten things out with Cohn.'

Shortly after, Davis hastily married a black girl, Loray White. It was a phoney marriage, but it was enough to have Cohn call off the contract. It may have saved Davis's life.

While Giancana, for whatever reasons, chose not to delve

further into the threats upon Davis's health and well-being and do something about it, he didn't balk when another came to him with the same kind of problem – only this was someone who promised something very special in return.

Joe Kennedy had risen high in America's political ranks. After dabbling in Hollywood and producing a few films starring his clandestine lover, Gloria Swanson, he had been appointed by Franklin D. Roosevelt as chairman of the Securities and Exchange Commission, and later as ambassador to England.

In 1956 Frank Costello finally lost patience with Kennedy for refusing to return certain favours which Costello believed had helped make Kennedy a rich and powerful figure. Despite all Costello's attempts to persuade Kennedy to reconsider, Kennedy had chosen to ignore the New York Boss.

In May, Kennedy met with Giancana in Chicago to explain the dangerous situation he was in.

'What the fuck were you thinking, insulting Frank Costello?' Giancana yelled at him. 'What do you think Frank's gonna do, for chrissake?'

'He's put a contract out on me,' Kennedy replied. 'Please, Sam, speak to him.'

'What makes you think I'd even want to help you?'

'Because my son Jack is moving up in politics and I hope he'll be President someday. You help me now, Sam, and I'll see to it that you'll have the President's ear when he's in the White House.'

Giancana saw his future suddenly mapped out before him. He wanted to own America. Now he had the chance to own a President. 'Let me see what I can do,' he said, and dismissed Joe Kennedy.

Then Giancana put through a call to Frank Costello and persuaded him to call off the contract. How he managed to dissuade Costello from having Joe Kennedy killed is open to speculation, but Costello was certainly distracted by his own problems.

*

On 2 May 1957, having appealed against the government's efforts to have him denaturalized, as well as appealing against numerous tax evasion charges, Frank Costello walked into his apartment house on Central Park West and was met by a man with a gun. The gunman fired at point blank range. Miraculously, Costello survived. The man who had ordered his death, Vito Genovese, retreated to his guarded mansion in New Jersey.

Just a few months later, on 25 October, Albert Anastasia walked into a barber shop for a haircut and shave. While he was reclining back in the chair, two men walked in and shot him dead. Even when his body had sagged to the floor, they continued to pump him with lead, just to make sure.

The following month, Genovese, who had announced himself as the new Boss of all Bosses, was arrested. He found himself sharing the Atlanta Penitentiary with Frank Costello who was on remand following the failure of his latest appeal.

Sam Giancana was suddenly the most powerful Mafia Boss in America. But despite the favour he'd done for Joe Kennedy, there was news in August 1957 that alarmed the Chicago Boss. Another of Kennedy's sons, Bobby, in his capacity as Chief Counsel to the Senate Select Committee on Improper Activities in the Labor or Management Field vowed to investigate organized crime.

18

More Blondes and Big Shots

In the spring of 1957 Johnny Stompanato, Mickey Cohen's trusted henchman, acquired the phone number of actress Lana Turner, recently divorced from Stephen Crane. He called her, dropped a few names she recognized as friends', and agreed to meet him. She knew he was connected but that didn't deter her from pursuing what turned out to be a passionate, though violent, affair, Lana's daughter, Cheryl Crane, approved of Stompanato because her mother seemed happy after a period of depression.

While away at school, Cheryl wrote not only to her mother but to Stompanato as well. 'Give my love to Mother,' she once wrote him. 'Write soon and be good. Love ya and miss ya loads, Cherie.'

In 1958 Lana and Stompanato were briefly separated when she went to England to film *Another Time, Another Place* with Sean Connery. She wrote heart-rending letters to Stompanato. In one, she wrote,

> I adore the way you write and all the truly beautiful things you say to me – so, please, please dearest, continue. Every line warms me and makes me ache and miss you more each tiny moment. It's true – it's beautiful yet terrible. But, just so is deep love ... we certainly are in tune 'all the way' ... Know how dearly I love you angel ... hold me dear lover mi macho.

Unable to be apart any longer, Lana bought him a plane

ticket. He arrived in England and they set up home in a London house. But by this time she was beginning to discover that he possessed a violent streak, and he began threatening her with violence if she so much as looked at another man.

One day he turned up at the studio brandishing a gun. Sean Connery told him bluntly, 'Keep away from Lana.'

Stompanato threw a punch, but Connery was quicker, and he sent the gangster sprawling on the sound stage floor.

When filming was over, Lana and Stompanato returned to her house in Beverly Hills where Cheryl was to discover his violent temper.

On 4 April 1958, Mickey Cohen heard the shocking news over the radio that Stompanato had been stabbed to death in Lana Turner's house. 'I don't believe it,' he said, 'they're saying it was Turner's teenage daughter did the killing.'

There were others too who thought it some kind of a ruse. Sean Connery was in Los Angeles at the time. He received a phone call at his hotel. A voice told him, 'If I were you, I'd get out of town.' There were some who thought Connery might be behind Stompanato's death. He took the advice.

But the fact was that Cheryl had killed Stompanato during a furious row between her mother and the gangster. Cheryl had feared that he was really going to harm her mother, so she grabbed a knife from the kitchen and plunged into him.

Mickey Cohen was asked to make a formal identification of the body, but he refused 'on the grounds that I may be accused of this murder'.

Cohen was outraged when it became obvious that Cheryl Crane was not going to be charged with murder. 'This was a great guy,' complained Cohen, and set about attempting to wreck Cheryl's case. He stole all the love letters the couple had written to each other and leaked them to the press. These letters were plastered all over the newspapers, and Lana Turner's love affair with the deceased gangster became public knowledge.

During the inquest, a man jumped up and yelled, 'This whole thing's a pack of lies. Johnny Stompanato was my friend. The daughter was in love with him, and he was killed because of jealousy between mother and daughter.'

Despite Cohen's attempt to sabotage Cheryl's case, he failed. The verdict was 'justifiable homicide'.

But it had a touch of irony, considering that Cheryl's father, Stephen Crane, had been a close friend of Bugsy Siegel who was Mickey Cohen's mentor who in turn was Stompanato's boss. Lana Turner had been yet another blonde to face tragedy through her Hollywood connections, but it was nothing compared to the fate that awaited the biggest blonde bombshell Hollywood has ever created – Marilyn Monroe.

Nobody crossed Sam Giancana or the Outfit and lived to tell the tale. He had proved this principle many times, such as with Willie Bioff. Now it was time to settle a score with Gus Greenbaum, the man who had taken over the Flamingo immediately following Bugsy Siegel's demise.

Greenbaum had certainly served the Mob well, with profits from the Flamingo under his management reaching $15 million. In 1952 when Chicago took control of the Riviera, Greenbaum was installed as manager. But as well as allowing Willie Bioff to work under his very nose, he had begun skimming off some of the Mob's profits for himself, and that was a worse crime. Meyer Lansky, responsible for many of the Mob's businesses, and Sam Giancana discussed the matter and agreed on what had to be done.

In December 1958 the mutilated bodies of Greenbaum and his wife were found at their Phoenix home.

Much of Meyer Lansky's time was now spent making money for the Mafia from casinos, not only Las Vegas, but in Cuba too. He had not forgotten favours given by George Raft, and he pulled a few well-connected strings to help out the struggling film star.

In the spring of 1958 Raft received a phone call from a old friend from his Broadway days, Jerry Brooks. He was managing the new Capri Hotel in Havana, although the real boss of the Capri was Charlie 'The Blade' Tourine, one of Vito Genovese's soldiers. According to Vincent Teresa, Tourine was a good friend of Raft's although the official story is that it was Brooks who offered Raft the job of hosting at the casino in the hotel. With little film work except for the occasional cameo performance, Raft accepted. It was at the Capri that Raft first met Vincent Teresa.

Teresa was there with a few friends. None of them paid attention to reports of fighting in the mountains nearby. On New Year's Day, 1959, Fidel Castro and his army of revolutionaries marched into Havana and took over the city. Teresa said that he was hustled onto a bus the next day and driven to the airport and put on a plane. Raft, in his account, said he was holed up in the Capri for fifteen days with the other guests because it was too dangerous to go out on the streets. On his last night there, Castro's men set themselves up at the nearby Nacional Hotel and began firing on the Capri. The next day, Raft said, he and Jerry Brooks were bundled into a car and driven to the airport where the revolutionary soldiers robbed them of all their money before putting them on a plane bound for America.

During 1959 Joe Kennedy phoned Sam Giancana, the first of several calls to the Chicago Boss designed to establish an understanding between the two men. Kennedy wanted Giancana's continued support for John 'Jack' Kennedy's race to the White House.

'That's all very well,' said Giancana, 'but what's all this shit with Bobby? He's spending all his time trying to prove a connection between the Teamsters Union and certain associates.'

'You've no need to worry, Sam,' Kennedy assured him. 'Nothing Bobby does will affect you.'

But Giancana didn't trust Joe Kennedy for a single moment. In an effort to guarantee Kennedy's protection, Mooney looked to Hollywood.

Giancana generally despised entertainers, calling them 'losers, prima donnas and assholes', although he had a genuine fondness for Frank Sinatra. And one of Sinatra's closest friends was Peter Lawford who was married to John Kennedy's sister, Pat. This brought Sinatra into the Kennedy fold, a close friend of both John and Bobby.

Giancana knew that both the Kennedy sons had inherited their father's penchant for sex. He figured that if he could gather enough dirt on the Kennedys, he could use it as a bargaining tool should either Bobby or John fail to live up to their father's promise to the Outfit. He got on to Murray Humphreys on the West Coast to see to it and Humphreys set about luring John Kennedy into various sexual traps.

Meanwhile Bobby Kennedy was unflagging in his determination to smash organized crime through the McClellan committee. 'We are dealing with organized crime and big-time gangsters and hoodlums as we had to deal with them in the days of Al Capone,' he said. His prime target was teamsters' leader Jimmy Hoffa whose connections with the Mob he described as 'a conspiracy of evil'.

Hoffa vehemently denied any connection with the Mob. Seated before Bobby Kennedy and the McClellan committee, Hoffa stated, 'You seem to have the impression that I am controlled by gangsters. I am not controlled by them.' However, Fred Otash, a private investigator later hired by Hoffa in an attempt to discredit the Kennedys, said, 'You can't be the head of the Teamsters Union unless you're approved by the Mob.'

In June 1959 Giancana found himself sitting before the McClellan committee, suffering a grilling at the hands of Bobby Kennedy.

'Would you tell us; if you have any opposition from anybody [do] you dispose of them by having them stuffed in a trunk? Is that what you do Mr Giancana?' demanded Kennedy.

Giancana chuckled and answered the same way he did no fewer than thirty-four times during the hearing: 'I decline to answer because I honestly belive my answer may incriminate me.'

'Can you tell us anything about any of your operations, or are you just going to giggle every time I ask you a question?'

'I decline to answer because I honestly believe my answer may incriminate me.'

'I thought only little girls giggled, Mr Giancana.'

Still Mooney thought that Joe Kennedy would ensure that Bobby would go no further with his investigation. But, taking no chances, Giancana decided to buy the Cal-Neva Lodge, a nightclub in Lake Tahoe which was frequented by the Kennedys, and ordered Hoffa to have the place wired up.

Towards the end of 1959, Giancana met three times with Joe Kennedy, Jack Kennedy and Mayor Daley at Chicago's Ambassador East. Their agreement was that if Giancana threw the weight of the Outfit behind Jack Kennedy's campaign to become President, the heat on him and the Mob would be turned off.

But, ever suspicious, Giancana didn't let up in his aim to get as much dirt on John and Bobby as possible. At least two actresses were involved, acting unwittingly as couriers between Giancana and John Kennedy. By 1960 Giancana was arranging for his influential showbusiness friends to back John Kennedy who, in November 1960, was elected President of the United States.

In 1974 when I interviewed Peter Lawford, he wasn't admitting to being involved in an affair between Marilyn Monroe and John Kennedy, but the fact was that Lawford arranged clandestine meetings between Kennedy and Monroe at Lawford's Los Angeles beach house. All Lawford said was, 'Marilyn was a close friend of mine, and Jack Kennedy was my brother-in-law, so they were bound to meet at some time, and sure, they both came to my home. It's still difficult for me to talk about Marilyn.'

Under orders from Jimmy Hoffa, private detective Fred Otash began bugging Lawford's house. Later, Giancana had Monroe's house wired.

Monroe was herself under investigation for her contacts with the Mafia. Late in 1959 two men from the Los Angeles District Attorney's office followed her when she left a restaurant on Sunset Boulevard accompanied by a young Italian gangster. Believing that the Mafia's intention was possibly to extort money from her, they followed. This stage of their investigation led to nothing, but the FBI were also tapping her phone. Later the FBI would learn that Monroe had more direct connections with Johnny Roselli and Sam Giancana, who for years had sponsored her in Hollywood.

In December of 1960, Bobby Kennedy was appointed Attorney-General. Feeling that Murray Humphreys had failed him, Giancana appointed Johnny Roselli to keep closer tabs on John and Bobby on the West Coast.

Bobby's appointment was even more baffling as Giancana was now giving assistance to the CIA's planned assassination attempt on Fidel Castro in Cuba, the notorious Bay of Pigs operation. Following the failure to eradicate Castro, John Kennedy's usual form of communication with Giancana – sending secret files delivered by a couple of young Hollywood starlets – stopped. Mooney began to realize that Bobby's assault on organized crime was not going to be halted, and that Joe Kennedy was intent on erasing all connections with the Mob.

In Italy, Charlie Luciano had tried to continue to rule, but he had been pursued from Rome to Palermo, and continually harassed by the police. He had enjoyed some solace in the arms of Igea Lissoni, a former nightclub singer and stripper. He missed his friends from his early New York days, so Meyer Lansky took passage on the *Italia* to visit him. It seems there was an ulterior motive for his visit. The Mafia were getting uneasy about the way illicit drug shipments from Italy were being seized, and Lansky was believed to have gone to Italy to advise him.

One alleged visitor of Luciano's in Naples was Frank Sinatra, who later denied that he and former boxer Hank

Sanicola ever made any such visit. The Italian police, however, said that they found a solid gold cigarette case inscribed 'To my dear pal, Charlie, from his friend Frank Sinatra.'

Towards the end of the fifties, Luciano suffered from angina. As the sixties swept in, Vito Genovese decided from his prison cell to put more pressure on Luciano by setting him up for a narcotics bust. Luciano, he hoped, would either keel over or go to prison. The Italian police unwittingly became the pawns of Genovese, and as they made intensive investigations into Luciano's activities, a fatal heart attack claimed the former Salvatore Luciana on 25 January 1962.

Frank Costello, out of prison now, celebrated the news that the Supreme Court had thrown out the deportation ruling on a technicality, and he settled down to enjoy a long retirement.

In March 1962 Marilyn passed from the arms of John Kennedy to brother Bobby. She apparently acted as a go-between for the Outfit and the CIA. Whether this was true or not, she certainly had knowledge of the Bay of Pigs affair. She told her friend (and husband for a fleeting moment) Robert Slatzer that Bobby had talked to her of the attempt on Castro's life and of the Mob involvement. She also told him that she tried reaching Bobby by phone but had been told she was no longer to call him.

In fact, the President had ordered Bobby to break all contacts with her, possibly because he was now aware that Giancana and Hoffa had been keeping tabs on his brother's and his own relationship with her. Angered and upset, she called Peter Lawford and said, 'I've been used. I'm going public with everything.'

She told Slatzer, 'If Bobby keeps avoiding me, I might just call a press conference and tell them about it.'

Slatzer advised her not to make any threats against the Kennedys. But she ignored him. 'If he's out there,' she said, 'I'll get in touch with him.'

Even Frank Sinatra had his connections with the White House severed. In March 1962, he invited John Kennedy to stay at his Palm Springs home. But Bobby Kennedy had been checking through old FBI files and three reports on Sinatra were drawn up. The final report, completed on 3 August, said:

Sinatra has had a long and wide association with hoodlums and racketeers which seems to be continuing. The nature of Sinatra's work may, on occasion, bring him into contact with underworld figures but this cannot account for his friendship and/or financial involvement with people such as Joe and Rocco Fischetti, cousins of Al Capone, Paul Emilio D'Amato, John Formosa and Sam Giancana, all of whom are on our list of racketeers. No other entertainer appears to be mentioned nearly so often with racketeers.

Available information indicates not only that Sinatra is associated with each of the above-mentioned racketeers but that they apparently maintain contact with one another. This indicates a possible community of interest involving Sinatra and racketeers in Illinois, Indiana, New Jersey, Florida and Nevada.

Consequently, the President was persuaded to dissociate himself from Sinatra. 'Frank,' said Peter Lawford, 'always blamed Pat and me for the break-up of his friendship with the President, which was preposterous because we had nothing to do with it, but he saw it as an act of betrayal. What betrayed Frank was his own friendship with Sam Giancana and that was enough to bring his association with the President to an end. Frank never spoke to me again.'

Late in July 1962, Monroe flew to the Cal-Neva Lodge. Her host there was Sam Giancana. At dinner that evening, Giancana and another of his guests, Peter Lawford, watched as she drank heavily, eventually unloading her problems on the Chicago Boss who listened with feigned sympathy.

'I've tried calling Bobby in Washington,' she told him, 'but he won't talk to me. I even tried calling him at his home but he just went into a rage.'

Giancana seemed happy to lend her a friendly ear.

'I've been nothing more than a piece of meat for Jack and Bobby,' she told him. Giancana decided that what the Kennedys had had, he could have also.

He took her up to his suite. She stripped naked and lay across his bed. He'd once said, 'I'll fuck her.' That night he did.

A few days later word reached Giancana that Bobby Kennedy was due in California on 4 August. Mooney summoned Needles Gianola. 'Monroe knows too much for her own good,' he said. 'I've a job for you. This should fix Bobby and Jack once and for all.

According to the authors of *Double Cross*, Gianola arrived in California accompanied by Mugsy Tortella. Two other assassins also landed that day, one from Kansas and the other from Detroit. From a selected vantage point, the four men listened in on electronic surveillance equipment set up in Monroe's home. They listened as Bobby Kennedy and a doctor arrived at her home and told her she was not to try to contact him again. She became hysterical and he had his doctor give her an injection to tranquillize her. Then Kennedy and his doctor left.

Later that evening, the four assassins entered Monroe's house. They found her still groggy from the sedative. They grabbed her and she struggled weakly as they laid her across her bed and taped her mouth. Then they inserted a Nembutal suppository into her anus. She was soon unconscious. They removed the tape from her mouth and left.

When Marilyn's own doctor, called out by Monroe's housekeeper, discovered her unconscious, he called for an ambulance. She was taken to hospital but doctors could not save her. Her body was returned to her home. In the meantime, Peter Lawford was called and he immediately arranged for Bobby Kennedy to fly out of Los Angeles by helicopter. The house had been thoroughly gone through prior to the police being called, and all evidence – including Marilyn's diary – was removed. Lawford was not, in 1974, admitting to his part in Kennedy's hurried exit from Los Angeles, sticking to the traditional story that Monroe had called him on the phone shortly before killing herself. He said he had always felt guilty for not rushing to her that evening.

'There is nothing worse in life than being unable to turn back the clock,' he said. 'If I could do that, maybe Marilyn would be alive today.' At the time of our interview, and to the day of his death, Lawford refuted any idea that Monroe was murdered. Yet the regret expressed in his voice was genuine, and in retrospect this was a man racked by guilt for knowing far more than he could ever say. It is possible that he never knew for sure who killed her. But it's likely that he believed Bobby Kennedy was involved.

As well as silencing Monroe for ever, Giancana also hoped that Bobby Kennedy would be accused of her murder. But the Kennedys were too well protected. A huge cover-up operation, including the removal of hospital records and the acquisition of all the wire recordings, resulted in Monroe's death being recorded as a 'probably suicide' by swallowing almost fifty Nembutal tablets.

Giancana had failed to destroy the Kennedys. But he swore to get his revenge.

The President was assassinated in 1963. Bobby Kennedy was assassinated five years later.

On 19 June 1975, Sam Giancana was shot dead at his home in Chicago. His family and friends suspected that Johnny Roselli was behind the killing. The following year Roselli gave top-secret testimony before the Senate Select Committee on Intelligence, where he disclosed the CIA-Mafia connection in the Bay of Pigs invasion and the attempt on Castro's life.

In 1976 Roselli was hacked to death and his remains dumped in an oil drum.

19

The Final Shot

'No matter where you went, the Mob had its finger in the pie somewhere and usually it was Meyer Lansky's finger,' wrote Vincent Teresa.

It was Lansky who had begun building a gambling empire in Cuba before the revolution. In 1949 he had invested in a television company, claiming his businesses were all legitimate. His partners in the company were Frank Costello and Joe Adonis.

He was also the brains behind the Colony Club in London. This casino was well known to Vincent Teresa who travelled the world on his 'gambling junkets' visiting casinos with parties of top-class gamblers. In London during the mid-sixties most of the casinos in London were 'off-beat', where the odds were stacked according to the people in the game. If there was a 'sucker' playing, the casino would rig the game to rip him off by thirty or forty thousand.

The Colony Club was 'the class casino of London'. It was controlled by Meyer Lansky, still active and earning millions for the Mafia. By the mid-sixties his role in the Mob was one of financial adviser, working with all the bosses and investing their money. With the Mob's money, he took control of countless casinos and gave the Mob their cut, making millions upon millions for them.

Keeping an eye on Lansky on behalf of the Mafia was Vincent Alo, better known as Jimmy Blue Eyes. He ensured that Lansky didn't short-change the bosses, and he also protected Lansky from anyone who thought to shake him down. But

Lansky was no Mafia boss. He was a Jew, and that meant he could never be a modern mafioso. He did, however, sit with the Bosses and probably had more money than any of them. He was a 'valuable friend', but if he'd ever stepped out of line and defied them, he would have been dead.

Jimmy Blue Eyes also checked out people to make sure they had Mob approval for Lansky to do business with. So before Dino Cellini, Meyer's top aide, could approach George Raft with a proposition to work as official host at the Colony, Jimmy Blue Eyes would have had to approve him. According to Raft, it was a British businessman who approached him in 1966 about the Colony. Raft admitted to being nervous about the offer, not because of any Mob connections – he claimed he didn't know that Lansky was behind the Colony – but because he felt that if his name was used so it became 'George Raft's Colony Club' and nobody came, it would be bad box office reflecting directly on him.

Raft said it took a number of phone calls to persuade him to agree to a meeting with Dino Cellini. 'This was the first time I met Cellini,' he said, 'although I'd heard of him in Cuba and the Bahamas as a guy who trained British dealers for the islands. Later I heard he was somehow connected with Meyer Lansky, but that wasn't important to me.'

That was a strange attitude for a man whose career had suffered as a direct result of his Mob connections. He had previously been refused a work permit by the British authorities in 1957 when he came to England expecting to make a film, and had told Logan Gourlay of the *Sunday Express*, 'This is a cruel business if you're sensitive. And Hollywood's a cruel place. The moment you start slipping, nobody wants to know you.'

Raft was understandably bitter towards Hollywood, but he still had friends in the business. Billy Wilder was among the directors who insisted on using Raft as a cameo star, and featured him in his 1959 comedy classic *Some Like It Hot*. Tony Curtis, one of the film's stars, told me, 'Nobody was more right for the part of a mob leader than George in that film. So he'd been friends with Bugsy, so what! A lot of actors were, so were the producers, and so were the studios' heads. I had an empathy with George because I came from the same environment. There but for grace of God, ya know. He was there when Prohibition was in force, and a lot of guys had a hand in it, a lot of ordinary guys who didn't have a chance in life. I don't know the exact background of George, but he got involved and that made it difficult for him to break away from it. He tried when he got to Hollywood, but once you're in that racket it's almost impossible to get away from it because there are a lot of people you maybe owe a lot of favours to, let's say. George had a lot of stories, but if anyone's gonna tell them, it should be him.'

Frank Sinatra was another friend of Raft's who came to his aid. 'Frank had an admiration for George Raft,' said Peter Lawford, 'and he saw to it that he got a part in *Ocean's Eleven* at a time when nobody else would touch him in Hollywood.'

With the chance to front the Colony Club, Raft laid down his conditions, insisting that the establishment carry his name, despite his initial reservations, and it became known as George Raft's Colony Club. He also asked for, and received, an apartment, a Rolls-Royce, and a 'good wardrobe' to add 'a feeling of class to me and to the place'. He also asked for 'a small salary, around $200 a week, and a few points in the club'. But he wanted nothing to do with hiring, firing or financing. He was given five per cent of the club and joined Cellini and fourteen other men as a stock-holder.

'At the Colony,' said Teresa, 'Raft fronted for Cellini and Lansky. He was there as an attraction to bring the suckers in.'

Each evening Raft arrived at about eight-thirty to check the kitchen, bar, entertainers and tables. He made sure the cuisine was the best in London. Each night, immaculate in a tuxedo, he greeted all the club's visitors, signed autographs and danced with women. The club was decorated in his own favourite colours – lush red velvet and gold. Everyone who worked there dressed in the sartorial style associated with Raft, such as red handkerchiefs in breast-pockets.

Teresa described him as 'a helluva drawing card, the best investment Lansky and Cellini made at that club'.

Frequent guests included Elizabeth Taylor and Richard Burton, Ari Onassis and Jackie Kennedy, Charlie Chaplin and even former Supreme Court Justice Earl Warren.

This was one of the few casinos where the guests could expect honestly run games. There were no marked cards, no fast mechancis operating behind the tables, and no loaded dice. Not even the Mafia received special favours, except when it came to reporting profits from gambling junkets to the Inland Revenue. Vincent Teresa, a regular guest with his games, would tell the manager, 'Don't put it in your records that we made $50,000 this trip. Put down that we only made $22,000.' Not only did he beat the American government on taxes but the British government too.

During one of Teresa's junkets at the Colony with fellow mobster Danny Mondavano, Telly Savalas, a friend of Teresa's since their early days in Boston, and actor Neville Brand turned up. Somewhat the worse for wear, Brand tried moving in on Mondavano's hooker, whose name was Dawn. Mondavano turned to Savalas and said, 'Tell your friend to keep away from Dawn.'

Brand failed to take heed of the warning, and Mondavano grabbed him by the collar and landed a punch that sent Brand sprawling. Two or three men came rushing over to defend Brand, and as one of them grabbed Mondavano, Teresa grabbed a steak knife and came to his friend's aid. He was just about to cut the man up when the manager grabbed Teresa's arm and said, 'Vinnie, for God's sake, that's a cop there.'

He was a plainclothes man from Scotland Yard. The manager had no choice but to throw Teresa and Mondavano out, but Telly Savalas stepped in and told the policeman that Neville Brand had begun the trouble. All was forgotten and forgiven, and a couple of days later Neville Brand very wisely apologized to the two Mafia men.

'One night,' recalled Raft, 'Darryl F. Zanuck came into the club with Charlie Feldman the producer, John Huston and Dino de Laurentiis. Darryl is a good gambler. He lost a size-able chunk of dough and wound up owing around $8,000. He was a little late in paying. I made a personal visit to his hotel to see him, in case he had a beef of some kind. He assured me that nothing was wrong and took care of the eight grand immediately.'

During 1966, news reached Raft about the widow of his late lamented pal, Bugsy. Virginia Hill was residing in a Salzburg hotel room in Austria which she shared with her fifteen-year-old son. For months they had subsisted on his earnings as an apprentice waiter. Her fortune was gone. She wrote that she was 'fed up with life', and after taking a handful of sleeping tablets, she walked into a snowbank and died. She was forty-nine.

There was even more shocking news for Raft in January 1967. He had returned to the States to spend the holiday season at home. During the first few weeks of the new year of 1967, the British Home Secretary, Roy Jenkins, decided that George Raft was *persona non grata* in the UK. The newspapers announced in their headlines: GEORGE RAFT BARRED FROM ENGLAND.

The first Raft knew about it was when a reporter phoned him in the middle of the night asking him if the story was true. 'You got some very wrong facts,' said Raft. 'I'm due back in London in a few days. As far as I know, none of what you've told me is true,' said Raft, and hung up.

Then he phoned Joel Tarlo, attorney for the Colony Club in London, who expressed surprise and assured Raft that the story was a hoax. But a few days later Tarlo rang Raft to confirm that he had been banned and that he was trying to do everything possible to get the British government to change their decision.

That day a group of newsmen cornered Raft and asked for the 'real story'.

'Is it true that you are affiliated with the Mafia?' 'Does

Meyer Lansky really own the George Raft Colony Club?'

Raft kept cool. He told them, 'What did I do? You tell me.'

In March, Raft made a statement for publication in the *Los Angeles Herald-Examiner*.

Somebody put the finger on me. They haven't accused me of anything; they've just barred me from the country without charges, without trial or anything. And just when I was about to start participating in the profits of the Colony. All I got was an apartment, the use of a car and a small salary until the investors were paid off. Now that they have been, I won't be there to collect.

I suppose the British had some information on me, and it must have come from the FBI. I'm going to New York this week to see about a job, and I plan to drop down to Washington and wait in Hoover's office until he sees me. I know him; once I introduced him to Aly Khan at the Del Mar race track.

I'm not a member of any mob, never was. Sure, I know some guys that are, but I know a lot of people. What am I supposed to do when those guys say hello to me – tell them to get lost?

What have I got to do to clear myself? I lead a quiet life. I don't ask for any trouble. I have never taken a drink. I don't get in any fights. If broads are an offense, then I plead guilty.

Raft didn't get to see Hoover, but through Walter Winchell he did write to the FBI, and on 4 April 1967 he received the following letter from FBI Director J. Edgar Hoover.

Dear Mr Raft

This will acknowledge your letter of March 28, 1967, concerning the actions of the British Government in excluding you from the United Kingdom. I am certain you realize that the FBI has no jurisdiction in England and had no control over governmental action taken by a foreign country.

In the event you desire to supplement your letter with additional data, you may be certain that such will be made a matter of permanent record upon receipt at this Bureau.

Raft wasn't the only American barred from Britain that year. Meyer Lansky, Dino Cellini, Charles 'The Blade' Tourine and Morris Lansburgh, owner of the Flamingo, were among a line-up of underworld figures refused entry into Britain by the Home Office.

Raft was bitter. He tried to play down, as he always had, his Mob associations. He said that the only reason he was barred was because he was guilty by association.

'Sure, I knew Benny Siegel,' he said. 'He was a guy who tried to imitate me. I met Meyer Lansky, but I never associated with him. I knew lots of people.'

He described what the British government had done to him as 'a kick in the balls', and wondered what he'd done to deserve it.

'In the twenties, the worst thing I could be accused of was being a guy who loved to dance. That was my life. I liked nothing better. And I made a pretty big success of it.'

But following the ban from the UK, Raft said, 'Sure, I admired Owney Madden. He was a big hero in our neighbourhood. The worst thing I ever did for Owney was help his boys move some booze from one place to another. In those days no one saw that as crime. It was a service.'

He complained about this bitter blow to Vincent Teresa. 'Vinnie, those were the best days I've had in years,' he said. 'I had a chauffeured Rolls-Royce, beautiful women with me every night, a beautiful penthouse apartment in the Mayfair area and $500 [contradicting himself – he said he'd asked for $200] a week. Who lived better than I did? What did I care about what was going on in the casino every night or who was involved? I never did anything wrong.'

Raft may not have committed any great crimes, but he had openly displayed friendship with, above all other crime lords, Owney Madden and Benny Siegel, and he had defended Siegel, a killer and extortionist, against prosecution. His days as a hood in New York prevented him from turning his back on his friend who came to shake down Hollywood, while Cary Grant dissociated himself completely from the underworld following Bugsy's death. Raft predicted that the gunshot which took out Siegel killed him too. The final shot for Raft had come unexpectedly from the British government.

Another of Siegel's associates, Howard Hughes, later had problems of his own with the Mafia, outside the film business, when he began buying clusters of hotels and casinos in Las Vegas, effectively wresting much power and influence from the Mafia. Frank Sinatra continued to associate with mobsters, notably Sam Giancana, Godfather of Chicago, but never suffered professionally because of it.

Meyer Lansky's years of freedom ended when Vicent Teresa's testimony brought him before a Grand Jury on Federal indictments. Frank Costello retired and died in 1973.

From time to time the Mafia has exerted its influence on Hollywood. During the sixties the Federation of Italian-American Democratic Organizations was founded by New York Congressman Alfred Santangelo, who immediately began a fight to get *The Untouchables* TV show off the air in America. He claimed he was doing this simply because the show gave Italian-Americans a bad image. But there were those who said that the organization was covertly initiated by the Mafia.

The show's producers and the network refused to cancel the show, so the FIADO organized a boycott against the show's sponsor, Chesterfield Cigarettes. Within a year, all commercials were withdrawn from the show and the classic series came to an end.

Around the same time pressure was put upon J. Edgar Hoover to ensure that the TV series *The FBI* did not feature characters with Italian-sounding names. In 1970 mafioso Joe Colombo succeeded in having the words 'Cosa Nostra' and 'Mafia' removed from the screenplay of *The Godfather*.

George Raft ended his days in 1980, broke and out of work as an actor. The Mob had given him further work in their casinos, doing what he did best in those latter years: being himself – a sharp dresser in fedora and spats, a street-wise hood from a tough New York background who was, in the public eye, as much as a gangster off screen as he was on. With all others either dead or in retirement, Raft's downfall in 1967 – that final shot – finally and irrevocably severed the Hollywood Connection.

Sources and Acknowledgements

A good deal of the information in this book was garnered from interviews I've conducted over the years, and from access to material supplied by or through friends and colleagues. To them all I am indebted.

Interviews were with James Cagney, on the set of *Ragtime* in the UK, 1980; Tony Curtis at his then home in London, 1974; Lauren Bacall on the set of *Murder on the Orient Express* at EMI, Elstree Studios, 1974; Helen Hayes, on the set of *Candleshoe* at Pinewood Studios, 1977; David Niven, on the set of *Candleshoe*, 1977; Peter Lawford, in London, 1974; Jesse Lasky Jr, in London, 1978; John Lee Mahin, by phone, 1974. I have sifted information regarding Jean Harlow, Clark Gable, Cary Grant, Gary Cooper, George Raft and Marilyn Monroe from interviews with Dore Schary, Van Johnson, Adela Rogers St John, Eli Wallach, Lee Remick, Shelley Winters and John Huston among others. A wealth of material on the life of George Raft was supplied to me by my late friend and colleague, John Kobal.

First-hand material was passed on to me through a trusted friend in the United States from a gentleman whom I refer to in the text as Mr Volonte. The name is purely a pseudonym to protect the gentleman's identity. I named him after the Italian actor, Gian Maria Volonte, who gave what is arguably the definitive portrayal of Salvatore Lucania in the film *Lucky Luciano*.

Special thanks to Karen Lambert for all her help. And to Jane to whom this book is dedicated.

Bibliography

Anger, Kenneth, *Hollywood Babylon II*, Arrow Books Ltd (London), 1986

Balsamo, William, and George Carpozi Jr, *Crime Incorporated*, New Horizon Press (US), W.H. Allen (UK), 1978.

Barry, Norman, *Film Greats*, Hodder and Stoughton Ltd (London), 1979

Berg, A. Scott, *Goldwyn*, Viking Penguin Inc (New York), Hamish Hamilton (London), 1989

Biagi, Enzo, *Il Boss e solo*; *Buscette, la vera storia d'un vero padrino*, Arnoldo Mondadori (Milan), 1986

Blakey, G. Robert, and Richard N. Billings, *The Plot to Kill the President: Organised Crime Assassinated J.F.K.* Times Books (New York), 1981

Carpozi Jr, George, *The Gary Cooper Story*, W.H. Allen (London), 1970

Davis Jr, Sammy, with Jane and Burt Boyar, *Why Me?*, Viking Penguin Inc. (New York), Michael Joseph Ltd (London), 1989

de Leeuw, Hendrik, *The Underworld Story*, Neville Spearman & Arco Publishers Ltd (US), 1955

Edmonds, Andy, *Hot Toddy*, Macdonald & Co. (London) 1989

Feder, Sid, and Joachim Joesten, *The Luciano Story*, David McKay Company Inc. (New York), 1954

Giancana, Sam, and Chuck Giancana, *Double Cross*, Warner Books Inc. (New York), Macdonald & Co. Ltd (London), 1992

Higham, Charles, and Roy Mosely, *Cary Grant: The Lonely Heart*, Harcourt Brace Jovanovich (US), New English Library (UK), 1989

Hurt, Henner, *Reasonable Doubt*, Holt, Rinehart and Winston (New York), 1985

Jacobs, Timothy, *The Gangsters*, Magna Books (UK), 1990

Kelley, Kitty, *His Way: The Unauthorized Biography of Frank Sinatra*, Bantam Books (New York), 1986

Kobler, John, *Capone: The Life and World of Al Capone*, G.P. Putnam's Sons, 1971

Marx, Samuel, and Joyce Vanderveen, *Deadly Illusions*, Random House Inc. (New York), Century (London), 1986

Messick, Hank and Burt Goldblatt, *The Mobs and the Mafia*, Thomas Y. Cromwell Company (New York), 1972

Scheim, David, *Contract on America: The Mafia Murders of John and Robert Kennedy*, Argyle Press, 1983

Sterling, Claire, *The Mafia: The Long Reach of the International Sicilian Mafia*, Hamish Hamilton and Penguin, 1990

Taylor, Gus, *Organised Crime in America*, University of Michigan Press, 1962

Teresa, Vincent, with Thomas C. Renner, *My Life in the Mafia*, Hart-Davis, McGibbon Ltd (UK), 1973

Wolf, George, with Joseph DiMona, *Frank Costello: Prime Minister of the Underworld*, Hodder & Stoughton Ltd (UK), 1974

Wolf, Marvin J. and Katherine Moder, *L.A. Crime*, Facts on File Publications (New York), 1986

Index